CREATION STORIES

CREATION STORIES

RIOTS, RAVES AND RUNNING A LABEL

ALAN McGEE

SIDGWICK & JACKSON

First published 2013 by Sidgwick & Jackson
an imprint of Pan Macmillan, a division of Macmillan Publishers Limited
Pan Macmillan, 20 New Wharf Road, London N1 9RR
Basingstoke and Oxford
Associated companies throughout the world
www.panmacmillan.com

ISBN 978-0-283-07177-5 HB
ISBN 978-0-283-07180-5 TPB

3 5 7 9 8 6 4 2

A CIP catalogue record for this book is available from the British Library.

Typeset by Palimpsest Book Production Limited, Falkirk, Stirlingshire
Printed and bound by CPI Group (UK) Ltd, Croydon, CR0 4YY

Visit www.panmacmillan.com to read more about all our books
and to buy them. You will also find features, author interviews and
news of any author events, and you can sign up for e-newsletters
so that you're always first to hear about our new releases.

THIS BOOK IS DEDICATED TO MY MOTHER,

BARBARA McGEE, R.I.P.

I would like to thank Luke Brown who has done an incredible job assisting me to pull my life story together. He was an amazing partner to work with.

PICTURE ACKNOWLEDGEMENTS

All photographs are from the author's personal collection apart from:

Page 3, top: © Paul Slattery / Retna Pictures
Page 4, middle: © Valerie Hicks; bottom: © Rex / Steve Callaghan
Page 5, bottom: © Dave Evans
Page 6, top: © Alastair Indge / Photoshot / Getty Images; bottom left: © Bleddyn Butcher / REX
Page 7, top: © Alastair Indge / Retna Pictures; bottom: © Kevin Cummins / Getty Images
Page 8, top: © Bleddyn Butcher
Page 9, top: © Suzie Gibbons / Redferns; bottom: © Retna / Photoshot
Page 10, top: © Grant Fleming; bottom: © Ian Dickson / Redferns
Page 11, top: © Michel Linssen / Redferns; bottom © Roger Sargent
Page 13, bottom: © Photoshot
Page 14, top: © Stefan Rousseau / PA Archive / Press Association Images; bottom: © Jill Furmanovksy
Page 15, top left and right: © BP Fallon; bottom left: © Dave Hogan / Getty Images; bottom right: photo by Eitan Lee, courtesy of Kate Holmes

Every effort has been made to credit all copyright holders of photographs in this book but where omissions have been made the publishers would be glad to rectify them in future editions.

CONTENTS

PROLOGUE

When you're a drug addict there's no such thing as jet lag. For years I'd fly two or three times a month between London and Los Angeles. The party in London would end when I dragged myself away from Noel or Liam, Bobby or Throb, and poured myself into a taxi to Heathrow. Neck some Valium on the plane, get an hour or two's sleep, then back into the action. You get off the plane, get drugs, get pissed and the same party continues. And it is the same party. They've all blurred into one.

That night in 1994 I was out with Primal Scream, who were rehearsing in a room in Waterloo. I think Oasis had left town the night before. This was before their first album was out, and they had a ferocious appetite for the rock and roll lifestyle they knew was theirs now for the taking. Every time they arrived in London it was the start of a two-day bender. I had the flu that night – I should have been in bed. But I was taking coke with Throb Young. He racks out lines as long as your arm. Almost as thick, too. Just before my taxi arrived, I made the mistake of doing one.

I was taking my sister Susan with me on this trip. I was going to show her a good time in Los Angeles, introduce her to my cool friends out there. It was going to be great fun. Creation Records was the most hedonistic good times rock and roll label in the world, and it was modelled in my own image.

In the taxi to Heathrow I began to feel unusual. I checked my pockets, looking for a Valium or a Temazepam. Shit, I'd run out. I took a deep breath. It didn't matter. I'd done this trip a hundred times before. Another deep breath. It would be fine.

It was the last time I would leave Britain for three years. It was the moment that everything changed.

1: GLASGOW

My father hasn't gone out of his way to help me much in life but he did give me one useful piece of advice when I was young: If someone tells you they're going to hit you, they're probably not going to. Don't worry about the ones who threaten you. It's probably all they'll do.

He was right about that. Even in Glasgow, in the violent 1970s, the mouthy dudes weren't the problem. It wouldn't be long before I'd become one of them myself. And that advice would stick in my mind years later when I was negotiating with the most powerful people in the music industry, people who were telling me they were going to take away everything I'd built up.

My father didn't give warnings. He gave me something else. From the day I left Glasgow I've never been scared of anyone, because I know what being scared really feels like.

I was born on 29 September 1960 in Redlands hospital, in the West End Road area of Glasgow. My father John McGee married my mother Barbara Barr in 1953. He was twenty years old; she was nineteen. They met when my mum was doing the books for the car mechanics where my dad worked as a panel-beater.

Both my parents were from working-class families. My grandpa on my mother's side, Jimmy Barr, worked in the shipyards in Govan, on the Clyde. I never met him; he died in 1953 from a heart attack. Members of my family tend to check out when they're in their fifties. A bit worrying for the fifty-two-year-old writing this book. But that's Scotland, the diet, the weather, the booze – I've put all that behind me. Grandpa Barr was, by all accounts, an abusive alcoholic. My mum says he made her and Gran Barr's lives a misery. From where I was standing, that was all too easy to believe. I've never met a more miserable woman than Gran Barr, and no wonder that after growing up with her my mother wasn't too happy herself. Gran Barr had been raised in one of the now notorious Quarrier's homes for orphans, founded in the nineteenth century by a Glaswegian shoemaker, William Quarrier. They were a byword for abuse. Her mother had died young of illness and then her father had been killed in the First World War. Gran Barr and her brother were sent to the Quarrier's home then. I didn't know much about this when I was a child and only found out about this later, when my father saw me putting money into an envelope to give to Quarrier's. '*Never* let your gran see that,' he told me. I never found out exactly what had happened to my gran in those homes. There was physical abuse; *that* I'm sure of. Gran Barr could be a vicious piece of work, but with a beginning like that, she probably didn't have much choice.

I never knew my dad's dad either. He was in the car trade, like my father, and died in his fifties before I was born. We didn't see much of Gran Gee, as we called her. She was slightly demonized at home, for reasons kept from me, and didn't have much of a relationship with my dad. She died when I was fourteen. My dad had one brother, who passed away not too long ago. He'd been shot in the head in Cyprus during the Second World War. It didn't seem to hold him back much.

My father was a seriously handsome man, with dark Cary Grant hair and piercing blue eyes. As a wee child he was my hero. He was strong from his work as a panel-beater. In fact one of my earliest memories is of him lifting me out of bed and carrying me downstairs when the roof of our house caught fire because of some dodgy wiring in the attic. The firemen arrived and saved the day; the house survived. As I grew up, I saw less and less of him. He was always at work. There was his day job at Wiley's, then he'd come home, have a quick tea, then be off to do a 'homer' – a cash job to sneak past the tax man – or to go to the Masons.

It was sometimes hard to keep track of what my mum looked like. She changed regularly, her hair a different cut or colour from one month to the next. She kept herself well turned out and was very thin. She was a looker herself, but probably not in the same league as my dad, and it wound her up to see the attention he enjoyed from other women. She smoked constantly, especially when one of her moods came on.

And they came on a lot more when Gran Barr moved into the house. This was just after we moved from Govan Hill in Paisley to 36 Carmunnock Road in Mount Florida in 1963, just around the corner from Hampden Park, the national football ground. Gran Barr had been burgled and was too scared now to stay in her house. With no brothers or sisters, my mum was the only one who could help, and so Gran came to live with us. The mood at home went rapidly downhill. I can imagine what a prison sentence it was to my parents, and how much they must have resented the sacrifice they had to make. That was when I was three years old, so Gran pretty much set the domestic tone for my whole childhood. I would live in this house till I was sixteen, when my dad made it impossible to stay there any longer. (We'll come to that later.)

My mum worked hard to make money as well as my dad. She worked wherever she could, in a sports shop as well as doing the books in the mechanics; she was a jack of all trades. She was the clever one in the relationship, but it wasn't in the days when it was possible for women to break through to a position of power. Not working-class women from Glasgow, anyway. I wish she'd been born twenty years later when she would have stood a chance to use her intelligence. She'd have found life much less frustrating. She argued all the time with my dad – she knew exactly how to wind him up.

Nevertheless, until I went to secondary school, I had quite a happy childhood.

I went to Mount Florida primary school 200 yards up the road. School was fun. My sister Laura had been born in 1963; too early for me to remember. To begin with she looked up to me, though our relationship soon became more competitive. I must still have been cute enough then not to annoy my parents, small enough for it to seem unreasonable for them to give me a belt. I loved football and we lived five minutes' walk away from Hampden Park. Dad would take me there as a treat to watch Queen's Park or an international against England. Those England games were the most exciting things on earth. They were just mental: 150,000 people standing, singing and swaying twenty yards to one side, twenty yards to the other – the Hampden sway. It was seriously dangerous, exhilarating. My dad would have to hold on to me to stop me from getting trampled to death. He hated it. Later, I supported Rangers, which was further away – thirty minutes to the west, just south of the shipyards where my grandfather had worked. I went on my own from the age of eleven, and saw them every second Saturday.

You can't get away from sectarianism in Glasgow. I knew as a Rangers fan I was supposed to hate Celtic fans, just because they were Catholic. But I had a lot of friends who were Catholic – it never mattered for a second to me. I don't even believe in Christianity, let alone the Catholic or Protestant creed.

But having said all that, there was something about the tribalism of the rivalry that made for an unbeatable atmosphere. They were great matches. The roar in the stadium was ferocious. The Rangers fans would be busy beating each other up, never mind the Celtic fans. But I was used to it; it never felt scary to me.

It was Gran Barr who gave me my first taste of violence in the house. She'd whack with a slipper to start with, moving up to her heels. They were big heavy things, and it gave my mum the idea too, so she started joining in.

The violence increased steadily from the time I was about nine. This was when my younger sister Susan was born. There just wasn't enough love in the house for it to be shared between three kids, and Laura and I were no longer a priority. Tempers frayed. There were a lot of us in the house now and we were on top of each other a lot of the time. My mum *was* a loving woman, but a frustrated woman. A busy woman too: she worked hard and as the woman in the house probably thought she needed to prioritize looking after the girls.

Gran Barr could take her shoe off in a split second and then I'd be on the floor, holding the lump that was growing on my head. She was a big woman. She had a strong swing for an old lady. You never knew what to expect from her. She was on all kinds of prescriptions and swallowed pills by the handful. Thyroid pills for certain but all kinds of others too – I didn't know what they did. My dad used to say if you shook her, she'd rattle. He did his best to keep away from her, and I suspect she was the reason he did so many 'homers' and became such an active Mason.

I assumed this was what life was like for everyone and I suspect for many people it was. Glasgow was a dismal place, an angry place. No one had any money where I was from and when people drank they took their frustrations out on whatever was nearest to them. And the older I got the more often that was me.

*

There was no choice about where you went after primary school, like there seems to be these days. King's Park Secondary it was, and that's where I met the boys who became the first incarnation of Primal Scream: Bobby Gillespie, Robert Young and Jim Beattie. I was a year above Gillespie who lived just round the corner from me. We're only nine months apart but he has definitely done a deal with the devil at some point; he looks twenty years younger than me, despite having caned it for years after I'd calmed down. Well, we've all done our deals with the devil, some more successfully than others. In the end, I didn't do too badly myself.

Bobby Gillespie is my oldest and best friend. We've known each other now for forty-one years. It's been an intense relationship. For some of those years we haven't been able to talk to each other at all, though in the end we always come back to each other. Certainly then, I couldn't have guessed he'd become the hippest rock star of his generation. He was just a normal lad, one of the pack, liked to blend in. Ran around the yard chasing a football, just like all of us.

There was something in the air in Mount Florida. As soon as we went up to secondary school the violence showed itself. I saw things no child should have seen. One day an older kid brought a hatchet in and buried it in someone's back in the playground. We presumed this was normal. The area wasn't terrible, not for Glasgow. But there were still knife fights in the playground and the occasional hatchet job.

I wasn't violent in those days at all. Robert Young from

Primal Scream, a few years younger, he liked a fight. He was small but really bolshie. We called him Throb later on. He was the heart-throb of the band. Even then, he may have got his confidence from his physical attributes. As Alex Ferguson said of Dion Dublin, you should see him in the showers, it's magnificent. Bobby was no fighter either, though he hung with guys who were. I'd only ever fight if I was forced into a corner. I wasn't soft – you had to be able to take a punch in my house, and I'd happily batter someone if they were going to insist. But fighting was not my bag: I was into Bowie.

I was becoming quite a music obsessive. I saw music as my salvation, it was that important to me. And straight away music and money were connected for me. I needed money to buy records, to take myself off to concerts, to keep some independence from my family. I started earning my own when I was eleven years old, shortly after starting secondary school. My pals were getting 50p pocket money a week so I asked my parents if I could have some too. I should have known the answer: there was no way they'd give me that. Well, they didn't *have* it to give me, they really didn't, they needed it all to feed us and pay the bills. I'll give credit to my dad in that respect: he didn't earn much and he had to work hard to get it but he brought home the money to raise three children. There was nothing left afterwards.

He was never going to give me pocket money, that was for certain. So I got a job with the *South Side News*, selling newspapers for 10p a copy on the streets. I got to keep 4p for every one I sold. That was okay, for a week, then I realized if I turned up at five in the morning rather than six, the papers had been delivered and there was no one else around. So, with an hour's less sleep, I could just help myself to them for free. I'd take 200 copies, sell the lot and make £20 in a week. Twenty quid was a fortune in those days, and not just for a wee lad.

This is when it all started. The love of having money in my pocket. The thrill of making it. There was no time to sleep if you wanted to get rich.

The music that my parents played in the house was nearly all terrible. It has always amazed me that so many people of their generation went through the 1960s, young enough to get what was happening around them, but they chose to stay at home and listen to Tony Christie. That's one of my few memories of my mum and dad being happy together, having a drink on a Saturday night, playing 'Knock Three Times' and banging the floor instead of the ceiling when Tony asked if they wanted him. The answer is *no*, I don't. I couldn't understand how they could like this stuff when they were living in the middle of a musical revolution. Of course, if they'd been hip, it may have thrown me a different way, so I shouldn't complain. They tolerated the Beatles, because the London Symphony Orchestra had done a version of their songs. And actually, they loved Simon and Garfunkel, were always playing 'Bridge Over Troubled Water' and that wasn't so bad. But other than that, I got into music by myself. I spent my money in the record shop at Battlefield. It was one of those shops that sold everything, TVs, stereos, but they had all the new records too. I'd be in there every week. Singles were only 50p, albums a few quid, but I only ever bought singles to start with. I'd go the library too and take out records then tape them at home. I got into the Beatles this way, taped both the red and blue singles compilations.

Glam rock was the first music that really got me going. This was 1971. I loved 'Get It On' by T. Rex. Then Slade, 'Coz I Luv You'. I bought both singles and played them all the time. My dad was very protective of his stereo so I bought myself a little Dansette mono record player with built-in speakers and this lasted me till I was sixteen. I'd never bought an album before I heard David Bowie. I thought albums were for grown-ups. After finding out about Bowie though, I went out and bought *Ziggy Stardust*. I still think it's one of the best ten albums ever made. I must have listened to it about two thousand times and I think this is when my dad decided there was something wrong with me. My room was covered in posters of him and he was all I talked about. He thought I was *in love* with Bowie. He was right. I *was* in love with him. I was obsessed.

I started going to rock concerts when I was about fourteen. I'd go to anything that was on at the Apollo. So I saw gigs by Queen, Santana, The Who, Alex Harvey, Lynyrd Skynyrd. I'd get crazily excited when the roadies just brought the amps on stage, there cheering them on at the front. So I'd been to loads of gigs on my own before I took Gillespie to his first ever gig. It was music that would make me and Bobby so close. I was fifteen, he was fourteen. He knocked on the door. 'Would you take me to Thin Lizzy?'

Would *you* take me to Thin Lizzy? I didn't really get it. I was thinking, Why don't you just go on your fucking own? I'd been going to gigs on my own for ages. It was one of the advantages of having parents who didn't care about me. They didn't give a fuck if I was in at midnight or seven o'clock. No one would tell me off on that level. They cared about what the girls were up to – they didn't want them getting reputations that would reflect badly on them – but they couldn't give two shits what I was doing. As long as the police weren't coming to the door – and they never did. I'd go and see the glam bands, on my own or with my mate Colin. I wasn't scared, but looking back, they were more dangerous than today's gigs. There was a header called General Jed who would just walk up to people and smack them in the face. You assumed it was normal and moved out of the way if you saw him coming.

I was doing other jobs by then. One was putting the jam into doughnuts in a bakery. It seemed to me then that Glaswegians ate a lot of doughnuts. Then on Saturdays I'd go round the houses, offering the leftovers from the bakers for sale. Anything left after that, I'd take home to my family.

By the time I was fourteen, I'd pretty much given up on school. I wasn't getting educated, unless a survival course in not getting your head kicked in counts for education. It was like that for most boys where I was from. Girls could show a bit more interest in learning than we were allowed to. If you were a boy and you showed interest, you were a swot and you were likely to get a kicking in the playground. If you were lucky. You never knew what people were carrying around.

I thought teachers were wankers then. I hated the place and so anyone involved with it was automatically a wanker to me. I learned how to add up, but after that, I can't think of anything I was taught that I've found useful. I thought it was all rubbish. I was always dobbing school, playing Bowie and Led Zeppelin records round my (appropriately named) pal Dobbins's house. In those days no one cared much about where we were. The fewer people in a class, the fewer to create problems. School didn't give a fuck. My parents kidded on they cared but I don't think they really gave a fuck either. They didn't see much hope for me and formal education. They didn't seem to see much hope for me at all.

As I got older at secondary school I'd become more and more lonely, more depressed. Home was miserable. I'd become too old to get hit by my mum or Gran Barr. I wouldn't stand for it. But the violence from my dad had started, and it was much worse. My mum and gran had always been in control of themselves, and not that much stronger than me. My dad was a strong man, and he'd completely lose it.

Laura watched Dad punch and kick me on the stairs one day. I had to go to hospital and have stitches in my head. I can show you the scar today. 'Don't tell anyone how this happened,' he told me before we went into hospital.

There's a part of me that doesn't want to make too much of this. One of the ways to cope is by making light of it. It was only what was going on around the country at the time, whether it was mates round the corner or Noel Gallagher in Burnage. It was a violent time – a drunken man's world – people were more accepting of knocking your kids about than they are now. There's been some progress, I guess.

But there's another part of me who knows what the violence did to me. I'm not talking physically, though when other people's dads hit them, they weren't ending up in hospital as far as I know. I'm talking more about the feeling I had of complete powerlessness and worthlessness. Wanting to run but having nowhere to go. It was a feeling I always had inside me but I could never explain what it was. It controlled me and I was running away from it as fast as I could, without understanding what it was, this feeling that made me so argumentative, hedonistic, self-destructive, provocative, and sometimes really nasty.

I was diagnosed as being clinically depressed when I was thirty-five, but I think then, at fifteen, was the first time I suffered majorly from it. It was the 1970s. I was in Glasgow. Of course it was undiagnosed. You'd never heard of depression at that time. But I knew that even in Glasgow it wasn't normal that I didn't leave the house once for the entire summer. It wasn't until I was thirty-five that I realized I had been clinically depressed for twenty years. No medication – except I supplied *a lot* of my own. I think it was the fact that I never confronted my depression which made me violent, argumentative, competitive to the point of being mental – probably all the reasons I made it in the music business.

My dad fucked me up you see, but you could say in quite a brilliant way – it formed my personality and led to the success I had. In the end, there's not much you can be scared of that's worse than your own father trying to really hurt you.

Punk changed everything when I was sixteen. It was a wake-up call. I remember when I first heard 'God Save the Queen', sitting my O-levels, still living with my parents. It was the end of probably the most depressing period of my life. The music was life-changing for me. I rushed out to buy 'God Save the Queen' by the Sex Pistols, 'Go Buddy Go' by the Stranglers and 'Sheena Is a Punk Rocker' by the Ramones, all on the same day. I was like, *fuck, I'm in to this*.

My first punk gig was the Ramones supported by the Rezillos. The Rezillos were amazing. I went with a girl I had a crush on. My mum's pal's daughter Caroline. I was too innocent then to even think about trying it on. I had only just left school.

The first thing for me with punk wasn't the politics or even the attitude, though there was a lot about the attitude that appealed to my hatred of bogus authority at home and at school. But first of all it was about the simplicity of the music, the way a few chords could sound so good, the way a singer with swagger could make music as good as a technically brilliant vocalist. It made me think that here was something *I* could do. Maybe *I* can be in a band. Before that, there wasn't one thing I wanted I believed I could get, you see. I wasn't thinking about running a record company or making lots of money or anything like that. But when I heard those songs I thought, I can do this, I could play guitar in a band like this. And maybe I don't have to turn out like my dad.

The music was so refreshing then. It was all Elton John and Rolls-Royces before that. And then you have Mick Jones arriving, saying he's never lived anywhere lower than the fourteenth floor of a tower block. And though I didn't live in a tower block, I thought *yes*, I understand *that*.

I wasn't surprised when I only got one O-level (in arithmetic). I'd never considered staying on for any more education and had always known that this would be the point in my life when I had to join the 'real world'. My parents thought I should become a tradesman. If I was really lucky, I might end up a taxi-driver, but they thought probably the best I could hope for was an electrician. So I got a job as an apprentice electrician and immediately hated it. From one set of bullies to another. They used to send me up on these moving scaffolding towers on wheels. I think they're illegal now – you had to climb up the outside of it. None of the men would do it. They'd say, you do it, you're light, but they only said that because they knew that anyone who climbed up on it stood a good chance of coming off it and dying. That or being in a wheelchair for life. I used to climb to the ceiling of a gymnasium, up a fifty-foot scaffolding, and then put in halogen lamps. Completely fucking bonkers. I wish I could say I got used to it, but each time it was terrifying.

I was only sixteen and surrounded by grown men, bullies a lot of them. They liked to do something nasty as an initiation for the new boys. Mine was that they pinned me down and painted my bollocks with bright red paint. And actually, it was pretty funny. I could take a joke. Then they tried to do it again another day. A big guy from Castlemilk leading the attempt. That was no fucking laughing matter at all. I picked up a metal bar and started swinging it at his head, chased him round the warehouse we were working in. I nearly caught him a couple of times when I threw it at his head. Good job I missed. It probably would have killed him. Maybe just maimed him. But it kept flying that frustrating inch or two just over his head.

It was understood after that that I was a bit of a head-the-ball. On a short fuse, supposedly. They never tried to paint my balls again.

My dad had always had a battered old acoustic lying around. He'd pretended to my mum he could play guitar to impress her, obviously without ever giving a demonstration, because he couldn't play a fucking note. When I decided I was going to be in a band I started to play around on it, working out basslines. Then, when I became an apprentice electrician I bought myself a crap Japanese Stratocaster imitation with a terrible neck. I think it cost £70. I had one or two lessons but didn't like them.

My relationship with my dad had got worse now I'd discovered punk. He'd always suspected me of being gay since my obsession with Bowie (I was so in love with Bowie I wondered if I was gay *myself*), and now I'd started to wear eyeliner when I went out. I was beginning to look like a

Buzzcock. He couldn't understand how he had managed to produce a man so completely unlike himself. I understand that: I've no idea how a man like him produced me either.

I didn't have to even be awake to provoke him. He'd get in from the Masons pissed and angry and come looking for me. He woke me up one time, my hands pinned below my sheet, and gave me five rabbit punches to the face. It was a Tom and Jerry-style doing. My head bounced back and forward against his fists and the pillow with my hands trapped and him staring down at me, furious about – about fucking what I don't know. It sounds comical when I tell the story now, and it's easier to tell it that way, but it wasn't funny then. You can't stay somewhere where you get assaulted in your sleep. I knew I had to get out. The next day I went round to Bobby's and asked if I could stay there for a few days. His dad, who I've always looked up to, took me in. He didn't judge my father: he knew the old man was frustrated, financially strapped. But he agreed to put me up, and he was an example to me of what a dad could be. Bobby's family were pretty far ahead of their time: the only parents I knew who didn't batter their kids.

After that I found a bedsit in the West End of Glasgow. I had no money, just enough to pay the rent and eat, but it was enough. At least I was safe when I went to sleep at night.

I hated my job and it was only punk that gave me hope of a different life. I wasn't getting on too well with learning the guitar so I decided to buy myself a bass. I thought it might be easier playing one string at a time. I bought myself a cheap cherry-red Gibson SG copy – a heavy metal bass, really, though a lot of punk bands used them too. Now I just had to find a band. There was a show on Radio Clyde I used to listen to, the Brian Ford show. This was the punk show and definitely the main thing I listened to on the radio. I listened to John Peel a bit too, but he seemed miles away from my life. I never thought I'd move to London then: Glasgow was still the world. On the show Brian Ford would read out adverts from bands looking for members and that's how I met Andrew Innes, who was looking for a bassist for his band the Drains. Even then, I thought, *What a shit name*. I think he was taking the piss. He's always been a satirical bastard.

The Drains was Innes on lead guitar and a posh guy on drums, Pete Buchanan. He was Innes's next door neighbour. From a private school. We bullied him for two or three months then kicked him out. We used to really wind each other up too, but we were tough little bastards and we could give as much as we got. Bobby would start coming round and hanging out with us on Friday nights in Andrew's bedroom. So putting those two together was the first of the many things I would do for Primal Scream, and they remain to this day the creative force of Primal Scream (now Throb's left the band). The three of us formed an imaginary band that never left that bedroom, called Captain Scarlet and the Mysterons. Me and Innes would drink beer and play Clash, the Sex Pistols, even Sham 69. We never had a drummer. We never played a gig. Andrew had a Les Paul copy in cherry red. Bobby would sing a bit and bang some boxes but mostly roll around the floor like Iggy Pop. I'd be on the bed, pretending to be Glen Matlock. We wanted to be at a punk gig every Friday night and because we couldn't we put it on ourselves. We were the audience and the band.

Innes was a brilliant guitarist. He could play all the songs, everything by the Jam, everything by the Clash. He could play 'Freebird'. He was a twisted fuck too, even at sixteen. He knew just what to say to me to upset me. But I knew just what to say to him to upset him.

It was nothing serious: he'd call me a ginger cunt and I'd call him a speccy wee shite. Gillespie and I didn't argue at all at that stage. Our music tastes merged into each other.

It was Innes who taught me how to play my bass. He'd point out where to put my fingers. He's a real musician; I'm a blagger. He taught me to be a punk bass player. It was the same with the Clash: Mick Jones taught Paul Simonon. All the punk bass players were taught on the job. Before too long I could hold my own in a punk band. We got a good-looking singer in, Jack Riley, and changed the band's name from the Drains to Newspeak. (I'd just read *1984*.) This was the dream. It was what kept me hopeful in those days.

I chucked the electricians after six months. I just made tea and risked my neck changing light bulbs. I was learning fuck all. My dad was pissed off that I quit, but I didn't have to listen to him so much any more now I'd moved out. Luckily, in those days there were jobs to be had and I managed to get one working for British Rail. This was pretty boring, putting wage packets together, but it wasn't unbearable and the people were a good laugh there. You didn't have to wear a tie, which suited the Buzzcocks-style Oxfam chic I was wearing in those days.

It was here I met Yvonne, my first wife. She was one of the supervisor's sisters, a couple of years younger than me. I met her at a work social event in the Pollokshields depot – she was selling cakes – and fancied her straight away but I didn't think I stood a chance of going out with her. She was beautiful, with dark Italian looks. A few months after I'd first met her, she came to work for British Rail too, and we became good friends. She had a boyfriend, so for nine months all we were was pals.

I turned eighteen in 1978. My father proudly gave me a form to fill in so I could join the Masons, like him. I was thinking, What the fuck, Dad? I'm a punk! Who ever heard of a punk joining the Masons? I enjoyed ripping up that form. That pissed him right off. And that pleased me enormously.

And then, incredibly, Yvonne and her boyfriend split up. I wondered if I'd ever have the courage to tell her how I felt. Somehow I managed to mumble it out. And incredibly she told me she liked me and kissed me and we started going out. She was so beautiful. I was walking around in a state of amazement. I was so happy! I had a job, a flat, a band, a girlfriend.

It was then that Andrew Innes told me we had to move to London.

2: LONDON

Andrew Innes, what a bastard. He wanted me to leave Glasgow just when life there was finally good. It had taken nineteen *years* to become good, and now he wanted me to start again in London!

Well, I could have said no and stayed where I was. A lot of people would have thought that was the sensible thing to do. I had a girlfriend, my own place, a steady job. But Andrew was going and I knew my best chance to make it in a band was to stay with him. He'd taught me everything I knew about how to play music. So I decided to go with him, and that was the first time I picked music as a priority over Yvonne. It wouldn't be the last. I think quite often about what would have happened if I hadn't followed Andrew. There'd have been no Creation Records, that's for sure. Maybe I'd have become a taxi-driver and fulfilled my parents' ambitions for me. Had fifty conversations a day about Rangers. When the heart attack arrived, I'd have probably been glad.

I said goodbye to Yvonne but we decided we would stay together and give long distance love a go.

I quit my job and caught the train down with Andrew Innes. I took nothing with me except a new Yamaha bass guitar bought on credit and a very small bag of clothes. We had no plan except that we would arrive in London and become pop stars.

We all lived in a bedsit in Tooting Bec, me, Andrew Innes and Jack Riley. It was survival of the fittest. Jack didn't last long. He came from a nice family. Well, you know about mine, and Innes was born a twisted and dark human being independent of familial influence. We're as acerbic as each other. Jack was a good-looking rich lad and had been having a whale of a time in Glasgow, living in his parents' nice house, shagging all the girls. He should have been in the Police. Now he had to live with two vitriolic cunts who informed him on a minute-by-minute basis how much we hated him. You know how it is when you're that age, or maybe you don't. We were cruel and we were nasty and we loved it. There was a bitterness in me, a rage at those who had had it so much easier than me. When you think the world doesn't want to let you into its club you can either give up trying or make yourself sharp like a knife and try to stab your way through. I'm sorry for it now. Jack was a bit soft and didn't stand a chance against me and Innes. Off he went back to Glasgow and Innes took over singing duties. We changed the name of the band at this point too, from Newspeak to the Laughing Apple (you'd have to ask Andrew why).

We needed a drummer and I found one, when I walked past this punk girl with bright pink hair and got chatting to her. Do you know any drummers? I asked. Of course she did, she had one on the sofa back at her place, a lovely guy but with a bad smack problem. He kept his kit in a squat on St Alphonsus Road in Clapham and when we ran out of money Andrew and I moved in there. It was really run down in those days. The place was full of guys who were on the run from the army, deserters. All of them with no hope, with the threat of military prison hanging over them. It was a heavy drug scene, the first time I saw people injecting heroin. I'd never seen any drugs until then. Bobby, Innes, me, we were all innocents in that respect.

I've always been grateful that it was there that I first saw heroin. It was definitely good for me. If I'd seen people shooting up in a more glamorous setting, I think I would have fallen for it later in life. I mean, I got addicted to every *other* drug going. I remember watching a guy inject in this horrible, dark, damp room in Clapham and thinking, No, that's not for me.

After a couple of months of that I'd had enough. I'd got a job working for the railways again. I was a stores clerk. It was the most boring job in the world. People would come in and ask for thirty-two bolts and then I was supposed to fill in a form and give them thirty-two bolts. But I'd never do the paperwork. I used to take it all home in my bag and dump it in the bin. I had to work with a guy called Tony who was a total div. He was the stores supervisor and OCD about everything. I don't think he liked Scottish people, and definitely not Scottish people like me. It was with great joy that I used to take home the entire week's paperwork and dump it. It was so boring. I couldn't face it. It took them a couple of years to find out it was all missing, by which time I was off.

When I left I used to torment Tony by sending him postcards from the Jesus and Mary Chain tours I'd go on. From Tokyo, New York, Paris. *Missing you Tony, love Alan*. I knew he'd receive them sitting in his horrible little storage hut, where he'd be till he got his pension, and he would *hate* me. I kept that up for a couple of years.

The job meant I had enough to rent a room in Clapham North. I was renting the room from a family and in some ways it was worst than the squat. The dad was mental, a head case. I remember playing my records in my room and him bursting through the door, screaming and shouting and telling me I had to get out. I was staying in his daughter's room, who he'd fallen out with, and now he'd made up with her and wanted to move her back in. He wanted me to leave immediately, and I'd have had to sleep on the streets. I'd paid till the end of the month, was going nowhere and told him so. I moved out soon enough though: I'd bounce around from one mad bedsit to the next, two months with one lunatic and two months with another. Yvonne and I would travel back and forward between London and Glasgow at the weekends – we both got tickets for next to nothing because we worked for British Rail. It took a year for her to decide to join me in London. Andrew stayed living in the squat. He was more interested than me in what was going on there.

We were playing gigs as the Laughing Apple wherever we could. We rehearsed at the squat and wrote our own songs. Andrew wrote the first ones and I learned from watching him, just as I learned everything about how to be in a band.

We played gigs at the Stockwell Arms and at a dive in Tooting Bec. We supported the UK Subs at one point. I loved playing the gigs at first, but as we got used to them the buzz of playing wasn't enough any more. It was desperate times, to be honest. I knew what I wanted but things weren't going my way. Music felt like a hobby, not an escape – I couldn't see how it was going to help me escape the destiny of a boring nine to five existence.

But I kept trying. The one gig everyone wanted to be on was the Hampstead Moonlight Club run by Dave Kitson from Red Flame. It was so hard to even get put on as third on the bill. Finally we managed it: I just wouldn't go away and they put me on so I'd stop hassling them. We were supporting the Scars, who were the coolest band in the world then. During the middle of our set on stage we put a record on the portable Dansette I'd bought with the newspaper money back in Glasgow – it was 'Jumping Someone Else's Train' by the Cure – then Andrew and I jumped into the crowd and started dancing around to it. The crowd were totally bewildered. 'I've seen it all now,' said Paul Research, the Scars' guitarist, as we danced past him. Once it had finished we got back on stage and started playing our instruments again. Total post-punk!

We were putting out our own singles too. I used to go to Mayking records and give them £500 for a thousand records. We managed to blag the money for the first one, 'The Ha Ha Hee Hee EP', from CND, which we paid back once we'd sold all the records. Bobby was working at a printers in Glasgow and he'd design the sleeves, print them and send them down to London where we'd fold them into a plastic bag. It was pure budget stuff, and that was my first experience of putting out records. We'd take them down to Rough Trade records and Geoff Travis would take fifty of them at a time and distribute them around the country through his Cartel shops. What an amazing concept that was he came up with there. We could take them into the shop and he'd get them out across the country for us, and for loads of other small indie bands. The Cartel was a collective of shops that offered small bands a genuine alternative to major label distribution. I don't really get on with Geoff Travis (and he probably hates me) but professionally and personally he'll always have my respect for Rough Trade distribution. It was completely idealistic and ultimately it failed but for a while it changed the landscape of British music. And being part of the Rough Trade scene, for all the things I hated about them, was a very important education for me when I started off.

We were aware too that just as we'd left Glasgow the music scene was really kicking off there, with Alan Horne's Postcard label and their biggest band Orange Juice. We didn't know them but we were connected through friends. In fact, they asked if they could borrow a Vox organ Andrew and I had bought together, and that's the organ on 'Blueboy' by Orange Juice. I've got a lot of respect for Alan Horne and Postcard these days (I was horrible about him in interviews when I was a loudmouth drug addict). He was as responsible for changing Glasgow into a music city as I was, as Bobby Gillespie was, Edwyn Collins and Teenage Fanclub. Before

1980 all we were famous for was Lulu and the Alex Harvey Band. Now it's perhaps the biggest music city in the UK.

Though Andrew wasn't paying any rent he certainly paid the price of the lifestyle in the squat. Within a year he'd caught hepatitis B and suffered kidney failure. He told everyone he'd got it from 'sitting on dirty toilet seats'. He lost a kidney – it was that serious. His parents had to come and pick him up to take him back to Glasgow. He was gone for a whole year. (When he came back he went to university and got a degree in chemistry, specializing in pharmaceuticals. It makes sense, he's the musical alchemist in Primal Scream. Though the thought of a member of Primal Scream opening up his own chemist's is scary, for sure.)

London was a lonely place without Andrew. I'd lost my guitarist and I guess that was a moment when I could have given up on my dreams of being in a band and concentrated on working for British Rail, getting enough together for a mortgage, having kids with Yvonne, being the normal nine to fiver she would have liked me to be . . . But I couldn't get the idea out of my head that the music industry was where I belonged, the only place I belonged.

It was good that I had music to focus on. Without that to occupy me, I don't know what I would have done. I was a really angry man. I was ready to lash out all the time. I'd be in a record shop and someone would say something and next thing I'd be threatening to throw them through the window. My accent was quite scary to some people and once

I'd realized that, I couldn't resist. I guess I thought all south-
erners were soft. I'm amazed I didn't get filled in more often.

With Andrew back recovering, we got Dick Green in as
a replacement guitarist in the Laughing Apple. Before Andrew
left we'd had to sack the drummer Mark Jardim when he
didn't turn up for the fiftieth practice in a row, and it was his
replacement Ken Popple who brought Dick along to the squat
one day to try out. He was a good guitarist too, played like
Will Sergeant from Echo & the Bunnymen. We let him in and
I'm glad we did because Dick has played such an important
part in Creation's story, though when we met him he was
working as a pensions clerk and it took him till 1988 to jump
fully on the Creation bandwagon. It wasn't all fun in those
days being in the Laughing Apple. Well, almost none of it
was fun. We did a miserable tour of England supporting
Eyeless in Gaza, playing universities. I really liked Eyeless in
Gaza – Martyn Bates had such a soulful voice. I think I was
the only one who did like them though. Someone stole my
bass from the last gig of the tour in Edinburgh and on the
drive back to London Dick hit some black ice and wrote our
van off. Yvonne got thrown through the windscreen. It could
have been a lot worse although she had pretty serious whip-
lash afterwards.

Yvonne had moved to London in 1981 and got a job at
British Rail at Euston. We got engaged straight away. Not for
very long; it seemed like the next minute we were getting
married.

The wedding was that December, at 3 p.m. in Brixton

register office. It was three o'clock and Yvonne's family were there but my parents and sisters weren't. It was quarter past and they still weren't there, and we had to start the ceremony. Typical, I was thinking. They can't even get here on time for their son's wedding. (They'd set off that morning and been delayed by snow on the tracks.) Yvonne and I made our vows and we were married. Andrew Innes was there and Dick Green. Ken Popple. I loved Yvonne and I was pleased about that at least, despite how annoyed I was at my parents. We hung around afterwards, waiting, in case my parents turned up. They wanted to shut the register office soon and go home. It was 3.45, 3.54, one minute past four and that's when my mum and dad dashed in and said, 'Have we missed it?'

Poor Mum, I think it broke her heart. My sisters were just bemused. Dad couldn't have given a fuck.

Yvonne and I lived in some terrible places after we'd got married. Ilford was the worst. The roof of our kitchen was a tarpaulin. It was the winter of February 1982, just after we'd got married, and it must have been the coldest flat in London. It wasn't fit to live in. Eventually, Yvonne managed to sort out a mortgage and we bought a little house in Tottenham on Beaconsfield Road. We were completely terrified of the £15,000 mortgage we'd taken on – it seemed like more money than anyone could hope to earn in a lifetime. I think we were on £70 a week then.

That was as close as I came to giving it up forever. I tried for a while to be Joe Soap. I was at home in the evenings, watching Paul Weller appear with the Style Council on *Top of the Pops.* I was still missing Andrew a lot. I never made many friends in London until I started running the Living Room club in 1983. There was one good thing about Andrew being gone though: now the responsibility all fell to me to get gigs, and I realized this was a side of the music business I enjoyed in a different way to being in a band. Particularly when I began to get us press as well as gigs. I got us a two-page feature in *Sounds* written by Dave McCullough: 'The band most likely to' and all this shit. Janice Long was a fan straight away and played our songs. She's always been a huge supporter of me. I wore John Peel down with persistence and eventually he played a single, 'Sometimes I Wish'. I was still talking to Andrew up in Glasgow and he was amazed by the press I was getting. You could be a manager, he was telling me.

I didn't understand then that I'd stumbled across my true talent. I was good at organizing people, at persuading them to do something, making things happen. I liked trying to get people to share my enthusiasm, making them believe me. I convinced people that the Laughing Apple were going to change the world! They stayed convinced for about five seconds, but even that was some achievement.

Pressing the Laughing Apple records had taught me a lot too. Because I didn't have anyone babysitting me, by default I had to learn how to do every stage of the process. It didn't seem intimidating to me. I'd had to work things out for myself my whole life, from the day I started selling newspapers to the day I realized it was much more profitable to steal them *then* sell them.

We weren't doing it to make money. We covered costs and made a little bit but it was never about profit. We were addicted to having our own records. My own record where I played bass on it! It was mind-blowing. The days of vinyl too – it had a mystique that CDs never had, even in the days before every PC could churn them out.

I'd found another band too that changed my life. The first time I saw Television Personalities was in 1982, supporting the Nightingales. Andrew must have recovered then, because he was with me. I liked the Nightingales but the TVPs were out of this world. It was March 1982, a Rough Trade concert. What a performance. There were about twelve of their mates sitting around on stage, wearing suits, smoking cigarettes through holders and pretending to be aristocrats. There was Ed Ball on bass, Dan Treacy singing and on guitar, and then Joe Foster ran on to sing 'Part Time Punks' really camply, before he sawed Dan Treacy's Rickenbacker in half! It was maybe a grand's worth of guitar. They were only getting paid about £50 for the gig! I saw them loads after that. Their live sets were always incredible: whimsical, camp, racing with the speed rush of the 1960s mod scene. I loved the first two albums *And Don't the Kids Just Love It* and *Mummy Your Not Watching Me*. 'Three Wishes', 'Part Time Punks' – brilliant singles. Treacy was like a cross between Jonathan Richman and Ray Davies.

There were two future Creation employees on stage that night too: Ed Ball and Joe Foster would play a big part in the story.

It wasn't just the TV Personalities' music I loved – it was their record label Whaam!. It was a pop-art label. I'd start going to visit Dan Treacy in his house on the King's Road. He was a bit suspicious of me, didn't know what I was after. I just wanted to be his mate, ask him for a bit of advice. I saw him as a kindred spirit – he had a club, a label and a band – and he was influenced by punk and psychedelic sixties bands too. I think it annoyed Dan Treacy at the time that we got so successful by copying his moves but we became good friends later in life. I have a lot of affection for him.

Discovering the TV Personalities reinvigorated me and I'd been inspired by the fanzine *Jamming!* too. It was a great fanzine which Paul Weller helped fund and Tony Fletcher, who went on to write Keith Moon's biography, put together. Tony Fletcher was even younger than me, and I was only about twenty-two when I started reading *Jamming!* He did this one brilliant issue that made me sit bolt upright: get up off your arse, form a fanzine, form a club, form a band. So I went and did all three.

Years later I told Tony Fletcher what an influence he'd been for me, and he was pissed off: 'Why don't you tell people that!?' So I'm correcting that now, Tony – thanks for the inspiration.

First I tried the fanzine. Jerry Thackray and I put *Communication Blur* together. Jerry Thackray was the Laughing Apple's biggest and, on dark days it seemed, only fan. He'd be the one dancing at our gigs, and we became mates. We nicknamed him The Legend, ironically. There was nothing legendary about him, but it was a good persona for him in the fanzine to let rip. We used *Communication Blur* to unleash our bile about everything we hated on the world. We pretty much hated everything, or Jerry did anyway. He was slagging me off by the end, for being too cosy with music journalists. I'd put adverts in the fanzine for the Laughing Apple singles, special offers, and I managed to sell a few doing this. But that was the last act of the Laughing Apple. We petered out that summer. As a band we'd never really found our own style, and I was tired of ripping off Joy Division.

Next up I wanted to try to run a club. My first club was the Communication Club in October 1982. I put on the Nightingales, the Television Personalities, the Go-Betweens. I ran it for eight weeks in Camden and no one was interested. I lost money every night – we'd get about fifty people there and it wouldn't cover the costs. It was depressing but I'm glad I did it: it was through putting on the TV Personalities that I became involved with Joe Foster. I remember the first time we spoke. He arrived up the club with hair and clothes like Bob Dylan in speed-fuelled 1966 and strode up to me.

'Are you Alan McGee?' he said.

'Yeah.'

'Good,' he said. 'You owe me eleven quid for the cab fare.'

Joe quickly became one of my best mates. The thing that I loved most about Joe Foster was that he was genuinely more mental than me. Six months after the failure of Communication Club, in June 1983, we tried to run another night together, this time called the Living Room. It was up in the Adams Arms on Conway Street.

The Living Room was anti-everything else that was going on at that time. Gigs were in set venues. There was no one else putting four good bands on in the upstairs rooms of pubs or if there was I didn't know about it. I think we were responsible in large part for starting that scene: not many people would put on unsigned bands at that time and after that, there were nights like ours everywhere. Bobby was running a similar night, Splash One, in Glasgow, but that was posh – he was hiring a nightclub. We just bought our own cheap PA and did gigs wherever we could find the space, whether it was a place normally used for old men to play dominos or if it was a place normally full of women who got paid to take their clothes off. Because the rooms were so small our cheap PA was fine. It was raw. We'd get the room cheap, pay the bands a reasonable amount and make a decent profit. Completely illegal in terms of regulations, and the police shut us down once.

Some nights we'd have two hundred people coming up the stairs. Big guys from the army would be trying to get in and Joe would decide he wasn't going to let them. These enormous hard guys and Joe would stand there telling them to fuck off. 'Come on then, we'll come down and we'll fight you now,' he'd say if they didn't like it. I'd be looking at these hard cunts and back at Joe and he'd be totally unafraid. I'm not scared of much but he's mental. Joe, I was thinking, we'll get our heads absolutely stoved in. But he was totally fearless. Everyone in the TV Personalities had told me he was mental, and within a week of starting the Living Room he was on the door telling trained killers they'd better fuck off or he'd come out and batter them. He couldn't give a fuck. The funny thing is he wasn't even hard! I found this out later when he drove me mental on a tour in Europe.

It's hard to work out why some clubs arrive at the right time and work and why some arrive at the wrong time. At the height of Britpop, when I was at my most famous, no one would come to a night Bobby and I tried to run. A couple of years later, people were queuing up for Death Disco. In 1982 no one cared about my Communication Club. In 1983 the Living Room took off immediately. We'd have two hundred people paying a fiver each and once we'd paid the bands Joe and I would have about £800 to split between us. It was completely nuts – to put it in context, I was getting only £70 a week from British Rail.

I got a lot of my confidence back then. The Television Personalities had really inspired me and I wanted to try to make music again. The influence of Joe Foster and Dan Treacy was definitely making itself felt when I started a new band in summer 1983. I'd been into the 1960s garage band the Creation since seeing their record 'Biff Bang Pow' on the inside sleeve of *All Mod Cons* by the Jam. Joe Foster and Dan Treacy were even bigger fans: I'd seen the Television Personalities cover 'Biff Bang Pow', and the amphetamine energy of the 1960s mod bands was a huge influence in the pop-art scene they were trying to create with Whaam!. We called the band Biff Bang Pow!. It was me on vocals and guitar, Dick Green on guitar, Dave Evans on bass and Ken Popple on the drums.

I'd write a lot of the basic melodies and then Dick would put the flowery parts on. And Joe Foster produced all the recording sessions for us and played on most of the songs, and then wrote a lot of songs with me, so it wasn't long before he was a fully fledged member too.

After a couple of months of Joe Foster and me drinking all of the profits from the Living Room away, the McGee work ethic kicked in and I decided with Joe to use the money to start putting records out. Running the club had been very useful too. Being on the door of the place everyone was trying to get into, I'd ended up getting known and made lots of new pals. The journalists were all coming along, and they all knew my face now.

We called the label Creation, after the band again, and with a lot of influence from Whaam!. The punk spirit and the melodies of 1960s psychedelic pop – that was the concept for the label. But the first record we ever brought out – in August 1983 – was by the Legend and it was fucking awful. I played the drums and Jerry chanted over the top. At the time I was shocked people didn't think it was a work of genius. We were crucified. My favourite fanzine *Jamming!* described it as 'totally worthless'. It took me six months before I dared attempt another record.

We did twelve singles before I found the Jesus and Mary Chain and we had our first hit. The Pastels, the Jasmine Minks, Revolving Paint Dream and the Loft all followed.

Of these, I thought the Jasmine Minks had the best chance of making it. They were the first band we took seriously in that respect. They were from Aberdeen. It was fronted by Jim Shepherd and Adam Sanderson and they both wrote songs. There aren't many bigger characters in the history of the label than Hans Christian Sanderson, as we called him: he was an incredible teller of tall tales. They were all great people. We released their records till 1989. Majors were sniffing around them but it came to nothing. They should have made it, and maybe they did make it, maybe making it is the joy in making the records you wanted to make and getting to tour them around Britain and Europe. They seemed happy with that – they weren't desperate to be pop stars. They had a punk ethos in that respect. Hans Christian ended up coming to work for Creation, answering the phones for a year, in the days of Hackney madness.

Revolving Paint Dream was just another name for Andrew Innes. He played most of the instruments himself, recorded one of my songs actually, 'In the Afternoon'. On one version I sing, on another it's his girlfriend. I'd steal songs from him and put them out with Biff Bang Pow! There was no preciousness about songs – we'd swap them all the time, not care about who got credited. 'Someone Stole the Wheels' for Biff Bang Pow! was one of Andrew's for example.

The Loft were fronted by Pete Astor. When I first met Pete Astor I thought he was a pretentious prick. He's a well-spoken posh lad, and we were all rough Scottish lads. You make snap judgements that are not really fair, because he's a lovely lad. Back then, I thought he thought he was better than me. I began to realize the Loft could play really well watching them at the Living Room and signed them. Just before they split up they were getting a lot of radio play from Janice Long for 'Up the Hill and Down the Slope' – that was a *tune*. Perhaps if they'd stayed together they could have ridden that momentum and sold a few records. But it was inevitable they were going to split up: because Pete Astor absolutely hated two members of the band. They seemed oblivious to it. I wasn't: he wouldn't stop telling me *how much* he hated them. The drummer always seemed stoned, which may be why he didn't annoy anyone or notice that the rest of the band hated each other, and when Pete split the band he came with him and formed the Weather Prophets.

We put out the Pastels too, though that wasn't much fun. I've got nothing against Stephen Pastel – he's coming from a good place, still busy with his shop and events and his band these days. But he always had such romantic ideas and it was hard to socialize with him then. In those days all the bands would stop with me and Yvonne in our house on Beaconsfield Road when they were playing London gigs. The Pastels were the most awkward people I'd ever met. I don't know who they thought me and Yvonne were but they seemed terrified of us. We ended up dropping the band twice. Stephen had fallen out with Geoff Travis at Rough Trade and left them and we released the Pastels' single 'Something Going On', which got some nice reviews. Then we put out 'I Wonder Why' and his guitar player called me and accused me of owing him £100 that I was sure I didn't owe him. It was all a misunderstanding but for that we threw them off the label. I think Joe Foster re-signed them after that to do an album but I heard that before they'd even gone into record the songs they'd had an argument and they and Joe Foster had gone their separate ways.

We made a formal deal with Rough Trade, who had been distributing and selling my records since I pressed up the Laughing Apple singles. It was a straightforward P & D deal (production and distribution). I thought it was shit. They took 25 per cent off the top, despite all their bullshit about being a workers' cooperative. Although I respected Rough Trade for what Geoff Travis had pulled off with the Cartel, I hated the ethos there from day one. The offices and the warehouse were up in Blenheim Crescent, off Ladbroke Grove. It was the most unsafe warehouse in the world: anyone could have wandered in off the street and stolen as many records as they wanted. While I liked the music fans on the warehouse floor I thought the bosses were preachy and hypocritical. You'd find out that they'd been to Eton, or that their dad was a merchant banker, and yet there was all this 'up the workers' crap and big bowls of communal brown rice for everyone to eat. It was pretend poverty. I had actually *been* poor; I didn't *aspire* to be poor. As soon as I could, I was going to be a champagne and sirloin steak kind of guy and there was no way I'd be ashamed of it.

I was getting better and better at handling the music press. There wasn't anyone else out there with my self-belief. By 1985 I was being quoted in *Sounds*: 'I run the greatest record label in the world.' Deep down I knew it wasn't true, but I knew there was no way you could *become* the greatest record label in the world without people believing you were. I'd use any trick I could to rise out of indie obscurity and I knew no one else had the balls to make these kinds of claims.

The music press had always found me amusing. I was a breath of fresh air after all the worthy brown-rice-for-tea bollocks the likes of Rough Trade would spout to them. They loved the cocky persona, certainly at first. And when they decided I was too cocky, roughly 1988–1994, I barely did any interviews with them.

It was beginning to feel to me like maybe Creation could do something. But it was only a dream then. It took signing my first great rock and roll band in 1984 for me to really start to believe that I could make that dream a reality.

3: THE JESUS AND MARY CHAIN

The Jesus and Mary Chain were Bobby Gillespie's discovery. You can't underestimate Bobby's importance to Creation. He's been like a member of staff at times, an unofficial A&R man. When Bobby first heard the band they were called the Poppy Seeds and Alan Horne at Postcard had turned them down. Everyone had turned them down. It was doubtful whether anyone had even listened to the demos. William and Jim Reid sent them out from their bedroom in East Kilbride and never heard anything back. Do you know East Kilbride? One of the new towns that people from Glasgow were shifted to in the 1960s when it had run out of places for people to live. It looks like Milton Keynes, a drab place, no character. Though whether the band would have been any cheerier if they'd come from somewhere more lively is another matter.

The way Bobby had come across them was a mad chance thing. They'd sent a demo taped on the back of a Syd Barrett bootleg to a promoter in Glasgow called Nick Lowe. Nick Lowe didn't think much of them but heard the Syd Barrett bootleg and knew Bobby would like it. When Bobby listened to the Poppy Seeds songs on the other side, he absolutely loved them. The tape had Douglas's number on and Bobby called him up at his mum's house and made friends with the band, started planning joint shows with the Jesus and Mary Chain and Primal Scream. After a while Bobby told them about me, about the Living Room, the club I ran in London.

On Bobby's recommendation I booked them for their first London gig in June 1984 – we'd moved venue again to the Roebuck on Tottenham Court Road – and they came down.

I remember the moment they wandered into the pub. They were punk rockers from East Kilbride, six years too late. Scruffy clothes, hanging together. The Reid brothers, William and Jim, they looked like a punk version of the Bay City Rollers. What I mean is, they looked like they were punks by accident, like they could easily have been something else. Don't get me wrong, they looked cool, but there was something wrong about it too, a small-town version of a movement that was dead. Douglas Hart, the bassist, was the most striking. He looked like a film star. He was only seventeen. Wandering round in motorcycle boots, tall as fuck and skinny.

So we said hello and told them when they were on and they sat down and started sinking pints. Lots of pints.

The demo we'd heard of the band was okay. Buzzsaw guitar, it sounded like the Ramones' fourth album. So I wasn't expecting wonders but when they got on stage they were fucking unbelievable.

A lot of that was down to Joe Foster. He was in control of the PA, which meant no one was in control of the PA. He didn't know how to work a PA! He said he did but he just used to fiddle around with the knobs and eventually turn everything up to ten. William had never played a gig before and had no idea how to control his amplifier. When they started playing the feedback was outrageous. Howling. I'd never heard a noise that visceral. But buried beneath that were these great pop songs. The crowd was absolutely bewildered. The band looked like they were about to have a fight. They played 'Vegetable Man' and 'Somebody to Love' and 'Ambition'. The feedback kept screaming, getting louder and louder. William was crouched by his amp with his guitar. It was hard to know if he was trying to stop it or make it even louder. And at the end of it they all attacked the drummer! Kicked his drums over and started kicking him round the stage. I loved it! As soon as they'd finished I ran up and said, 'Can I sign you?'

At that time I didn't really think they'd sell loads of records but I did think we might get them as big as the Cramps, who they really loved.

They were all very shy at the beginning. I had different relationships with all of them. I became very good friends with Jim, the lead singer. He wasn't as temperamentally miserable as William, but he must have felt he had to be out of family duty. His brother William, well, William didn't really get me. We've never really got each other. We had such different personalities. William's probably a lovely guy if you can tune into him – I could never understand the controls on the television. He was the shyer one. He gave the impression of being really annoyed we were imposing on his life of being a hermit in East Kilbride. William is the better guitarist, better songwriter, the original talent – he'd write two songs for every one of Jim's. He was a genius guitar player, and I don't mean that lightly. No one else sounded like him. He wasn't good in the conventional technical sense; there was only one band in the world he could have played for, and luckily he did. Jim was more of a natural rock star than William. In his head he probably thought he was the Lizard King. Jim was the best rock star, the most charismatic; William the best musician. Neither one of them will want to see it like that! But the best bands normally have that rub, that personality clash, that combination of different skills.

Bobby wasn't originally the drummer. We drafted him in to replace Murray Dalglish. Murray's dad was advising him he should be getting £100 a gig! And they were playing for £50 a night in London to twelve people! No wonder they liked to assault him on stage. When he left we got Bobby in. Bobby knew exactly what kind of a drummer he'd be. One snare, one floor tom, playing a simple beat standing up like Maureen Tucker out of the Velvet Underground. He looked cool as fuck.

The first thing we had to do was record them but that was harder than it sounded. For one, the sound that I'd signed them for had been a complete fluke of circumstance caused by Joe Foster's ineptitude and a dodgy sound system. Their sound had been created then and there at that gig by an alchemy of fuck-ups and now the band needed persuading that *was* their sound. William and Jim weren't having it at all. We had to get Douglas Hart and Bobby Gillespie to

convince them. It had been pure alchemy at that first gig, the
feedback and their pop songs combining together in a way
that was absolutely magical.

We recorded 'Upside Down' in September 1984 at Alaska
Studios under a railway arch in Waterloo. It was a typical
Creation recording session of that time. The cheapest you
could book was for an overnighter, starting at midnight,
normally dead time for a studio. We didn't have a promising
lead-up to the session. Before they'd come to London they'd
played a gig in Glasgow where they'd been thrown off stage
in less than five minutes and down the stairs of the club with
their equipment following behind them. We'd had the band
playing gigs all week in London, one a night, and they were
going to be getting the coach home in the morning after a
week of heavy drinking and on-stage fighting during which
they'd managed to break their drum kit. So, in the studio, Joe
Foster had to break into the locker of another band's and
steal theirs. ('Why didn't you just ring us and ask?' they asked
him later. 'It was one in the morning,' he said. 'I didn't want
to be rude.')

Joe Foster was the producer of all the sessions back then.
But when we listened to the recording, it was too clean, too
weak. Joe mixed the feedback too low. So me and William
went in and turned the feedback right back up again, arguing
all the way with the engineer who kept telling us we couldn't
do what we were doing, that it would sound awful, that it
broke every rule in the book.

He said it would be impossible to master. We ignored him.

I thought the end result sounded amazing. As close as you could get to the live sound. The Reid brothers unsurprisingly thought it was shit to start off with. They thought everything was shit to start off with. If they won the lottery it would put them in a bad mood.

And then it was the first tour for the Jesus and Mary Chain, in Germany. It was November 1984 and it was them, us (Biff Bang Pow!) and the Jasmine Minks. We hired a bus and off we went. The plan was to swap the headliners every night but after a couple of gigs we all got together and agreed the Mary Chain had to be the headliners. It was awful to follow them; they were just killing it every night. It would have been like having a Mini headline over a jumbo jet.

I first started getting into drugs on that tour. Joe Foster was on the bus still thinking he was Bob Dylan so there was a lot of speed there. We'd be washing it down with Polish vodka.

When we got back from touring Europe there was a great review by Neil Taylor in the *NME*. The Jesus and Mary Chain were the new Sex Pistols, he said!

I met Jeff Barrett for the first time then. They were the days we all wore leather trousers. Ours were fitted but Jeff's were ahead of his time: he had the Happy Mondays look, in leather. Jeff had booked the Jesus and Mary Chain to play in Plymouth immediately after they'd got back from the European tour. We found it hard to get audiences for the band in London so I didn't really believe he'd get any people to show up. But he did a brilliant job promoting it. First he rang the local radio station to wind them up. 'They're blasphemous, you know, they incite riots. They're coming here!' That sort of thing. I was doing it myself too. The local newspaper got hold of it and the gig sold out. There were cops, reporters, and loads of teenagers. Yeah, I thought, I like your style. Jeff was a brilliant guy, an enthusiast, believed in what we doing in the same way we believed. 'What the fuck are you doing down here?' I asked him, and it wasn't long before I'd invited him to join the gang in London. He ended up working as our publicist, before he set up and had great success with Heavenly records.

'Upside Down' took a while to get going. Number 34 in the indie chart in its first week. Bobby had printed the sleeves for a thousand copies and sent them down from the printers he worked at in Glasgow. Then the press coverage of the gigs started and the radio play on John Peel's show every night and suddenly Joe Foster and I were banging speed up our noses in my house and desperately trying to fold sleeves for thousands of records. Bobby would have more sleeves printed and sent down; we'd fold them into little plastic bags with the records. Fifty thousand records in the end – it was incredible numbers. We couldn't fold the sleeves fast enough and as soon as we'd done a box someone at Rough Trade would whisk them away and onto a lorry.

I knew then that we weren't big enough to keep the Jesus and Mary Chain, but I was their manager as well as their label. (I don't remember asking to be their manager, I don't remember them asking me to be their manager, I just somehow *was* their manager.) I had a job to do and a commission to earn by finding them a good deal on a bigger label. Geoff Travis at Rough Trade had a new label, Blanco y Negro, which acted like an indie but was a puppet label of Warner Brothers. Whether he wore sandals or not, Travis was an A&R man for a major label. The meeting took place in Glasgow, in my mum and dad's front room. I've seen this written up as me trying to provoke Travis by insisting he travel to Scotland. But the band lived in Scotland then, it was convenient for them! The truth of the matter is, I hadn't been on a plane in a while and I fancied going on one to see them. It wasn't me being Malcolm McLaren, it was me being a kid who wanted to go on a plane! The meeting went okay. The brothers were typically upbeat, staring at my mum's carpet as if their own mum had just died, but Geoff said the right things. They saw him as a good halfway house: someone with indie values but the power of the corporation.

So he won the race and things started to move really quickly then. 'Upside Down' was still climbing, 12 to 6 on the indie chart at the start of December. Before Christmas they went into the studio to record a single with Stephen Street, who'd produced all the Smiths records. It was a disaster, and it wasn't the last disaster one of my bands would have with Stephen Street. He wanted to rub off the edges, turn down the feedback, record the instruments one by one. The Smiths were technically brilliant musicians; my bands were punk and relied more on energy than precision. We abandoned those recordings and went back to Alaska, this time with an engineer called Noel Thompson. He did what he was told, left things visceral and screaming, and the recording was just right.

The comparisons with the Sex Pistols had inspired me and now I was really playing up to being Malcolm McLaren, trying to generate cash from chaos. Douglas Hart had brought me a video down of *The Great Rock 'n' Roll Swindle* and I watched it over and over. (The band liked the idea of having their own McLaren, it wasn't just me.)

It was a way to justify my behaviour in some ways. I liked provoking people and the idea that you could sell records this way enticed me. We did things just to wind people up.

The last event of the year was 29 December, when the Mary Chain were booked to play the ICA. When they got on they were pissed as usual and the sound was awful, pure fucking white noise. There were loads of delays. The band didn't want to go on, and then when they did they were too pissed to operate their equipment. I remember someone shouting at me that he wanted his money back.

'How much did you pay?' I asked him.

'Three fifty.'

'You're a fucking mug then,' I shot back.

The crowd were all football chanting: 'What a bunch of wankers.' I hadn't ever seen a band create such an intense reaction from a crowd. I had no sympathy for people moaning about the lack of professionalism, the short sets. They were great gigs! The sound was awful, they didn't go on for long, everyone was pissed, they probably wouldn't even finish a song, but fucking hell, it was some spectacle. That's why more and more people were coming to see them. I loved the gigs. This one at the ICA was too small for the crowd's anger to feel threatening, but I knew now we were going to be heading for bigger and bigger venues.

We brought out our own Biff Bang Pow! album at the start of 1985, *Pass the Paintbrush, Honey*. People like to have a pop about me being in bands. Like I'm a failed musician. But at that stage it was never about us trying to become pop stars. We booked a cheap studio for five days and made the record for £500 with Joe Foster at the controls. It was the same with all the records we did. It might turn out shit or it might turn out okay. Most of all, it was fun – and actually most of them did turn out all right. It was a fun record to make. There's three guitarists on it: I play the chords, Dick plays the lead, and Joe plays the noise. There are some people out there who think we were better than we were, there are some people out there who thought we were awful – I think the truth is, we were okay. As indie bands from the mid-1980s go, we weren't that bad.

Being in a band was a laugh but it was running a label and managing bands that gave me the biggest sense of purpose in 1985. Creation had been a hobby up until then but now it was real. I may have lost the Jesus and Mary Chain from the label but I was managing the most exciting up and coming band in Britain. They were number 2 now in the indie chart. We did a publishing deal for £40,000 with Warners.

We were doing a tour starting at the end of January but the first date was cancelled the same day that the *Sun* ran a story in the morning claiming the band had smashed up Warners' offices and been thrown out by security. It was a massive exaggeration. What had actually happened was that Douglas was the most clumsy motherfucking seventeen-year-old alive and while walking down the corridor had leant against the wall and managed to knock off loads of gold and silver Simply Red discs. The venue in Sheffield read the story and cancelled the gig! Annoying, but great publicity, straight away. More gigs got cancelled. I began to quite like it when they did. They used to have to pay us the money, and then they claimed it off their insurance. And obviously, I'd be on the phone to the *NME* and *Melody Maker* and *Sounds*, stoking up the fires. We went to number one in the indie chart in February.

My time with the Jesus and Mary Chain was a good introduction to managing bands because it was such a hard way to start. They were just totally depressing people. Douglas was bullied by the brothers. The brothers would just moan the whole time and whatever they were moaning about would be my fault. Sometimes, it would *actually* be my fault, and that would be depressing too. (Thank god Bobby was there, with his evil sense of humour, to take the piss when it all got too much.) So I assumed that managing every band would be like that: miserable. Later, when I toured with the House of Love and Primal Scream, it was a great surprise to me. Then I was like, *wow*, rock and roll can be fun! That was a delicious surprise. You could even say it went to my head.

But a Mary Chain gig in those days was designed to give no fun to the crowd at all. An average set wasn't much longer than quarter of an hour. It would be a shambles. They didn't play their hit single! The interviews they did before their first big UK tour had them calling the audiences sheep, saying they were thick as shit. William's biggest ambition, he said, was 'to be murdered'! I'm surprised he's never achieved it. The crowds on that tour were furious. The tour finished in Brighton. A great crowd to start with. Cheering after every song. Seventeen minutes later, gig's over, and the crowd go mental. Jim Reid starts waving money at them and next thing Bobby's girlfriend was hit by a flying glass and we had to take her to hospital. A hospital that's full of members of the audience who've also been hit by flying glass. A girl started going berserk at us. 'What's wrong with you?' Her boyfriend had been cut up quite badly.

We were excited when the band was booked for *The Old Grey Whistle Test*. The producers were worried the band would turn up drunk if they put them on early and so they booked them for eleven in the morning. I took that as the challenge it was, woke them up at six and had them drinking by seven. And they were at their best: confrontational, screaming feedback, each of them looking every inch the rock and roll outlaw. They watched it that evening after sleeping off their hangovers.

Miserable bastards or not, the Jesus and Mary Chain were growing bigger and bigger. The second single, 'Never Understand', came out on 22 February 1985 and entered the national chart at 47. With all the hype I managed to book a well-paid gig at North London Poly in March. It would be their biggest yet.

The Reids moved down to London then. Bobby was still living in Glasgow so he found it hard to make practices. Who cared? Who needed them? They did without. The chaos of the gigs continued. The new Sex Pistols tag got mentioned more and more. The band had the spirit of punk and their gigs were dangerous and confrontational in a way that gigs hadn't been for years. As the gigs got bigger and bigger there were a lot more heckles from the audience. They'd go on late, drunk, shouting at them to shut up, that they hated them, that they were wankers. The sets stayed as short as they had always been.

When we turned up for the London Poly gig we realized they had got the fucking band's name wrong on all the posters. So I started daubing abuse all over the posters for a laugh. It was a horrible atmosphere that night. They'd oversold tickets massively, and loads of people were outside who couldn't get in. Bobby Gillespie being Bobby Gillespie decided to kick the firedoors open and let them in that way. Then the police got called.

We should have known what was going to happen eventually. When the band finally came on, Joe Foster was stood at the side of the stage, winding up the audience, mouthing abuse at them. He had to dive into the moshpit to rescue Jim when he got pulled in by one of the crowd. And then they did their usual and cut the gig after twenty minutes. You can see it on YouTube. When the crowd realize the band aren't coming back on, they start smashing the place up. There was an OAP in charge of security there and he got completely overrun.

Geoff Travis came out, got on the microphone and told the crowd to calm down. A bottle sailed through the air towards his head. He left as the crowd invaded the stage. They ripped the PA apart. Then the man who I'd hired the PA from nearly ripped me apart!

That was the first gig that got written up as being a riot. It was scary, yeah, but exhilarating too. It was 1985 and I was managing the only band in the country who could cause riots at their gigs!

I released a statement. 'The audience were not smashing up the hall, they were smashing up pop music. This is truly art as terrorism.'

Soon after that Jim got attacked and beaten up in the crowd of a Birthday Party gig. That was my fault (despite the fact that Jim used to scream 'you're all a bunch of cunts' at the audience when he was on stage).

The band's mood took a turn for the worse, which I would never have believed possible if I hadn't seen it with my own eyes. They'd drink after gigs for a bit then William would have a nervous breakdown and start smashing bottles. The first time I saw him do that was in Denmark. We were on the way back from our first trip to New York together, where the band had played two nights in a row in the Danceteria. We'd been brought over by a brilliant promoter, Ruth Polsky, who showed us an amazing time and was very keen on Douglas Hart. (She died a couple of years later, far too young, hit by a taxi while she was standing in a queue to get into the Limelight club.)

So we headed back via Denmark and Bobby and I were having such a great time but then William started losing it in the dressing room. Bottles of beer were sailing over our heads and smashing against the walls. Jim and Douglas made a dash for it. Bobby and I stuck around, laughing at him, encouraging him. Just gawping really. Voyeurs. I don't know what that says about me and Bob. There's always been a sick humour that connects us. All of Primal Scream pretty much have it, certainly Andrew and Throb. The black humour, sarcasm and sheer verbal nastiness when we get together is quite a test for anyone hanging around with us. The ones who can put up with it – well, you can imagine why Primal Scream have a reputation for a ferocious entourage. Our humour was very dark. All of us from Cathcart in Glasgow. Andrew was nasty, Bob and me were worse, and Throb was the worst of all – because while we were nasty, he was nasty and hilarious at the same time. Innes was funny too, but a bit kinder than the rest of us.

Once William had run out of things to smash and we had stopped laughing, he calmed down for the night.

I was having the time of my life back then handling the band's press. I made stuff up and fed it to the papers, who were happy to print whatever I said. 'Arrested on a bus for drugs!' 'Banned from Warners' offices for stealing Rob Dickins' wallet!' Rob Dickins was the chairman of Warners – he liked that last one.

I'd lowered their ages too: they were all teenagers in the press releases. (Jim was 24; William was 27.)

It would have been easy to forget about our other bands then, but we were still releasing records. The Loft were reaching the peak of their popularity with 'Up the Hill and Down the Slope' and in June we released the very first Primal Scream single, 'All Fall Down'. Primal Scream were always going to be on Creation; from the day I started the label I knew I wanted to put out whatever records Bobby would make. (He was still in both bands then: Jesus and Mary Chain and Primal Scream.) Bobby wrote the songs at that point with Jim Beattie, another friend from school, who played a twelve-string Rickenbacker that gave them their 1960s Byrds pop sound. The band had had a false start with a recording session in Edinburgh but we got them down to London and in Alaska studio with Joe Foster, and we recorded two songs quickly and put them out in June 1985. The press preferred the B-side 'It Happens', which they always did with the first few Primal Scream singles.

It wasn't a good time for me and Yvonne though. It was a terrible time actually. Yvonne was supportive of Creation to begin with but it wore her down. Having the Jesus and Mary Chain and Primal Scream constantly staying on their floor would drive any sane woman up the wall. But the bands had no money, what could I do? Yvonne would be stepping over them to leave the house early to go to work. I'd quit my job when the Living Room took off, borrowed a thousand pounds from the bank which made me eligible to sign on for Thatcher's Enterprise Allowance Scheme. Creation was full time for me now and we were already beginning to live incompatible lives. I realized that year that we shouldn't be married. Our lives didn't fit together any more. Yvonne hung out on the Creation scene too, and she was very well liked by everyone, but it must have been weird for her with me at the centre of it. She was so beautiful that for years I'd felt like I was punching above my weight, and the balance of power in the relationship had been in her favour. Now I was flying high with managing a top band, giving interviews to the music press and having everyone want to know me and be my friend. I loved being at the centre of things and what we wanted from each other was becoming more and more incompatible. We broke up for a few months in 1985. She finished her job and went back to Scotland.

We moved into our first office in August 1985, on Clerkenwell Road. The broom cupboard. It had room for one desk, Joe Foster on one side and me on the other. It was just the two of us – most of the time it was just the one of us. Joe Foster would wander in about four in the afternoon and start to do speed. Helpful. No, it actually was. He'd get a lot of work done after that.

Yvonne came back and we had another go at it. For that year, it was better. She came to work at Creation for a while.

A great thing about that office was that Factory Records'

London office was upstairs from ours. I made sure that I met Tony Wilson. Because I was managing the Jesus and Mary Chain he was quite interested in me. He had a respect for independent music, for people who did things on their own.

The Jesus and Mary Chain toured again in September. I remember bouncers beating Jim up in Edinburgh after he was sick on one of their shoes.

Then, at the Electric Ballroom in Camden, one of the few venues in London who would agree to put them on, we had the worst riot yet. This was serious violence, like Chelsea v. Millwall. I'm not sure if it wasn't literally Chelsea and Millwall hooligans who'd heard this was the place to have a fight. Because of their reputation, people were turning up on purpose now just to smash stuff up. It was a shock when the riot happened at North London Poly but when we saw the mood of the crowd here we realized it was going to be a shock if there wasn't a riot. The sound was awful and the band went off early, even earlier than usual. The audience invaded the stage straight away. There were glass bottles flying through the air. Lights smashing, raining broken glass. The bouncers couldn't cope and the crowd smashed up the amps, the PA. One of the security guards we'd employed got brained with a metal bar.

That's when we decided it had gone too far. The band weren't up for continuing the provocation in the way we'd been doing. If they'd wanted to continue, I would have, but I thought they did the right thing. It wasn't like we bottled it, like someone claimed in the *NME* – we turned back and got on the right road after having been on the wrong road for a while. When you had Jim being battered in clubs, people ending up in hospital – in the end, it was pop music, not war. And we realized we'd been naive thinking we could charge people a tenner in the mid-1980s for ten or fifteen minutes of songs. And when we realized that we had to change the nature of the gigs, the band had to focus more on the music.

We employed more security for the next tour. But security were as dangerous as the crowd. By the end of the tour they wanted to kill me. What was provoking them? Me! They hated me. Whenever I asked them to do something for me they'd normally threaten to kill me or one of the Reid brothers. I can't imagine what I did to annoy them.

I liked touring abroad most – going to Portugal, America – it was all good fun. For me, anyway. Yvonne was finding it difficult. She wanted me to be home, with a regular job, a normal guy. I was out with the Mary Chain trying to create rock and roll history, as crazy as that sounds. I was thriving on the attention I was getting. It's hard for it not to go to your head.

I gave Jeff Barrett his first job for Creation as the manager of the Jesus and Mary Chain's next tour of Germany. That one tour was enough for him. I asked him for the tour accounts afterwards and he dug into his jeans pockets and pulled out this enormous ball of crumpled paper made out of receipts and handed it to me. I'd thought that *I* was unprofessional. Tour management and Jeff Barrett parted ways forever that day. We hired him as Creation's publicist instead.

In October that year the Jesus and Mary Chain recorded 'Just Like Honey'. We dropped the intensity of the feedback from this record, aiming to let the pop melodies come through more. Then their first album *Psychocandy* came out in November. It was everything I hoped it would be. I knew they were going to get bigger and bigger.

Joe Foster went mad pretty early. We'd released a couple of his singles that year under his alias Slaughter Joe. I basically wrote the first one, 'I'll Follow You Down', though he'll claim it as his own. Same for 'She's So Out of Touch', which he definitely did claim as his own and registered with a publishing company. So he claimed all the royalties for it being used on the Creation documentary. Which I thought was quite funny, if inaccurate.

By the end of 1985 the amount of speed he was doing had sent Joe crazy, paranoid, psychotic. He wasn't the only one on occasions. We were on another tour in Germany and had both taken so much. Joe was annoying me so badly that I tried to hit him over the head with a bottle. Bobby Gillespie caught my arm when it was about a foot away from his head. Joe and I were always fighting on that tour. I had to whack him a few times, though that was the only time I tried to do it with a bottle.

But if I was getting bad, then Joe always outdid me. I lost it on drink and drugs by about 1994. Joe was the precocious one – he had lost it by the end of 1985. I was in Canada when I got the call from Yvonne.

'Joe Foster has to go, Alan.'

'What's he done now?'

'He's punched out the head of Rough Trade distribution.'

'*Oh.*' I thought for a minute. 'He probably *has* to.' That was unacceptable, even by my venomous standards. I told him then to take a break. I didn't know the break was going to be seven years. We needed the break by then, though I don't want to underplay how important he'd been to Creation in those early years. He'd been the one in the studio, getting our records done quickly, capturing the energy of the bands so that the low budgets (£150, a lot of the time) of the sessions didn't matter. He got great results. But he'd also fall out with band members at the drop of a hat. By the time we temporarily parted ways at the end of 1985, the bands were getting confident enough to want to control their own recording sessions, and so he wasn't missed as much as he would have been in the beginning.

I'll save the story of Joe's return to Creation for later. Most people wouldn't have employed Joe then, or later. I think I'm one of only a few people who can deal with his madness. Well, some people think I'm madder than Joe – which is scary. I hope to god they're wrong.

4: SACKED

Psychocandy was out now in America after we toured it in late December. The people there said we shouldn't tour then because all the students would be on holiday. I knew from the momentum we had that we'd sell out, that this wasn't just a band for students, and I was right. Americans got the band straight away. Full crowds everywhere. We flew back on Christmas Day.

The Jesus and Mary Chain had some New Year resolutions for 1986. They wanted to be taken seriously. They were sick of the violence, of the amateurism. The songs were getting better and better. They were learning how to play their instruments properly. They consented to soundchecks. Sets were beginning to clock in at almost forty minutes as their first tour of the year started in January.

At the start of 1986 Bobby Gillespie decided to leave the band to focus on Primal Scream. I admired him a lot for doing that – it took some courage to leave a band having that kind of success – and for a band who wouldn't experience success for many more years. He didn't take any of the advance offered to the band when they signed to Blanco y Negro.

Creation had started to get it in the neck from the music

press. At the end of 1985 we'd lost the Pastels and the Membranes, who had a certain amount of indie credibility. It wasn't a financial decision. We weren't capable of that at the time. It came down to a coin toss with the Membranes and Pastels as to who would headline on a night we were all playing. Joe won, but they claimed he'd cheated. There was an argument and the Pastels were dropped, and then the Membranes left out of solidarity. Up the workers again. So we were seen as the bad guys for that. (It was one of Joe's final acts for Creation in the 1980s.) But we weren't interested in pleasing the indie purists – the Jesus and Mary Chain had shown me that if Creation combined my favourite punk and psychedelic influences it would be a rock and roll label first and foremost.

In those days, rock and roll was a dirty word for some journalists. They didn't like the leather trousers Primal Scream and Pete Astor and me were wearing. How dare they play a guitar solo. That sort of bollocks. You weren't supposed to reference anything before 1976. There was no point trying to please those cunts. It was more fun to annoy them.

The whole indie thing wasn't a philosophical choice. We recorded on a budget because that's what we had to work with, and we were lucky that it suited a lot of our bands. But if recording on a budget was fine for my band – we weren't doing it to smash the charts open – I knew that it wasn't enough for Primal Scream or the Weather Prophets if we had real commercial ambition for them. If they wanted to move beyond the indie charts I knew we needed more money for studio time, for experienced producers.

Primal Scream's second single came out in April 1986. 'Crystal Crescent', the A-side, was backed with 'Velocity Girl' on the B. Bobby had wanted to have another go at recording the A-side but there wasn't the money available for a second go. The B-side in fact grew much more popular than the A-side when the *NME* included it as the opening track on their *C86* tape. This was a compilation of jangly indie pop, which launched the supposed C86 scene and found the band a lot of fans they'd quickly alienate with their next album. The single climbed up the indie chart and when they came back to London, this time we filled the University of London Union.

Running the label and managing the Mary Chain was becoming exhausting. We were stepping up the releases. I'd just signed Felt. This was a real coup for Creation at the time. I'd been a fan of the records they'd put out with Cherry Red. I was amazed we could get Lawrence – who would never tell anyone his surname – to come to Creation. Felt were number one in the indie chart with the single 'Primitive Painters'; he was a pop star to us. We didn't chase him at all – Lawrence just called up and told me he wanted to sign with us. He was the singer and wrote all the songs for Felt. He wanted to be on a cool label and we had one of the coolest reputations at the time. The first album Lawrence gave me was insane. There was no singing on it at all. Loads of brilliant organ by Martin Duffy, who later joined Primal Scream. It was called, get this, *Let the Snakes Crinkle*

Their Heads to Death. With Lawrence I thought you had to let him do what he was going to do. He was very creative.

So we were really excited about Felt and we also had 'Almost Prayed' about to come out by the Weather Prophets, a pure pop single we had high hopes for.

That's when my legs gave up on me. I just couldn't walk on them any more. It turned out I was seriously ill, with sarcoidosis. I was very unlucky; about one person in every ten thousand gets it and it was incredibly painful. It took me six months to recover, so from then on I had to take a less hands-on role in the day-to-day management of the Jesus and Mary Chain. I think it was me being away that gave them the courage to do what they next did.

Just when I was getting better I went to see Felt in a club on Portobello Road. Warners were quite interested in signing him at this stage. Lawrence took an acid tab that Douglas Hart had given him and had a freak-out right on stage, demanding that everyone stop looking at him! Then he legged it off stage. I tried to calm him down, persuade him back on. And he totally blew it, came back out, freaked out, told the crowd to ask for their money back and ran away again. It was quite clear to me then that Lawrence belonged on an indie label.

In May 1986 the Jesus and Mary Chain headlined Hammersmith Palais. We were bricking it beforehand. It was the first London gig since the Electric Ballroom rampage. It went well. They toned down the feedback, which created less sound problems, though I thought it also made the gig less visceral, less atmospheric, less frightening.

Warners had a lot invested in getting the next single right. 'Some Candy Talking' was an expensive recording, backed with an expensive video. The band's playing was still a bit limited. Dick Green had had to play Douglas Hart's bassline on the single. None of that mattered. When it was released in July it entered the charts at number 20 and by August had gone to 13. It was the first chart hit for a band of mine and I remember feeling so proud of it.

Then Radio 1 banned it from the breakfast show – 'Candy' was a reference to drugs apparently. Everything's a reference to drugs if you want it to be. I got ready to make a fuss about the establishment trying to censor the music the kids wanted to hear.

But no – I wasn't allowed to. The band and Geoff Travis were sick of controversy. Just ignore it, I was told. There was to be no more provocation.

And then in September I was called in for a meeting in the usual venue, a Wendy's burger bar on Oxford Street. It was William who told me the news. I was fired.

It was cruel, but I wasn't really surprised. I knew William and I didn't understand each other. Geoff Travis had probably shown them when I was ill that they could do without me. I don't know whether he ever suggested as much to them – he certainly wouldn't have missed me. We never going to be great mates, me and Geoff: he's a rich kid and I'm the son of a panel-beater. But I absolutely loved Jim Reid though, and thought he loved me, and that made being sacked hurt terribly. They said I was unprofessional. Probably right! But what the fuck did that matter? At this time they were in the Top 10, these depressives from East Kilbride! Who looked like they'd fallen out of an Oxfam shop! So I wasn't doing that bad a job. They'd been on the dole for five years before I signed them. I'd made them believe they were as big as the Sex Pistols, because *I* believed that myself. *I* believed they were the revolution and with me *they* believed they were the revolution. So they sacked me. And after that, though they may have had their business taken care of more professionally, I think a lot of their self-belief walked out the door alongside me.

I had a moment, I admit it, when I thought, what's the point in going on with the label? I was absolutely gutted. I didn't know how I was going to pay the bills, and I got paranoid wondering who else was going to betray me.

Primal Scream were important to me then. I tried to imagine them abandoning me and I couldn't. I knew Bobby would never let me down. So I kept going when I wanted to give up by holding on to my defiance. I decided then and there that I would make Primal Scream into stars.

At the same time I wanted to know what I would have to do to get to a stage when I would have been able to keep the Mary Chain at Creation and never have had to involve Geoff Travis. How I could do what he had done and get the major labels to work for me?

5: ELEVATION

The Jesus and Mary Chain may have sacked me, but my reputation had grown after I had found them and managed them into the big time. I had a profile now and the music press loved me. I thought I could use my success to get me into a partnership with a major label. I picked myself up and decided to try again. After all, I'd only just turned twenty-six.

The first thing I did was to sign a new band, a band who would completely transform my fortunes again. I'll come to them in the next chapter. First I started a new record label with backing from a major.

It was Rob Dickins who had brought Geoff Travis to Warners. I'd always liked him. He'd seen the appeal of the Jesus and Mary Chain straight away and supported Geoff Travis in his bid to sign them. He didn't mind when I made stuff up to the press about the Reid brothers nicking his wallet and trashing his offices. He's been unpopular with the Mary Chain, Echo & the Bunnymen, with other bands. But do you know what? He just told the truth. I don't think there's anything wrong with a guy who just says *I like it* or *I don't like it*. In my book that's all you can ask for from a record company: the truth.

Interest in Pete Astor's new band the Weather Prophets had been building steadily. I was managing them as well as putting out their records. Their first single 'Almost Prayed' was brilliant pop, and Dickins came to me and offered a £75,000 advance to sign them to Warner Brothers. I had a better idea – he could fund me to start an offshoot label of Creation that was distributed by Warners. It would be for the bands on Creation with the biggest potential once they were ready to make a jump to the top division. Rob Dickins liked the idea and I managed to negotiate a deal for Primal Scream too, getting him up to £55,000. It meant the bands could get a wage, spend more on recording. But it also meant they'd no longer be eligible for the indie charts and would have to make it on a less forgiving stage. I called the label Elevation, another psychedelic name to go alongside Creation.

I'd tried to get Felt a deal too but what they offered was minuscule, and I knew Lawrence would be better keeping his independence. This was at the same time Creation released their *Forever Breathes the Lonely Word*, one of the best records I think we ever did, Creation's equivalent to the Smiths' *The Queen is Dead* or *Low-Life* by New Order. It was too muted to be commercial, too art to go pop, too pop to go art – but it was a perfect combination of all my influences, all that I loved about music at the time.

Lawrence was a minor-scale indie celebrity. He thought he wanted to be famous, but at the same time he wanted to stay in the underground. They were incompatible urges he never reconciled, and so he was never sure of himself. Danny

Kelly loved him at the *NME*. He was famous for his clean living, for having this meticulously hoovered house in Birmingham, hovering by the bathroom when journalists came to interview him in case they had the cheek to try to shit in his toilet.

Warners just didn't want him enough – he'd have sunk without a trace there. There was an advantage to being on an indie label – he wouldn't alienate his core fans and he'd continue to qualify for the indie charts and get noticed that way.

The Weather Prophets went straight into the studio with Lenny Kaye – their first major label recording session. They were used to recording all the instruments at the same time, playing live in the studio essentially. But Kaye stripped it down to one track at a time, standard procedure on the majors. You get a cleaner sound this way, but if you're not very careful you lose the energy.

They'd finished the record by the end of the year and Warners were really happy with it. Graham Carpenter, who was the guy at Warners I worked directly with, loved the record. The signs were great. Pete called it *Mayflower* and they loved the title. There was something in the back of my mind though telling me the record wasn't quite right. I was too inexperienced then to put my finger on it instantly, and so I joined in with the optimism.

Recording the first Primal Scream album was a much harder experience. Warners were really keen on Stephen Street, though

I should have known from his experience with the Mary Chain that he wasn't temperamentally suited for working with bands who weren't technically great musicians. Punk had shown the world you didn't need to be technically great musicians to have great musical ideas and record great songs – but not everyone had got the message. We booked Rockfield studios in Monmouth and the whole of the Scream decamped to the Welsh countryside, not so far from where I live now. Street was a hotshot producer at the time; he'd just produced *The Queen is Dead* by the Smiths. But the Smiths were experienced musicians, and Street couldn't get past the fact that Primal Scream's drummer Tam McGurk couldn't keep time. Street also insisted on recording one track at a time, the way you recorded session musicians. He was trying to enforce early starts, early to bed too: it's hilarious he tried that with the Scream. You should have seen the way they lived in Glasgow.

Andrew Innes wasn't in the band at the start of that recording, though he was by the end. When the sessions began, the line-up was Bobby on vocals, Jim Beattie on twelve-string guitar, Tam the drummer and Throb was then the bassist so we had another rhythm guitarist in Stuart May. He wasn't very good. No one was *very* good then. Things got ugly when they came in one morning and Stephen Street played them a guitar part he'd written and recorded for the song they were working on. Jim Beattie took the tape and wiped it, told him to go and record his own LP if that was what he wanted. After that, they were very wary of each other. A horrible atmosphere.

Graham Carpenter drove us there for the first time three weeks into the recordings. The recordings were shit. Street was hung up on recording one song – 'I Love You' – over and over. The band were complaining straight away. I was tempted to sack Street. But I thought I should give them a chance to work it out on their own and Graham drove us back to London.

Street called me back soon afterwards. The band were losing it. The drummer was holding everything up with his inability to keep time, and the band were beginning to take it out on him. It was obvious to everyone that Street didn't have enough belief in the band's musicianship. Bobby was having a particularly bad time with the vocals. I assumed it was because although Bobby was a natural singer he had no confidence then – it took him a decade to really get comfortable with his voice. He wanted to record it one word at a time.

I drove up with Yvonne. When we got there at first it seemed like Street was exaggerating. The band seemed fine to me. But as the day wore on they grew more and more angry. That night Bobby, Jim and Throb locked themselves in the room next to where Yvonne and I were trying to sleep and played fucking Burundi drums until seven in the morning, at which point we drove off. That was their way of letting me know they were unhappy.

I thought it would be a good idea to bring Andrew Innes in. A musician who knew what he was doing, who Bobby knew already and would trust. For a while that seemed to help, not least because he immediately realized why Bobby was having problems. The keys were all based around Jim Beattie's twelve-string guitar riffs. The band hadn't noticed any problem live, but when they tried to record they were impossible for Bobby to sing to. Andrew changed the keys; problem solved. Andrew's a great musician and a kindred spirit. From there on in, he was in the band.

Then I got another call from Street. Bobby had vandalized the studio. Fucking hell, so off I go again to Monmouth, with Yvonne again and this time with Christine, Andrew's girlfriend. The girls thought they'd combine the trip with an outing so they headed off on a pony trek.

The idea that some people were going to have some fun during the recording seemed to provoke the band. It was when we arrived that they really lost it. Bobby, Jim and Throb barricaded themselves in one of the cottages with mattresses and threatened to pour a bucket of boiling water over anyone who tried to get in. It was all getting a bit medieval now. I'd forgotten to bring any siege enginery so I had little choice but to leave them to it. They never left the cottage again, until one morning, five days before Christmas, they watched Stephen Street take the master tapes, load them into his car and drive away. It was the very last they saw of him. It was going to be interesting to see if the band would have the balls to come back from this.

We needed to do something so we sacked the drummer. There was only one song that was useable from weeks of recording.

We'd used three-quarters of the advance on that one song! I now had to tell Rob Dickins that we were scrapping the album and starting again. He was underwhelmed by the recordings he'd heard, but he hadn't lost faith yet. I don't remember being particularly stressed about it, except it meant that the Primals were going to be staying on my floor a lot more when they came to London, and that really wasn't going to help my relationship with Yvonne. For about three years Primal Scream and the Jesus and Mary Chain were regularly sleeping in my living room. I think that would be enough to break any marriage up.

We went into the studio again to record a single, 'Imperial', this time with Clive Langer. First thing he did was hire a session drummer, the guy from Prefab Sprout, and things went a bit more smoothly, though by the end of the session Langer was drinking a lot of vodka.

Meanwhile, the money situation at Creation was typically desperate and Yvonne wasn't helping. She was wandering into the office at 4 p.m. going, 'I've just been down to Boots and spent forty quid on the credit card.' Things were getting worse and worse between us. I'd be trying to make her see how desperate things were and she'd just think I was trying to boss her around. We weren't happy together in the office or at home. It had become a toxic relationship and I think we both knew in 1987 that we should have gone through with the split in 1985, when Yvonne had gone back to Glasgow for a while. We'd been together now for eight years, and we'd completely changed. We made the mistake of trying to carry on when deep down we knew we couldn't. We were both too scared to split up. I was twenty-seven, she was twenty-five. I was pretty unworldly; she was the only girlfriend I'd ever had. And I understand why she didn't want to give up on a marriage at the age of twenty-five. There was no winner in this situation. I'm sorry for any hurt I caused her because I really did love her. But we'd grown too far away from each other.

It was during my time at Elevation that I met Bill Drummond, later of the KLF. With Dave Balfe (who later set up Food and released Blur's records) he'd managed the Teardrop Explodes and Echo & the Bunnymen. Now Rob Dickins had offered him an A&R job in Warners.

Neither of us belonged there, really. He loved the Mary Chain but was working with Stock, Aitken and Waterman on trying to make massive-selling chart pop. And his bands just didn't work out. When he quit, still in his early thirties, he decided to record his own solo album and asked me if I'd put it out on Creation. He was disgusted with the industry. He wanted to say goodbye to it with an album that he'd write in five days and record in five days and thought I was the only one who'd be mad enough to put it out. Even so, I think he was surprised when I agreed without having listened to a note. I just thought the guy was probably a genius and he was offering to cover the cost of recording himself. There was nothing to lose, I thought. He delivered me a country folk album with him singing on it in a thick Scottish accent. We put it out, it got great reviews, sold fuck all, but I was proud of that album.

With money going from bad to worse, I needed to try something new at Creation and I came up with the idea of Baby Amphetamine. The charts were full of formulaic girl-group pop – I thought we could play this game and subvert it at the same time. I explained my idea to Nick Currie, otherwise known as Momus, who we'd just signed, and he helped me develop it. Then we decided to go and find our girl group in the Virgin megastore on Oxford Street.

We picked the three best-looking girls and I bought them all leather jackets. I wrote the lyrics as a rap and we went in and recorded them over a hip hop beat. 'Chernobyl Baby (Who Needs the Government)' – a great title but not the best song in the world, I'll admit.

Now I had the band and a single I needed to put them on the cover of the *NME*. Incredibly, Danny Kelly went for it. And then the girls started to slag me off in the interview! Which was fine, that was the plan. It went wrong when they decided they were real artists. They might have been right, they might have been wrong: it wasn't the point.

There was never another single. Everyone hated Baby Amphetamine except for Bill Drummond who started dancing around and punching the air when I told him about it. Two months later he told me he'd formed a new band, the Justified Ancients of Mu Mu, and he was going to get in the Top 10 sampling Abba records. Abba's lawyers put a stop to that. But it didn't keep him down for long . . .

We released quite a few records by Momus. He talked a good game. One of my biggest regrets from the Creation days was from that period. Primal Scream were on tour with him. It was before the wall had come down in Berlin and there was a corridor you could stop off in between the East and West, where you could buy Polish vodka. The Scream had gone to get themselves some of that good stuff, with Momus in the van. Bobby rang me up.

'Alan, can we leave Momus in No Man's Land?' He'd been driving them nuts on the bus. They couldn't stand him.

'Please don't do that,' I said.

'Alan, please, can we just leave him here?' Bobby asked again. He was surprised: he thought I would have been up for the idea. He really wanted to. I don't know why I wasn't more supportive. It could have been amazing, he could have been locked up for a couple of years . . .

It was so much fun hanging out with Primal Scream in those days (if you weren't Momus). They just drugged and partied their way around Britain and Europe. All you had to do was get on the bus, and then everything was great. If nothing else, they'd learned the first rule of rock and roll: have fun!

The Weather Prophets' debut album *Mayflower* came out in April 1987: a busy month for Warners. They were putting out new records by Prince, Fleetwood Mac and Simply Red, all at the height of their fame. You can't blame *Mayflower*'s failure purely on this, but it definitely didn't help.

It only charted at 67. This would have been great on Creation but it wasn't nearly enough for Rob Dickins to be interested in, and of course, it was no longer eligible for the indie charts and so there'd be no word of mouth that way.

It smashed me for six. Everyone had been so bullish, and me more than anyone. There was a whole world between what I thought would happen and what actually did. Now I can hear immediately that it was produced terribly, that the sound was too flat. But at that time I didn't have enough experience to know instantly what was wrong with it. By the time we got to *Screamadelica*, *Loveless*, *Definitely Maybe*, I could spot what was wrong, and what was right, much more easily.

The band had started to hate the album too – they thought it was too sterile. The major-label method of recording albums in the 1980s was more suitable to high-gloss pop than to real rock and roll – and it was in the latter direction that Pete Astor had been trying to take the band.

At the same time the Jesus and Mary Chain flew straight into the Top 10 with their next single, 'April Skies'. No comment necessary. And it was about then that I stopped talking to the music press. People had stopped taking Creation's music seriously after all my antagonistic statements about the Jesus and Mary Chain, and I wanted attention to be focused on our music now. I'd been overwhelming that with my personality.

With the Weather Prophets performing so badly, Elevation's future was in the hands of Primal Scream. We went into the Greenhouse studio with Mayo Thompson and Pat Collier at the controls. I think Bobby was still trying to record one word at a time, but the band hit it off with Mayo Thompson and we finished the recording.

'Gentle Tuesday' came out as the first single in June. It didn't even reach the Top 75, and nor did 'Imperial' when we put that out in September. Though Warners didn't give up immediately on Elevation they lost interest in Primal Scream straight away. They offered another £70,000 to record another Weather Prophets album, but they wanted control over the producer and Pete Astor said he wanted to do it himself.

That was that: they instantly dropped the band.

The first Primal Scream album *Sonic Flower Groove* came out in September 1987. Number 61. Warners weren't interested, did nothing to promote it. Graham Carpenter left the company and was replaced by a guy called Malcolm Dunbar. He told me Primal Scream would never make it. I was fucking furious and if I'd believed him, they might never have made it. Luckily I ignored him. Well, I did more than ignore him – I told him exactly where to go. Now I can see he wasn't such a bad guy, but at the time I couldn't see past my rage. He was surprised at how aggressive I was to him. He caught two years of my frustration with major labels straight in the mouth. When I called him a cunt, I was really calling Warners a cunt. I was probably trying to provoke him into hitting me so I could hit him back. I knew I was going to have to go but there was no way I was going to go in a rational way. I wasn't rational in those days. But there was no glory in it for me, that was for sure.

Then there was the crunch meeting with Rob Dickins. Who've you got for me next year, Alan? At the time, all I had was Momus. When that was all I could offer him, he pulled the plug and that was the end of Elevation.

I won't pretend I wasn't shattered by how badly things had gone. Tony Wilson was a big help then – this was when we really bonded. He took me to one side and gave me a huge fatherly talk for about two hours. Not about my personal life, which was falling to bits; just about the label. He told me to forget about the majors and gave his biggest band New Order as an example. 'You have to hang on to your bands,' he was telling me. 'If you make Creation big enough, then the majors can't fuck with you.' I'll always remember that chat and it's why Factory were the only label I really felt an affinity with. I'd go in to see Geoff Travis at Rough Trade and he'd accuse me of ripping off bands I'd never heard of. 'I see what you've done with the Loft,' he'd say, 'ripping off the Raspberries.' Pete Astor and I had no idea who the Raspberries were! With Geoff I always got a sense of rivalry, a feeling that he was trying to get one up on me. Tony never seemed to be threatened by Creation – he saw us as on the same side. Geoff talked to me like a schoolteacher whereas when Tony spoke to me it was like listening to a naughty big brother.

I was glad of Tony's friendship then because I wasn't just

losing Elevation and the Jesus and Mary Chain, I was losing my wife and my house. Yvonne and I couldn't share the same space any more. In the end it was she who suggested it first: let's break up for good. When I said yes, she said, I didn't mean it. Too late: it was out there and it couldn't be taken back. It was obviously what needed to happen, we just didn't want to face it. We broke up that September and I moved out. Within the space of a year it felt like I'd lost everything: my big band, my new label, and now my home and my wife. It was inevitable but it was still shattering.

I went off the rails that winter. We went on a Biff Bang Pow! tour with Felt in Germany. I drank a bottle of vodka a day. I blacked out. People told me I'd chased a promoter around a venue until he had to lock himself in an office. I put my foot through dressing-room walls.

And I moved to Brighton. I needed to put some distance between me and Yvonne. The singer in Blow Up – one of our bands – found me a room there with two old gay guys. And there I was, miles away from the office, and not really bothered at all about what was going on there.

6: HOUSE OF LOVE

House of Love became Creation's saviour over 1987 and 1988, though I would never have expected it when I first heard them. Guy Chadwick had been sending us demos for a while and Dick Green had rejected the first one. Jeff Barrett refused to put them on at his club night. In fact, my colleagues never ever liked them, even when they were single-handedly propping up the business. I hadn't thought much of House of Love either at first, but then I noticed that Yvonne kept playing one of their songs, 'Shine On'. I began to see they had quite a bit of potential, that their songs were really catchy, so I went to see the band play at the start of 1987. I told it to Chadwick straight afterwards: your songs are too long, too fiddly, you don't look right, buy some leather jackets, go away and work on everything and then come back and we'll do a single and that single will be 'Shine On'.

Guy Chadwick actually seemed to like being talked to in this way. He was ruthlessly ambitious and I guess he saw the same quality in me. He wasn't precious about his art – he wanted to be massive, as big as U2, and so despite coming from completely different worlds we became a good partnership.

They were an unusual band for Creation. Chadwick, the leader, was an aristocrat, the son of a major, high up in the army. He'd been in bands before, and had publishing deals, and I found out later he'd pretended to us all that he was younger than he was. Well, I'd played that trick before with the Mary Chain. His band were much younger than him. He'd picked them up from squats in Camberwell. There was Terry Bickers, a genius guitar player, Chris Groothuizen, a good bass player, good-looking, a bit of a space cadet, and Pete Evans on drums. Bickers and Chadwick were the strangest match. Chadwick – this was what I liked most about him – wanted to be Bono. Bickers, on the other hand, hadn't just lived in a squat out of necessity – he'd believed in it, you know, as a philosophy, in communal living, opting out of the world of money. He was a hippy, a punk hippy, but still a hippy at heart.

Chadwick wrote all the music – he'd had songs saved for years for this – and all of Bickers' guitar lines, but live you could still see what a great player Bickers was. Seeing them on stage was a different proposition to listening to them on record, when Bickers would turn everything to ten and really rock out, guitar hero stuff.

Their rise was slow. We put out a couple of singles that didn't work. But meanwhile, they'd become an amazing live act after touring Europe with Echo & the Bunnymen. Jeff Barrett put them on in the end in Camden and the crowd were loving it. You could sense something was brewing, that they had momentum.

I used money from my own bank account to fund the recording of their first album. I'd given them a budget of £4,000 to start with, but they were sounding like a big-stadium band and they needed more money to get what they were after. So I gambled and threw everything I had left at it.

Just before Christmas 1987 I was in London at a Primal Scream gig – they were supporting New Order at Wembley – when I got really ill with food poisoning. Yvonne was there and took pity on me and invited me back to the house so I wouldn't have to travel back to Brighton. We were lonely and had a brief fling on the third night, flirting with the idea of getting back together. It was a tough time. My heart was breaking. I felt like such a failure. It was a very short reunion and ended as soon as it started but it had serious consequences. In January I had a call from Yvonne. 'Alan, I've got something to tell you.'

See, when a woman says, 'I've got something to tell you,' it's going to be one of two things: *You're dumped* or *I'm pregnant*.

She was pregnant and she wanted to have the baby. I understand why now. We decided we'd have one last go at staying together for the baby's sake. I came back for a week. It lasted until she said this memorable line to me: 'You can't afford to divorce me.' Whenever someone tells me I've got no option but to do something is when I'm at my absolute worst. I pretty much always do the opposite. So I walked out the door and never came back.

That's Daniel, my son, who I'm talking about. Yvonne remarried in 1991 and her husband adopted him and so we don't know each other well, and that's a genuine regret. When he was eight I got back in touch with Yvonne, and contributed financially, but she thought it would unsettle him if I came into his life again at that time. We met when he was sixteen and, though we both tried, we didn't know each other and it didn't work out. I wish him the best of luck with his future and I'll always be sorry I wasn't able to be around for him when he grew up.

Just after I'd found out Yvonne was pregnant we went on the final Biff Bang Pow! tour in France, with Momus this time. It was shit. We were playing in shoeboxes to almost nobody. I was arguing again with promoters: just incredibly, furiously angry with the world. We drank and drank and drank and by the time we'd done ten nights we abandoned it. It wasn't fun any more. In the past touring had been an escape, a chance for me to live like the bands in a way I couldn't back home with Yvonne. There was nothing stopping me now and what I found I craved was the comfort of my own bed. I couldn't afford to waste time like this any more – if I wanted success in the music industry I needed to focus on the record company now. And that was the last time I went on tour as a member of a band.

Back in Brighton I made a discovery that would change Creation for ever: ecstasy. I'd started hearing about this new drug and was curious. I found a guy who could sell me six and phoned a girl I fancied and asked her to come and take them with me. It was nothing about the clubs then. We just sat on a hill.

We did one each and I felt this incredible empathy for her. I did another, and for some reason we moved to a burger bar. So I remember sitting with a coffee about six or seven at night and saying, 'I think I've fallen in love with you,' and she was the same, 'I think I've fallen in love with *you*.'

And then I did one a few weeks later with Ed Ball, and it was the same – I'd fallen in *love* with Ed Ball – and it was then I realized how powerful the drug was.

Ed Ball was in many ways the soul of Creation Records, and it was around then he came to work for us. I met him in 1983 when he was in the Television Personalities. I had the first album he'd recorded as The Times, *Pop Goes Art!*, and I loved it. Ed was one of the most enthusiastic guys I ever met, and he came to be the engine room of belief in the idea of Creation, just as much as me. He really believed in our purpose (and so, unfortunately, he was very upset when it finished). We did so many records with him, in so many different genres. He was so talented: he made some of the most amazing acid house records as Love Corporation, then the next minute he'd be doing a death metal record with the guy from Extreme Noise Terror. But to begin with, his involvement was helping out in the office. He used to come down to Brighton to see me after everyone else had written me off, and try to convince me that there was work we needed to do, that Creation was

Aged eight months, with my mum Barbara, in May 1964.

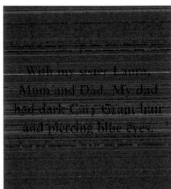

With my sister Laura, Mum and Dad. My dad had dark Cary Grant hair and piercing blue eyes.

Posing happily for the camera. I'm five and Laura is three.

In Bobby Gillespie's bedroom, 1980. Bobby's my oldest and best friend.

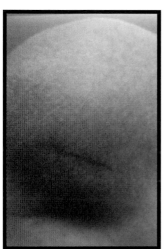

As The Laughing Apple, Andrew Innes and I put out singles through Mayking Records. Bobby designed and printed the sleeves.

The back of my head today, complete with scar.

Yvonne and me on our wedding day, December 1984 with Mum and Dad.

Above: One of the bands that changed my life: Television Personalities in 1981. From left to right: Dan Treacy, Ed Ball and Mark Sheppard.

Right: Communication Blur! 1983, the fanzine through which Jerry Thackray and I unleashed our wit on the world.

CREATION PACKAGE
JASMINE MINKS
BIFF BANG POW!
The Jesus and Mary Chain

PLEASE NOTE
THE JESUS & MARY
CHAINS'
SET TIME IS
12 MIDNIGHT—12:20 AM
THEY PLAY
A TOTAL OF
20 MINUTES

Above, right: A Jesus and Mary Chain poster from 1984. Twenty minutes? More like fifteen!

Above, left: November 1984, Germany. It was the first tour for the Jesus and Mary Chain and after a couple of gigs trying to follow them, we agreed they should be headlining.

Left: With Bobby on tour in 1985. By now I was the Mary Chain's manager.

Below: Jim Reid, William Reid and Bobby at the North London Polytechnic March 1985, before the bottles started flying and the gig turned into a riot.

Above: On the road with the Mary Chain, trying to create rock 'n' roll history. I enjoyed the overseas tours – in this case America 1985 – most of all. *Below:* Relaxing at the Franklin Plaza Suite in LA in 1985. From left to right: me, Bobby, William and Jim, and Douglas Hart.

Primal Scream: 1985. Bobby, Robert Young and Andrew Innes (who joined in 1987) were also from Cathcart. We had the same nasty sense of humour.

The Weather Prophets in 1985. From left to right: Pete Astor, Dave Morgan, David Greenwood Goulding and Oisin Little.

Posing for a cardboard cut-out to be hung up in record shops, 1988.

Above: The Pastels (Katrina Mitchell, Annabel Wright and Stephen McRobbie) would stop over with me and Yvonne at our house.

Below: We signed My Bloody Valentine in 1988, and by the end of the year they were on the road to greatness it seemed. From left to right: Kevin Shields, Colm Ó Cíosóig, Bilinda Butcher and Debbie Googe.

Above: Biff Bang Pow! in 1989,
in the hallway outside Creation's office
on Clerkenwell Road. From left to right:
Dick Green, Ken Popple, Alan and
Phil King (on the floor).

Right: Performing at the 'Doing it for
the Kids' concert in 1988.

important and that it could also be fun. I owe him enormously for that because it helped me a lot, and we came roaring back with a fantastic year in 1988 with House of Love and My Bloody Valentine. In that late period of the 1980s, and later too, he was like a blood brother to me.

Dick Green also really came into his own while I was pulling myself back together. He'd quit his job as a pensions clerk in 1987 and joined the crew signing on to the Enterprise Allowance Scheme in the office in London. I only worked from the office half-time – the rest I was doing from Brighton or wherever I happened to be. Jeff Barrett was there in the office too, doing press for us, for the House of Love. He hated the House of Love's music but he was doing a good job on the press. It was a good atmosphere in the office then. Ed Ball would be there too, sort of answering the phone, helping do the PR, getting what needed to be done done. We all pitched in with everything – there wasn't such a thing as a job title, unless we were taking the piss. I called myself 'The President of Pop' if anyone ever asked.

The House of Love just kept getting better and better live. Bickers was really challenging Chadwick by now for star of the show. We scheduled the album for the start of May and I really believed that we could make it work.

But when it came out it was disappointing yet again. Middling sales in the first week and the tour to go alongside it didn't sell out.

What made the difference was a John Peel review in the *Observer*. He'd never really supported our bands before but started playing the House of Love every night on his show. 'Destroy the Heart' came out in June and the album started to sell really well.

In Brighton I'd begun to cheer up. I'd moved in with Bobby Gillespie's brother Graham, and we began to run riot. We took all the drugs we could get hold of and went after every woman we could find. For the first time since I'd started Creation there was no hindrance to me living the life of the bands.

Bobby and his girlfriend Karen Parker arrived in town then, shortly followed by Andrew Innes and Robert 'Throb' Young. Jim Beattie stayed in Glasgow and that was the end of Primal Scream for him. That was sad – we'd all grown up together – though him leaving might have been best for the band's musical progression. If you have a twelve-string Rickenbacker player, you have to use him, and your songs are going to be defined by that sound. Now you had Throb and Andy armed with Les Pauls, and the music changed direction, became more raucous, straight-out rock and roll, influenced by the Stooges, by MC5, New York Dolls. It was totally unfashionable dirty rock music. I didn't know what they were hoping to achieve and it was clear to me the new direction was really unfashionable. Having said that, they were a better band live. Innes could really play and he was rocking the whole band. They went from being a fey indie band to rocking like animals. It was great fun. Innes was the real energy, and Bobby was getting off on it. There was no point me trying to step in and guide them at that point. They were finding themselves. My philosophy with Primal Scream was always to let them do what they wanted to do and see where they ended up.

I've always been grateful to Primal Scream for being such great friends in those Brighton days. I had been so sad and they picked me up, made me see that life could be fun again. They made me remember why I'd founded Creation in the first place. I wanted to make them famous.

Three months after the House of Love's self-titled album came out we were selling a thousand copies a week. I was trying not to think about the inevitable but it happened in July 1988: Guy Chadwick turned round and said, 'We're leaving.' I knew Guy's ambition was too big for him to be happy with Creation now he was big enough to interest the majors. They were already beginning to circle. I didn't do contracts so there was nothing stopping my bands from leaving Creation.

At the time I was fatalistic: 'Big surprise – every other fucker's left me, Jesus and Mary Chain, Yvonne – why shouldn't you?'

But then Chadwick asked me to be the band's manager and I cheered up (much as I'd rather have kept them on my label). They'd asked other people to manage them, I found out later, but Chadwick's ambition had frightened them. The other candidates had thought that the size of the advance he was seeking was unrealistic and that, even if someone would give it to him, it would put too much pressure on the band.

I was as ambitious as he was. I'd helped them secure a good publishing deal for their songs that June, playing one of the interested parties off against another and getting a much better deal than they'd first offered. To be a good negotiator I think you need courage and cunning. You can't be scared they're going to take the money off the table, whatever they say. Don't worry about the ones who threaten you.

Because I'd done so well for them, even when I wasn't taking a cut, Chadwick must have wondered how good a negotiator I'd be if it was also my money I stood to gain. They decided I was the ideal man to broker a deal to the majors for them, and unlike the other potential managers they'd spoken to, I was extremely ambitious about the money they could get. The more the better! We wanted the world. Chadwick and I were beginning to be a dangerous team.

The House of Love had restored my sense of purpose. Creation's reputation was on the up again. We were having fun with the marketing then, playing on my public persona. We did a special 99p offer for 'Christine' by the House of Love and 'Hollow Hearts' by the Weather Prophets with an advert in the *NME*: 'our president still loves the kids'.

I was back on top form, out all the time, a prominent figure even if I still wasn't doing interviews. We made lifesize cardboard cut-outs of me and sent them round the record stores before organizing a one-day festival in August, 'Doing it for the Kids' at the Town and Country Club in Kentish Town. We put out 'Destroy the Heart' by House of Love to coincide and put them on as headliners. I even considered flying around the stage on wires – thank god I thought better of *that*.

Primal Scream played in the middle of the line-up. They'd lost a lot of their jangly indie fans with the change of direction – it was a real transition period for them. Just below House of Love we put on a band we had signed recently called My Bloody Valentine.

I had first seen My Bloody Valentine in 1987. Joe Foster had recommended them to me after a label called Lazy put out a single. I went to see them at a gig Jeff Barrett had put on and they were absolutely rubbish. They really wanted to be on Creation, Joe told me, but there was no way I was having any of it.

At the start of 1988, they'd offered Biff Bang Pow! a gig supporting them in Kent. Supporting them? I thought. Supporting *them*? They're fucking anoraks. They're like a bad Pastels. A bad Pastels; can you be a bad Pastels? Anyway, fine, I said, but we're headlining.

That was a mistake. Kevin Shields magnanimously said, okay, we'll go on first. And they went on and they absolutely *destroyed* the place. They were playing out of their skins. Dick and I were watching them and turned to each other. The power was so amazing. It was so raw. The feedback hadn't emerged yet, and they sounded like a psychedelic Motörhead (and in fact none of their albums sound like they sounded that night). We were shocked at how good they were. So when we went on to headline Biff Bang Pow! sounded distinctly underpowered in comparison. Quite embarrassing. As soon as we got offstage we offered them a deal and they accepted.

That night at our Town and Country showcase My Bloody Valentine were incendiary, the best band on, but it was House of Love who headlined and they didn't let themselves down at all. Professional as ever. Anthem after anthem. Terry a guitar hero, Chadwick a great singer and front man. We had found some stars who everyone in the industry now agreed could be massive. Well, such is life. Now it was time to sell them to another label.

I decided I would conduct the auction for House of Love in style and checked into a suite in the Waldorf with my new girlfriend Belinda. I meant business, I wasn't some naive indie chancer – I was there to discuss money, and I wanted to discuss *a lot* of money.

Belinda was a mate of James Williamson, a friend of mine and Bobby's who lived in Brighton. James is an entirely diabolical human being but we had great fun with him at the time. Belinda was incredibly beautiful, and James was really into her, so I was very pleased when I realized it was me she was interested in.

I didn't normally stay at such a posh hotel but I didn't let on when the record labels came to visit. We were having the time of our lives, doing coke and speed, drinking champagne.

They nearly all came to see us: EMI, Phonogram, Columbia, Siren, MCA . . . Graham Carpenter, who I'd worked with at Warners on the Primal Scream album, and had now gone to

Polydor, was interested. No sign of Rob Dickins or Malcolm Dunbar though.

I was asking for £80,000 to start off with. That got rid of MCA. The other four kept talking. Guy Chadwick and I wanted a firm two-album deal, to make sure that if the first didn't work for whatever reason there was a second chance.

I was there in my suite with my beautiful girlfriend while the major labels came and told me what great taste I had. It helped me put my time at Warners in perspective. The money would go up £50,000 every week. We were talking about £200,000 in the last week.

After three weeks we checked out of the Waldorf. I'd done my job there. The auction was feverish. Graham Carpenter drove down to Brighton to see me, tried to get me to promise it to him, for old times' sakes. Well, I'll do my best, I said.

But I'd been very impressed with Dave Bates at Phonogram and his Fontana label. He was a real music fan, and an unashamed capitalist too. He'd signed some awful shit – Def Leppard, Tears for Fears – but he'd also signed Pere Ubu and Julian Cope. He made enough money with the awful shit to give him the power to sign whoever else he wanted. He was a maverick – he didn't toe the corporate line, said exactly what he meant, no matter how rude it was. I suppose I saw him as an example of how I could be successful without giving up on who I was. He was one of the few people I met at the majors who you could speak to like a human being. And when I said I wanted House of Love to be as big as U2 he understood exactly where I was coming from, that I didn't care about indie values at all, whatever they are. I wanted House of Love to be massive, sell millions of records and make us all loads of money.

He offered £400,000 plus the costs of recording. Carpenter surrendered in shock. He hadn't come close to that kind of money. But by playing on his interest I had driven the other two contenders right up.

Chadwick loved Columbia, and CBS offered nearly a million but, crucially, with the recording costs and expenses having to come out of that money. Chadwick wanted to go with it. (I hadn't let that lunatic anywhere near the hotel by the way, just reported to him at the end of the day.) But I just didn't like CBS as much. Bates seemed to know more about America – he had Def Leppard at number one there in the singles charts.

During this time Jeff Barrett did a really fucking cheeky thing and pretended to both the *NME* and *Melody Maker* that they were getting exclusive interviews with the band in the same week. We had two front covers in the same week! Perfect timing.

It took nearly two months to finalize the deal. There was a very high late bid from EMI but in the end we went with Dave Bates at Phonogram and his Fontana label. I'd just made £80,000 personally, and we were set to make House of Love the next big British band.

The thing we didn't predict was that the band would go completely fucking mental.

Both Chadwick and Bickers lost their minds. Kids from

military backgrounds, they're fucking nuts when they start taking drugs. I'd have that confirmed fifteen years later when I managed Pete Doherty. The drugs drove Guy mental. While we were still negotiating the deal House of Love were on a European tour and Chadwick completely lost it, ripping all his clothes off and trashing a dressing room, winding Pete Evans up till he was chasing him round a fairground trying to kill him. Jeff Barrett was there with a *Sounds* journalist and had to get him to hush it up.

With Terry, it was different – there was something wrong there that couldn't withstand the madness of touring, the pressure of recording the album and justifying that massive advance. I didn't know what to do. People from Glasgow didn't get depression. How would you tell if they did? I just didn't have the vocabulary to comprehend it. Or the experience. If only I'd known then what I later came to understand.

Meanwhile, we were getting very excited about putting My Bloody Valentine on record. They were living in squats in Kentish Town at that time. Pretty sordid places, I hear. I knew enough to go nowhere near them, not that I was ever invited. The band's line-up has always been the same: Kevin Shields, Bilinda Butcher, Colm Ó Cíosóig and Debbie Googe. The first album was unbelievably easy to get off them. We did it in two sessions. Kevin Shields had two kinds of song then. The Jingle Jangle Pastels sounds I hadn't really liked. And then he had what I called *the weird stuff*, the strange droney noise he was getting out of his guitar with the tremolo and some weird tuning. The only thing I ever did to A&R My Bloody Valentine was to ask Kevin for some more of the weird stuff. Red rag to a bull: he came back with *loads* more weird stuff! *Isn't Anything* cost £7,000 to make. It was done in six weeks in 1988 and released in November of the same year. It went silver quite quickly and continued to sell steadily. Straight away the journalists loved it. We got a lot of credit for reinventing the band which we didn't deserve – the truth was that they'd reinvented themselves. It looked like they were going to be big.

7: MANCHESTER AND ACID HOUSE

I ended 1988 in what became for me the best place in the world to take ecstasy: Manchester. I was aware of the acid house scene, going to Shoom in London a bit with Jeff Barrett, who was well into it. All sorts of characters were in there, everyone really friendly, asking how you were, what your name was, what you were on. But at Shoom I never went in the house room. House music just hadn't clicked for me yet. It had clicked for Jeff Barrett. You should have seen the dancing he got up to there. It was like he was digging a road with a pneumatic drill. I've always wanted to ask him about that dance. It was the weirdest dance I'd ever seen. So, *he* got it, but me – I just went there to get the drugs. A lot of the time I'd head somewhere else to take them.

That night in December New Order were playing the G-Mex and there was an after-show party going on at the Hacienda. A night called Disorder. I'd been going to Manchester for a while. I loved the Happy Mondays. I loved ecstasy. The Happy Mondays had loads of ecstasy. It was a great arrangement. I got on with Shaun Ryder really well.

I was Eed up that night when I made a great mate for life, Debbie Turner, who completely randomly and cosmically is in a way responsible for my greatest ever success. But that came years later. We got talking that night when she came up to me and said, 'Why are you wearing sunglasses inside?'

'Because I've got cancer of the eye,' I said.

She nearly broke down and went back to her mates. 'I'm gutted. Alan's got cancer of the eye.'

'You soft cow,' they said, 'he's taking the piss.'

She was a pretty Manchester girl, five years younger than me, and we became great buddies. We were lying around in the corner of the room when I had an epiphany.

'Debbie,' I said. 'I want to marry you.'

'You're already married,' she pointed out.

'Oh, yeah. I hadn't thought of that.'

I'd taken a lot of pills already that night but then I made the mistake of asking Shaun Ryder for another one. He only gave me a half but it was the strongest pill I ever took. That's when Debbie's face became a giant green diamond and I had to wander off. I was overheating, had to lie on the floor. When I got up I was walking through the basement, looking at the beams in the ceiling, green diamonds and blue tessellating shapes. It was beautiful. Tony Wilson was there, in a shining white suit, like God, or a king. I found Debbie dancing and suddenly I was dancing too and I understood what the music was about. It was something new, something incredible. It felt like it was going to change everything.

The new year started with Dave Bates rejecting the single 'Safe' we'd recorded and planned as the next House of Love single. He had a fixed idea of what an album that would sell millions was going to sound like and our recordings were too 'indie'. Chadwick and I should probably never have mentioned being as big as U2 – it was all we were beginning to hear now from Dave Bates. But we'd been glad to take the money – or Chadwick and I had, anyway – so we had to send them back into the studio, this time with Tim Palmer producing. He'd just produced a single by Texas. The band were instantly in a different recording world from Creation's.

Bickers immediately couldn't handle it. He was a hell of a guitar player and all of a sudden he didn't believe he was. He'd been worried about the deal from the start, about the pressure. He just wasn't motivated about money in the way Chadwick was. He started to play up badly. He'd walk out, have screaming fits. Despite this, we got two songs done, and chose 'Never' as a single for the spring.

I remember going on tour with My Bloody Valentine at the start of February 1989 and Kevin Shields telling me he wanted me to be the sound engineer. We did this gig at ULU. Kevin was always sacking the soundman at this point. The Kevinitis was beginning to show itself for the first time, and it would only get worse. Professional soundmen had their own ideas, and Kevin didn't like that. He didn't want anyone to interfere with his vision. He knew I'd do what he told me.

I was on magic mushrooms. I'd come up from Brighton with a girl and we'd eaten handfuls on the train. I had no idea what was going on. My way of mixing the sound anyway was just to turn everything up on the desk when it got to a loud bit. It was probably perfect for a My Bloody Valentine gig. I was tripping my head off, decked out in leathers, mad red hair, sunglasses on, blasting the audience with volume – Kevin and I were loving it! He knew I was on mushrooms when he asked me to do it.

They had a section called 'The Holocaust' which would make the audience run for cover when they heard it. It was probably dangerous. I think he gives them earplugs these days.

(I don't know how I managed to avoid getting tinnitus after all those years at gigs. Noel Gallagher's got it now, I heard. He once told me his guitar at Reading was as loud as a plane engine. No wonder the lunatic has tinnitus if he stood next to a plane engine every night!)

Being assaulted in the way they were didn't stop the fans from coming to see My Bloody Valentine. The tour was a great success. We were very pleased with *Isn't Anything*. Solid sales and unanimous respect. We couldn't wait for the follow-up.

While this was going on I had turned into an acid house fanatic. I really wanted to have a dance song. It would take me till February 1990 for that, so there was a bit of an incubation period. Grant Fleming played an important role in that. He had been the merch guy for the last House of Love tour. The band were such hard work at the time, most of them on drugs and going nuts, so I always travelled with Grant and the merch. Grant was great, a big West Ham fan who had a real joy for life. At the age of sixteen he'd been the tour manager of Jimmy Pursey and Sham 69. We'd drive around the country together listening to acid house records and after the gig we'd get on an E and track down the best club we could find. Whatever was going on me and Grant would be there. I think we took an E on every night of that tour.

At the end of the tour I asked him if he wanted to start an acid house label, and he started laughing and asked what we'd call it.

Creation, of course, I said.

People really don't remember us as an acid house label but we were serious about it. There's a great compilation from us around that time, with Primal Scream and Fluke and Hypnotone and Love Corporation. It's a fucking great acid house record and it was Grant who was the cheerleader for all of that. He was the one going round the shops on Saturday afternoon with the white labels.

Before Creation could fully embrace acid house I had to convert Bobby Gillespie to ecstasy and the clubs. I'd been telling him how great ecstasy was, how great Manchester was, and he came up with his girlfriend. I bought three Es off Shaun that night. They were twenty quid a go then. I bought two for me and one for Bobby. He was new to it: that would be more than enough for him, so I thought. I forgot, though, how dysfunctional Bobby's system is. The first one didn't touch the sides. He never came up at all. I was high as a kite. He had to have two to come up – I had to give him my other one, much to my disappointment! Bobby was a bit cautious about the scene to start with. He'd come to the clubs – there was a Brighton scene beginning; we started going to a club called Escape. While we were dancing around Bobby would sit on a wall with his legs dangling like a Ramone, off his face on E. That's Bob – he waits a while to make up his mind, dips his toes in the water before he plunges in completely. It was the same with punk – he got into it a few months after me, though that was independently of me, and the thing that really cemented our friendship. And it was the same with drugs in some ways too. As I was getting out of addiction in the mid-1990s, floating to the surface, Bobby was jumping in with both feet and waving at me on his way down as we passed each other.

In London we were going to Shoom and Spectrum regularly now. All the bands were there. House of Love – Guy taking his clothes off, always taking his clothes off. Kevin Shields, not saying anything to anyone. Bobby, vaguely talking to people, a rock and roller in winklepickers and tight trousers and despite that managing to look more entitled to be there than everyone else in the room. The Stone Roses – they were recording in London at the time.

Andrew Innes understood acid house straight away. The Es were just opening everyone up, to other people, to new ideas, to collaborations. Robert Young, the degenerate rocker, hated it. Really hated it. I understand why – they were about to record a classic two Les Paul rock and roll album. He was the happiest he'd been with his role in the band since it had started. He wanted Primal Scream to be the New York Dolls and didn't need acid house interfering with that.

Creation was expanding. *House of Love* was still selling. *Isn't Anything* by My Bloody Valentine was selling. Dick and

I hired James Kyllo at the start of 1989 as a business manager. He'd just quit Cherry Red, and he was working in a Record and Tape exchange. We needed someone who had experience of doing royalties, of using computers, of the systems you needed to run a record label that was getting bigger. We still didn't have contracts in those days – just a handshake and an agreement for a fifty-fifty profit share with the band. It was time to think about protecting our interests – though it was years before we signed anyone up to a proper contract.

The shoebox in Clerkenwell was far too small. To make things worse, it was full of band members lying on the floor. They'd wander in to hang out, drugged out of their heads. It was a tiny fucking office, two broom cupboards now, four of us sharing two desks and Primal Scream and the Weather Prophets lying on the floor in leather trousers while Jeff Barrett tried to write his press releases. They'd come in there and take acid. We didn't need that. I asked James Kyllo to find us new premises, somewhere far enough away for the bands not to move in, and he found us a place in Westgate Street, Hackney. We were moving out from central London to a place where, at that time, no one in the music industry went anywhere near. It was rough. It had no tube. I knew if we moved there, the bands would be too lazy or scared to come by. Bobby Gillespie has it that the reason I moved there was so it would be harder for people to come in and get the royalties they were owed. It was 1989, Bobby: there weren't any fucking royalties! It was only the Valentines who were selling any records in those days, and House of Love.

We waited for six years for Primal Scream to have a hit single. Anyway, we moved to this big office in Hackney, with tons of space, under the railway arches next to London Fields. Hackney's trendy nowadays but it wasn't then. No fucker would go there. You'd get mugged! It was perfect for us.

I was still living in Brighton. Graham Gillespie had moved out after managing to miss paying rent to me for fourteen of the twenty-six weeks he lived there. So I replaced him with Lawrence from Felt, who wanted to get out of Birmingham. That's when I found out the truth about his tidiness. It's bullshit that he's tidy. I'm tidier than Lawrence! He was a messy fucker. He was just playing up to journalists. When Lawrence moved in I knew for a fact that he would never pay me any rent, so I just said, 'Lawrence, it is your job to answer the phone and take messages for me.' Which he managed to do. We were actually good flatmates. He was part of the Primal Scream gang. They took to him immediately. All my experiences of Lawrence face to face were really positive.

I needed Lawrence as an answering service as I was beginning to spend a lot of time out of Brighton back then. Debbie Turner in Manchester was my new best mate and I began to spend weekend after weekend up there. Mainly, if I'm honest, for the drugs. On the weekend we met Debbie had taken me round various houses and I'd never seen so much ecstasy. I was thinking, This is amazing, this man's got a thousand Es in his fridge. The next thought was, Why don't I get a flat

here? I told Tony Wilson I was coming up and he arranged
for me to rent Alan Erasmus's place, one of the Factory direc-
tors. Debbie moved in and we split the rent. We were never
boyfriend and girlfriend. I'd jump on a train north every week
at some point. There was only one place then you wanted to
party and that was Manchester. Once I was there, I'd think,
Fuck the record company, and I'd stay a few days. I had that
place for about six months and had such great times there.
The Mancs were really friendly, to me anyway, though they
didn't like cockneys much. I met Mani Mounfield and the
Roses, and they admired me for being a headcase, for moving
up at the drop of a hat to go to raves. I think it got Creation
a lot of respect actually, me being in the middle of the action.
London wasn't music's creative centre then, if it ever has
been, and I was on hand to see it for myself. Tony Wilson
asked me to come on the regional news show he presented,
Granada Tonight. I think he thought I was going to be a
passive interviewee – because he was my hero – and, of course,
I wasn't.

'Why've you moved to Manchester, Alan?'

'A better class of drugs, Tony.'

Noel Gallagher saw that interview. I think the whole of
Manchester saw that interview. I went on and I was a rotten
cunt. I think Tony quite enjoyed it.

I suppose I'd lost interest in rock music temporarily. Not a
good thing for the manager of 'the next U2'. But far more of
a problem for House of Love was the fact that Terry Bickers

was getting even worse. I had no experience of what to do. None of us did. We thought he was just throwing tantrums for a while but it became clear there was something really wrong. It seemed he was clinically depressed. What did that mean though? The thing I came to realize much later is that I was clinically depressed too. And I was self-medicating like crazy. I wrote myself a prescription of ecstasy, speed, acid, coke or Jack Daniel's almost every day. I was the worst person to help him.

Before long the new Hackney office was the scene of some of the heaviest parties in London. So much for getting rid of the bands. We threw an opening party and everyone came. We introduced the *NME* to ecstasy that night by giving it to two of their journalists, Danny Kelly and Helen Mead. There was Primal Scream, the House of Love, My Bloody Valentine, the Weather Prophets.

One thing I wish is that I'd never introduced Guy Chadwick to ecstasy. Though he would have got hold of it without me anyway. It was not his scene at all. He couldn't take it without getting naked. It was so embarrassing. Every time. That's what the drug was for him – an excuse to take his clothes off. Made no impact whatsoever on his music. You'd see him neck a pill and think, *Christ*, we're in for it now.

'Never', the first single on Fontana, came out in May and charted at 41. I thought it was a terrible choice of single but Bates overruled me. It hadn't worked with Tim Palmer and they ended up using lots of other producers, including Stephen

Hague who'd just done 'True Faith' by New Order. But none of it was working and the recording was growing out of control. It was all the band's fault. They seemed completely deranged most of the time. Drugs didn't suit any of them, and definitely not Bickers and Chadwick. You didn't have Bono getting off stage and taking nine Es in a night. No wonder they were going crazy in the studio. No one could control them, not Dave Bates, not me. I'd begun to give up trying to.

The parties in the office were happening all the time. It was one big party really, which lasted from 1989 to 1995. It was still going on for a year or so after I'd finished. (It was one of the reasons we had to move offices!) I'd buy a lot of Es then and give them out, so I'm known as this big ecstasy evangelist. But I was no more of an evangelist than Bobby Gillespie or Jeff Barrett. We were all on that trip. Everyone was. We'd never been part of anything like it. You couldn't keep it to yourself.

For the first six months in 1989 when I wasn't in Manchester I pretty much lived in the office. I decided there was no point going back to Brighton. I'd just go to the clubs then come back to the office and crash. You can imagine I was pretty smelly in those days. I've always been grateful to Guy Chadwick for pointing that out. He phoned me up after we'd got a taxi home together once.

'Alan,' he said. 'I need to tell you something.' *Here we go again, what have I done wrong now* . . . 'You smell.'

'What do you mean?'

'Well, Alan, when you got out of the taxi, a really bad smell left.'

So I immediately borrowed someone's bath and tried to remember to do that more frequently. If I wasn't careful I'd find myself spending weeks taking drugs, not washing and sleeping on the office floor.

I wasn't the only one in the office who'd had his head turned by Manchester. We'd agreed that Jeff Barrett could start working as a publicist for Factory as well and he was promoting Happy Mondays and New Order. We were up there all the time – I'd go to every single New Order gig. Bernie Sumner, by the way, rivals Jeff Barrett for the strangest dance ever. I became good friends with him and I used to end up at parties with him at six in the morning. He'd stand on one leg and sort of bend over sideways and bounce about, like a flamingo coming up on mushrooms. It was worth the price of admission and an E just to watch Bernard dance.

House of Love were becoming a disaster. The money eventually spent recording that first Fontana album was mental – four to five hundred thousand.

The minute Chadwick got the wedge from the deal, he moved straight into a posh house in Camberwell and had everything going on, bar the butler. And he was trying to get the butler!

It wasn't just hiring the studios that was expensive, or the fact that nothing got done there. It was like a competition to see who could spend the most money. They blew £10,000 on taxis in a matter of months – god knows how. We thought a session with Daniel Miller might be more suitable for them but Terry Bickers lost it there, smashed his amp, threw his guitar at the wall. Another wasted session; they'd started recording at the start of 1989 and it was already July now. It was going to take years for the album to make a profit, if it was ever finished.

And there were big new bands on the scene. The biggest – surprise, surprise – from Manchester. In May the Stone Roses album was in the shops and soon they were playing to thousands of people. They had the euphoria and the rhythm of house, mixed with classic melodies and harmonies. House of Love were in danger of becoming yesterday's news.

It was the same with Primal Scream, whose second album *Primal Scream* came out in July. It was not of its moment at all. It was MC5 and the Stooges. I never understood why they made that record. There were some good songs on it but it was really not the right time for an album like that to catch the imagination. But I could never tell them what to do. There's no point telling Bobby Gillespie or Noel Gallagher or Kevin Shields or Kevin Rowlands what direction they should be travelling in. They know what they want. If they're feeling polite they'll listen to you and ignore you. If they're being impolite (more frequent) they'll tell you to fuck off, at length.

My favourite song on *Primal Scream* was 'I'm Losing More Than I'll Ever Have', a ballad, a break-up song. It proved they could write timeless classic songs. I still believed in them. I knew they were so talented, that they had more than talent, they had the spirit, the genius. And now we were all getting into ecstasy I wondered how we could channel that genius into something completely of the moment.

It was Andrew Weatherall who made the difference. Barrett was introduced to him first, I think. Weatherall was a DJ upstairs at Shoom, and didn't just play house records but mixed them in with New Order, old funk and soul. Bobby and I first met him at a rave in Brighton. He had hair like Marc Bolan. We danced all night – Bobby still dressed in his classic sixties gear, but that's what the scene was like – everyone was allowed in. Everyone was welcome.

Weatherall ran a magazine called *Boy's Own* and Jeff Barrett sent him the Primal Scream album to review. He loved it, loved the ballads. Thank god someone did. There weren't many around who did. What I found interesting was that it was someone coming out of that club culture who loved the band. Maybe there wasn't such a big divide between Primal Scream and acid house after all.

Terry Bickers got a girlfriend, which calmed him down for a while. We eventually got a couple more tracks for the album recorded with Stephen Hague's engineer, Dave Meegan. The rest of the album was to be recorded at Abbey Road. Apparently it got really stupid then, drinking all day, playing up – I was sick of it all by then and stayed away more. The wastage was stupid – I mean, I like money, I like spending it myself, but not on nothing. They recorded enough tracks but to what extent they really tried to make a great album, I don't know. Bates rejected the lot. He hated them. It was such a disaster. The only sessions that had worked were with Meegan. We went back to him for one last try. Finally, seven weeks later, the album was done after being completely re-recorded.

We'd been really worried about their appearance at Reading that August. Guy had suggested to me that we fire Bickers on a couple of occasions, but I knew he was the world-beater on the team and I persuaded him against it. In the end, they were really good. Bickers was in a good phase – the crowd loved it, their biggest gig by miles. Bickers celebrated by taking too many drugs, becoming feral and disappearing into the night.

I was backstage, off my face too. Apparently the office cleaner introduced me to her boyfriend Noel Gallagher that day. I certainly don't remember it.

I had one of the last fights of my life that summer, with James Brown (the features editor of *NME*, later editor of *Loaded*, not the godfather of soul). It was a House of Love gig and he said something snide to me, so I told him I'd slept with his girlfriend (I had and, well, what I said was nastier than that). He just lost it. I wasn't scared of him so I just chucked my beer over him and walked off. He came up from behind and got a really good punch in, staggered me. More punches were flying in and so I realized I had to fight back. But I wasn't winning. Luckily we got pulled apart.

After that I tried to slow down a little. Belinda moved to Birmingham and I gave up the flat in Manchester to move there. Except, I'd only go there for a weekend to chill out. I'd get to hers on a Friday night and I'd be flying after a week in London. She would sober me up and keep me around till Tuesday before I'd run off to get fucked again.

The rest of the time was spent running riot in London and sleeping in the office. If I slept.

Dave Bates needed to restart the momentum of House of Love, and suggested a long tour. I agreed, and to this day I wonder whether things would have been better if I'd resisted. It was on tour that Guy and Terry's sanity was most tested. We had seventy days booked in Britain and Ireland stretching from October to March in 1990. The idea was to have three singles come out during this megatour, and the tour would promote them into the Top 20.

The album was finished and it had cost well over half a million quid. But it was an okay album, a commercial sounding album that hadn't gone too far and ruined the band's individuality. Dave Bates was happy.

We just couldn't understand it when the next single 'I Don't Know Why I Love You' only charted at 41 again. Radio 1 had been caning it. It was a good song, a good single. The next week both the Happy Mondays and the Stone Roses were on *Top of the Pops*. I think I knew then in my heart it wasn't going to work for them.

It was time for a change. Jeff Barrett had been a brilliant publicist but he was overstretched between Creation, Factory and the House of Love, and I wanted someone committed to every band on Creation. He was gutted to have Primal Scream taken away from him – he believed in them as much as I did.

Primal Scream were very unpopular then. The anoraks who'd got into them as part of the C86 bullshit didn't like them any more. *Ooh, they've rocked out!* Namby pambies, we were glad to lose them. In principle. But we needed to sell more of their records.

I think it was Andrew Innes' idea to get Andy Weatherall to do a dance remix of 'I'm Losing More Than I'll Ever Have'. They'd recorded the song to a click track so it was perfectly in time. Weatherall had never remixed anything in his life but this was completely in the spirit of Creation. He had great taste and a good attitude and he knew what made a dance floor go off. The sample at the start of that record from Peter Fonda in *The Wild Angels* totally encapsulates the attitude we all had. We wanted to be free. We were going to have a good time, and we were going to get loaded.

Still, it didn't go smoothly. There was a lot of back and forth. I thought we needed to have a Bobby vocal on it. Bobby disagreed – he and Innes wanted Weatherall to be more brutal, to do what he wanted. Innes was in the studio with him – it was an artistic collaboration, not just a straight dance remix. It dragged on. In the end, I realized they were right and that we didn't need Bobby on the track.

When the year closed, it seemed like it couldn't get any worse for Primal Scream. Their big gig in London at Subterranea was half empty. Creation's flagship band was almost irrelevant now.

Then a week later Andrew Innes went with Weatherall to

watch him play 'Loaded'. They'd just finished it and had never heard it played on a dance floor. At three in the morning Weatherall dropped it in Subterranea – and the place went crazy. Innes rang to tell me. Everyone was going nuts in the background.

In one way House of Love's massive tour worked out well. The album came out at the beginning of 1990, landed in the Top 10 and went gold. But in the process we lost the lead guitarist and fucked the band.

Throughout November 1989 I'd been hearing horror stories from the House of Love tour. Chadwick was lashing out at Bickers, blaming him for what was going wrong, for being out of it earlier in the year. He kept trying to throw him out of the band but I wouldn't let him.

At the end of the month I flew out to America with Dave Bates to meet Phonogram's people who were going to try to break the band over there. This was just the opportunity Chadwick needed.

While we were out of the country Bickers managed to get hold of a carrier bag of mushrooms at a gig in deepest Wales. They all had terrible bad trips in a haunted house. Bickers smashed his room to bits. No one was talking to him. He wound Pete the drummer up – a sweet guy – until he ended up punching Bickers in the face and running away in a service station and saying he'd left the band.

Guy didn't let Pete Evans leave the band. He saw his opportunity and sacked Bickers instead.

I remember taking the call, about half eight in the morning

in the Chateau Marmont hotel in LA and thinking, Great, we've thrown out the centre forward. I knew that the dynamite team was Guy and Terry. Bickers was just a killer guitarist. It's not very cool to say it, but he was the only guy around then who was challenging the Edge as a guitar hero. Guy's songs were great but it was Terry's playing that made them shine. You don't throw a guy like that out of the band, it's insane.

I know it wasn't easy dealing with Bickers – he was having a genuine breakdown – but kicking him out of the band was throwing in the towel. Things hadn't been going well but given time and luck they could still have become one of the biggest bands in the world. Sacking Bickers removed any chance of that. They had to find a way of rehabilitating him somehow if they wanted to be successful.

I did my best to persuade them to take him back. I was furious. I was probably too honest. I told them they couldn't survive without him, which was a blow to their egos.

They'd mostly recorded the Butterfly album (called *House of Love* like its predecessor, but known for its butterfly sleeve artwork) with Terry playing on it, but he didn't tour it. They brought in Simon Walker who was actually a very good guitar player, but he wasn't right. In a different way, a jazz way, he was arguably a better guitarist than Terry Bickers. But for me that's what's wrong with jazz – players who think they're more intelligent than other players because they understand the chords better. (Some journalists have that problem too with punctuation if you ask me. No, it's about the message unfortunately.) He was trying to educate the masses when what they wanted was a killer guitar line. When I first saw them play with Simon, I knew they'd blown their chance for good. He just didn't have the presence of Bickers – you turned up to watch the band and it had become the Guy Chadwick show with a backing band. Getting rid of Bickers got rid of the rub that makes the best bands. Often it's a brother thing. You look at Kasabian, at Tom and Serge, you look at Oasis, at Liam and Noel. The Libertines, Pete and Carl, and the Reid brothers. Great bands have got that rub. Even if they're best mates, they've got that rub.

Interestingly, it's not the same for record labels. Record labels work because they're one man's vision. It's about Ivo at 4AD, or Laurence at Domino, or Jeff at Heavenly.

I used to talk about running Creation with a fascist state of mind and people thought I was a cunt for saying it. But it's the only way to do it. You have to believe in your own vision and if people challenge it you have to have the courage to say, Fuck off, this is the way we're doing it. Otherwise you never take risks and you never move quickly enough.

But bands aren't like that. You need Bobby and Andrew. You need a spark against each other. We needed Guy *and* Terry.

I lost all belief in House of Love at that moment. It was just as they began to work in the charts too. The album came in at number 8, they sold out the Albert Hall. That was okay. But I had convinced myself that they were going to be superstars, and I couldn't delude myself about that any more.

8: LOADED

You could make an argument that My Bloody Valentine were the most influential of all the Creation bands. I'm sure Oasis and Primal Scream would have something to say, but you could still make the argument. We certainly saw a lot of bands who'd been influenced by *Isn't Anything*. The most successful of these we signed was Ride.

They were just kids. Teenagers at art college in Oxford. I'd first heard them in 1989, in the middle of my acid house obsession. This had manifested itself for a while in me managing the Grid, who had signed a major label deal with Warners with a guy called Cally Calloman. I was round his office and he played me a tape of a band called Ride he was thinking of signing. Very trusting of him. I was nodding non-committally. They're not that bad, *I suppose*.

But really I'd loved what I heard. It was a Creation band through and through, influenced by Valentines and House of Love but younger sounding, more romantic I guess. I left the office and got straight on the phone to them. They didn't sound like a major label band to me – I thought they wouldn't get through the bullshit, the marketing people's distrust. I hoped Cally would have trouble getting Rob Dickins and

Malcolm Dunbar onside. He really wanted to sign them but was having to do it almost secretly, funding a recording and an EP through an indie label to keep the music press sweet and because his bosses wouldn't take the risk of signing them properly.

They *weren't* signed so there was nothing to stop me from talking to them. They came to a meeting with me and didn't seem to understand what I was saying. The Glasgow accent's a problem for middle-class bands from the South. But they were big fans of the label. They didn't want to be hustled into a deal, they were wary, so we just talked about the music. Other labels were scaring them, but they liked my attitude. My unprofessionalism, I guess! It wasn't always such a bad thing.

I followed them around on tour for the next two weeks, all around the country, went to every gig. They were supporting my mates the Soup Dragons. They were great. Mark Gardener was an amazing front man, Andy Bell a great guitarist. I loved the drummer Loz Colbert. I wasn't so keen on the bass player. He was one of those guys who read the *NME* back to front every week and thought he knew everything about the cynical practices of the music industry. He was an idealist. They all purported to be idealists, but the other three were really more interested in being rock and roll stars. They were at all the Creation parties, surrounded by women.

I took them to see the House of Love. We were having a good time. I thought it was Mark's band then. We used to go out and do Es together. He was the spokesman and seemed to be the leader. We assumed he wrote all the songs and he never corrected us so we took that as the case. And then they signed with us.

We released their first EP *Ride* in January 1990 and it took off straight away. (It was actually the recording Cally Calloman had paid for but didn't own; he never spoke to me again.) We sold out in three days and the music press went wild for them. Seymour Stein, who was a legend, appeared at the end of January to watch them play. The list of his bands was incredible: he'd put out British bands like the Smiths and Echo & the Bunnymen; and his American acts went from the Ramones to Blondie to Talking Heads and even Madonna on his label Sire. I'd met Seymour back in 1986 in Cannes when I was hanging out with my friend Luc Vergier, who was a music promoter then and later went to work for Sony. When I'd been introduced to Seymour then he was a bit rude to me – 'Ah, the new Brian Epstein,' he said, and he must have been taking the piss. I didn't realize that was his style, that from him it was a compliment. So when he tried to sign My Bloody Valentine I refused for a year as a matter of principle. I told him to fuck off fifty times before he wore me down. Classic Creation: he was trying to give me money and I was more interested in winning an argument he wasn't even having with me. My Bloody Valentine were the first band he signed from us; the next was Primal Scream. Selling bands to him and other labels in America was the way that we survived financially for a couple of years.

But I didn't have a deal in place for world rights for Ride. Part of the way I'd managed to sign them at all was by not being pushy, so I couldn't do anything when Seymour Stein and his A&R man Joe McEwen offered the band a direct deal for America on Sire. Joe McEwen had really reinvigorated Sire. They'd had the Smiths and Echo & the Bunnymen but no big bands for a while and Joe signed Dinosaur Jr, Primal Scream, My Bloody Valentine and (annoyingly) Ride.

Despite all the excitement around Ride at the beginning of 1990 I still hadn't given up on my ambition to put out a brilliant dance record on Creation. Ed Ball was busy knocking out dance records, and had a bit of success with Danny Rampling remixing a tune called 'Palatial'. But it was 'Loaded' that was really beginning to cause a stir, and we ended up having to switch it to the A-side and demote the original song 'I'm Losing More Than I'll Ever Have' to the B-side. That was the moment everything changed, when the crossfader got flicked and *Primal Scream* became *Screamadelica*.

Everyone from the *NME* to *The Face* was mad for the song. The calls started to flood in to Laurence Verfaillie, who'd taken over Jeff Barrett's job. She was Jim Reid's girlfriend. She showed up the very first time they ever played Paris. On that night we'd only had ten places on the guest list and she barged her way to the top of the queue to order me to put her on. I thought she was German at first, she was screaming and shouting at me, 'I must be on zee guest list now! You imbecile man!' I thought: You're turning me on, I'm putting you on the list. And she got together with Jim that night. She was so pushy, just what you needed for a publicist, I thought. We always employed people on their personalities rather than their experience.

Bobby Gillespie started doing his interview routine, slagging off all the shit bands of the moment. Radio 1 playlisted the single. It hit the Top 40, in at 32, then 24, then it became our first Top 20 hit when it reached 16. They were booked for *Top of the Pops*. I'd had bands I'd managed on *Top of the Pops* before, the Jesus and Mary Chain and House of Love, but never for a record released by Creation.

Of all the successes Creation ever had, 'Loaded' was the one I enjoyed the most. House of Love had had a Top 20 hit, but that wasn't Creation. House of Love weren't Primal Scream, my best friends, and the band everyone had been telling me for years would never amount to anything. We'd worked for so long for this and it had happened. They'd gone from a joke to the hippest band in the land. It seemed like a number one, it was such a big record. One of those records you heard everywhere, that defines the era. I wanted to run around the streets jumping up and down. I wanted to march into Malcolm Dunbar's office with Bobby and dance on his table together. I wanted to get loaded, and have a party. Go way baby, let's go!

I set Ride up as House of Love's support band for three nights in Europe in April – I always managed to set them up with Creation acts as support. Ride's second EP was about to come out and Chadwick was scared stiff of them, hanging around by the mixing desk trying to turn their sound down. Ride were playing out of their skins, with pure euphoria, whereas the House of Love were now very paranoid and nervous and missed the dynamic presence of Bickers. I didn't help their nerves by constantly buying champagne.

'What's the celebration?' Guy would ask eagerly.

'Primal Scream are at number 16,' I'd say, and watch his face fall.

The major label pressure was destroying any harmony within the band. Their new single 'Beatles and the Stones' was coming out in about a dozen formats to try and rig the charts and Dave Bates wanted them to film a big budget MTV-friendly video in LA. All of the band except Chadwick refused to be in it. In the end Dave Bates forced them to do it. It never got played on MTV. The single only made the Top 40 for a week. 'Play' by Ride went in at 32, with almost no marketing spend. It was looking really bad for the House of Love. But at Creation we had never had it so good. I thought of Tony Wilson telling me not to quit, to do my own thing. This was what I was good at, I realized now. It was the best time of my career so far. Suddenly we had hit records. I wanted more of them.

It's an amusing myth that waiting for My Bloody Valentine to deliver their second album *Loveless* turned Dick Green's hair grey. The other myth, less amusing, is that all our houses were put on the line. Well, not quite, but very close.

No one really knows what went wrong between *Isn't Anything* and *Loveless*. Maybe Kevin Shields was smoking a lot. Perhaps it was the weed that sent him mad. Who knows? How could we tell if someone had a drug problem? We all had drug problems and so we normalized and excused each other's behaviour. Everyone dealt with their drug abuse in a different way. The Primals took drugs in a really obvious, Rolling Stones-madness way – champagne and cocaine and heroin. Maybe My Bloody Valentine did it quietly and internalized it all. You didn't see the signs – you just didn't see the second album.

A year earlier, at the start of 1989, we'd been keen to see some progress but Kevin wasn't letting us near the studios the band were recording in, and the sessions were dragging on. They spent six weeks in one studio just recording drums! They were still at it in October.

So by the start of February 1990 Dick Green and I had pretty much no idea what they'd been doing for the last year. They wouldn't let us hear anything. I had to beg Kevin and, eventually, in one of the twenty-one studios he ended up using, he let me hear one song. If he hadn't I would have been close to pulling the plug on the recordings – the cost was creeping up and up. It was a clever move because the song was 'Soon' and I absolutely loved it. It was the Stooges meets the Mondays. The beat was amazing, the guitars were amazing. It was perfect for the moment too, an obvious single. From then he had me hooked.

We managed to get more tracks and released them as the

Glider EP in April 1990. It was so hard getting even this out of him. Shields insisted on moving studios every week. Nothing was ever right for him. He was getting paranoid, lost in his head. He insisted on recording all night long, always overnight. Which limited the options for engineers slightly.

Glider was amazing – blew everyone away. But we needed the album. We were spending what was beginning to be a fortune on it. Money we just didn't have. We were always ambitious and so any profits got swallowed with recording cost and promotions, and we were always on the verge of going bust.

My sisters and I found out my mother's cancer was terminal two weeks before she died. Mum wanted to believe she was getting better and somehow that was the impression we had too.

While she was ill I'd been seeing her every couple of months, like I normally would. I wish I'd spent more time there with her. I didn't realize how little time there was left, but it was my own fault I didn't go back more then. I was so busy with the label and taking drugs that the time slipped away without me noticing.

I found out she was about to die imminently in the middle of a Lilac Time tour. I was managing them for Dave Bates (who thought I'd done a good job with House of Love now the record was selling well). I had been due to go up in a couple of days, but I told their singer and songwriter Stephen Duffy I had to go immediately and headed off. I was in Birmingham and I'd got as far as York before I answered a call on my mobile, one of the first ones, for which everyone (correctly) used to give me abuse and call me a champagne Charlie when I whipped it out.

It was Dick Green on the phone. He told me my mother had just died. I'd missed her by two hours.

My sisters saw it all first hand. They said it was horrible to see her go. They both had a hard time for a few years afterwards coming to terms with it.

I arrived in Glasgow and a minister came round to talk to us. He said a lot of clichéd Christian things I didn't believe in and that really annoyed me, that seemed really false. My dad was trying to keep it together. My gran was heartbroken to have lost her daughter. After a couple of days I went back to London but returned soon for the funeral, with Ed Ball and Belinda.

I couldn't grieve at the time. I felt really disconnected. It hit me hardest when I got sober in 1994. The amount of drugs I was taking until then stalled the process and distanced the grief.

There was a notice in the paper about the church funeral. Someone must have read that notice and realized our house would be empty, because when we returned for the wake the house had been burgled. They stole my mum's jewellery, the stereo, nothing of much financial value. It was probably a desperate junkie, and it's a good job he didn't get caught. It was a big crowd at the funeral and there was a dark element to my family. The thief would never have made it to prison. He'd have been showing up in tins of dog food.

It was a tragedy Mum died so young. If only she'd had a few more years and could have seen the rest of the 1990s. She would have loved Kate. She would have loved my daughter Charlie. She'd have loved the fact that I had it away and sold millions of records. I could have bought her her own big house. She never got to see any of that.

Or who knows? Maybe she was sitting next to me the whole time. The only thing you know is that you don't know.

Over the next few months, if I started to feel pain over the loss of my mum, I distracted myself by working hard and by the frantic life I'd always lived. It was work and drugs separated by sleep and not so much of that, and it had been like that for years by then.

That year I ended our relationship with Rough Trade and signed with their main rival Pinnacle. We were about to be out of contract with Rough Trade and in typical Rough Trade fashion they used that as an opportunity to try to raise the percentage they charged us.

I'd always hated Rough Trade's attitude, their indie values which just seemed like hypocrisy to me. I liked Pinnacle for not indulging in any of that bollocks and for treating it honestly as a business about making money. They were really keen to sign us, particularly as George Kimpton, Steve Mason's old partner at Pinnacle, had now taken over Rough Trade. We played them off against each other until they were both offering ridiculously good deals, down from 28 to 12 per cent. That was incredibly low, no one had a percentage deal like that. But for years I had felt that Rough Trade hadn't given us the respect we deserved. It wasn't a problem with Geoff Travis, it was a company-wide thing. They still treated us like we were chancers. Now they were desperate to show us how much they wanted us but they'd left it too late. We signed with Pinnacle and I bought a lot of bottles of champagne that day.

We'd never had a formal contract with Primal Scream but after having lost out on Ride in the US I thought it was about time we did. We formally signed them for £15,000 and waited to hear the next Weatherall collaboration, 'Come Together'.

It wasn't an easy record to get right. It came close to breaking up the band at points. We were doing two mixes of it, a Weatherall one and a Terry Farley one. The Weatherall one was superb. But one big problem. He'd taken Bobby's vocals off it completely. They didn't fit with what he'd done, an epic house track. Bobby understood what a phenomenal song the Weatherall mix was but felt totally redundant. Robert Young had walked out too because his guitars had been taken off. Both of them were thinking there was no point in them being there if they weren't on any of the records. We knew we were going to have a problem with Robert Young. Throb got into ecstasy and acid house around summer 1990 when the scene was pretty much over. Before that he wanted Primal Scream to be the New York Dolls and was threatening to leave all the way through the making of *Screamadelica*. Funnily enough, if Throb had left, it would have been a disaster for the album. If Throb hadn't been resistant to the new direction, I think

Bobby and Andrew would have taken their experimentalism too far. I think Throb reined that in, kept the link with the band's past and future as a rock and roll band.

But we were more concerned about Bobby than about Throb. To everyone in the world, Bobby Gillespie is Primal Scream. His vision for that band is absolutely essential to it being what it is.

Then to compound the situation, Farley's vocal mix wasn't working and he sent a new version that didn't have Bobby on it at all! Bobby heard it and was really pissed off. It wasn't a good mix anyway. The band had written a great pop song with a brilliant melody, and we had to have it in one version or what was the point? So I phoned Farley and threatened him. I told him to put Bobby back on the mix or he wasn't getting paid. I kept on at him until he got it right and to his credit he pulled off an amazing mix, great percussion, piano high in the mix, gospel singers dropping out for Bobby to sing clear over the top of it, completely blissed out. (There might even be a little bit of Throb's guitar at the very end of it. The band certainly made it up to him with the next album, anyway.) I actually prefer the Farley mix to the Weatherall one. Weatherall's version is great but here's no hint of the original melody left there.

Bobby was strutting after that. Front cover of the *NME*, head to toe in white, like there had never been an issue. We had the two bands of the moment. We were becoming the hippest label in the UK. We hit the Top 30 with 'Come Together' in the summer. A bit disappointing, but it was time to build an album around those two singles now.

9: SHOEGAZING

Ride had a good manager, Dave Newton. He was in his late twenties and protected them, asked the right questions of me and of Sire. Allowed them complete creative freedom, even when the commercial arguments were opposed to it.

The band were no problem at all to begin with. The ticking time bomb was the tension between Mark Gardener and Andy Bell. They credited the whole group for the songwriting but we all thought it was Mark Gardener. Mark was nineteen years old but could have been twenty-nine, one of these guys who was just confident, an equal. He was the most outgoing, the most charismatic on stage. He was less shy than Andy, got more involved with the parties in the office – just made himself visible in a way that Andy didn't. Then one day Andy Bell came up to me and asked why I never spoke to him.

'You don't talk to me,' I said.

'Do you know I write the songs?' he asked me then, which surprised me a lot, because I didn't. Maybe Mark wasn't telling us he wrote all the songs himself but he certainly wasn't correcting us. Andy and Mark were both really talented, that's the thing. At the start they wrote songs as a band and worked on each other's songs, the McCartney and Lennon, Richards and Jagger model. Mark was just an amazing frontman, a really great producer, really underrated. He seems to be going out again on the road now and doing acoustic gigs, which I'm really pleased about. Mark was one of my favourite people we had on the label.

They were all nice lads but that didn't make for great press. Laurence was always trying to work out how we could make them say something more nasty, more quotable, but they just weren't that sort of lads. So we tried to promote Mark perhaps a bit more over Andy as the frontman, as the pin-up – and that was probably a mistake, because then the jealousy set in when Mark appeared on his own on an *NME* cover.

The album, *Nowhere*, went in at number 11 in October, which was the highest chart position we'd ever had at that point, and went gold. In the space of a year they'd gone from playing the upstairs of pubs to headlining to over a thousand people a night. Everything was great at that point.

Ride were not the only band we signed around then who had been influenced by My Bloody Valentine. Slowdive were Creation fans, still at school when we signed them. They were sixteen years old, very Valentines influenced. They were a very good band. I recently listened to their third album *Pygmalion*, which is terrific. By the time they'd got to this point they were sounding like Talk Talk. That album came out at the time Oasis and Britpop were going through the roof so it got completely overlooked. We got them a deal in America. We should have kept going with them for another album but it was towards the end of Creation, and again, it was unfortunate timing. So much of success in the music industry can be about luck. I really liked them as people, Rachel and Neil.

Swervedriver were a brilliant group – I was a big fan and still have a lot of love for them. I saw them a lot in America. They hit an anglophile audience and had more success out there than here. England had gone Britpop but America still had more of an audience for a harder rock sound.

In a book like this it's easy to pass quickly over the bands that didn't sell as many records as Oasis and Primal Scream but I've always been very proud of these bands. We didn't bring out records by bands unless someone in the office loved them.

From the beginning of 1991 Ride were trying to break America. That was Seymour Stein's responsibility now. They didn't have the greatest of times but then most bands don't. America's so much harder than England and my bands have always been pretty terrible at it. You really have to play the game over there. British bands were always too cool to do the meet and greets, to tell the guy from Boise, Idaho that his wife was fantastic and it was an honour to be on his show. As soon as my bands left Los Angeles and New York they were in trouble.

If anything, it went wrong for Ride when I started playing them Byrds and Beatles records after a couple of years. They started dressing like the Byrds and trying to write songs like them. They were more original at the start. They were bloody wonderful: the My Bloody Valentine who actually made records! I think they'd have sold more over the long term if they hadn't changed their sound so drastically – perhaps I could have got another five shoegazing albums out of them. That was probably a more transferable sound to the US, a more distorted, college-friendly sound for the rock fans.

I had four 'shoegazing' bands with My Bloody Valentine, Ride, Swervedriver and Slowdive. The music press called it 'shoegazing' because the bands didn't look at the audience and spent a lot of time hitting effects pedals. That was my sole contribution to creating a musical genre, and, anyway, it was all Kevin Shields' fault. Though they weren't all big bands in the UK market they were lifesavers for Creation. As usual, we were about to go bust. The way I managed to keep things going in those days was flying to America and selling one of our bands over there. Dick Green would tell me we were fucked unless I jumped on a plane to America and sold a band. It was exhausting and stressful but I loved the excitement of flying over to America and incredibly I normally managed to do it. I kept myself going with booze and drugs. Whatever's about to go wrong, try not to think about it: that's how I coped. There was a lot I refused to think about, a lot that would bite me on the arse in the near future. We got a $250,000 deal for Swervedriver. It was the only way we managed to keep our heads above water.

My Bloody Valentine's progress was so slow it was killing us: 248 nights of recording took place during 1990 and 1991. I had to go and borrow money from my father – money from my mum's life-insurance policy – to complete the album.

Kevin never understood. He was a perfectionist genius who couldn't see past the problems he'd set himself. I remember putting my mum's death money into the account, paying for another studio session and having Kevin shouting at me because I was only thinking about money. That was the breaking point for me. I'd borrowed money that had made me ashamed to ask my dad for, and Kevin was still talking to me like I was trying to rip him off.

My relationship with My Bloody Valentine didn't end officially that day, but in my mind I probably knew it couldn't go any further.

I don't blame Kevin now for his behaviour. I don't think he had any idea how far in debt we were getting. He was obsessively creative – he could only consider his own creative problems. It's the price you pay to work with geniuses. Kevin was erecting tents in the studio to get a special guitar sound only he could hear in his mind, experimenting relentlessly. He was a pure pioneer of sound.

I don't think our bands could have made the albums they did if they weren't on the edge. They're psychedelic master-pieces. They're extreme records. The people who made them were pushing the envelope.

I've always been proud that I managed to squeeze two albums out of Kevin Shields in five years, which no else ever managed to. Even if I knew I couldn't put myself through working with Kevin again I refused to give up on *Loveless*. But I really had to resort to desperate measures. They were always asking for more money for more recording. I had to cry down the phone to him.

I wasn't really crying. Well, maybe on the inside. It was the only way to make him understand what he was doing to us – otherwise he was too wrapped up in his perfectionism.

He let us hear more songs. Exceptional songs. We put them out in February 1991 as the *Tremolo* EP, and it went straight into the Top 30, their highest position yet. They were getting bigger and bigger just through word of mouth and live gigs and the fact their records were undisputedly incredible pieces of music.

We could never pull the plug because we were always so close, because there was never a second's doubt that when it came the music would be mind-blowingly good.

But if it didn't come soon, we'd go under. There were times when I nearly couldn't pay the wages to my staff. If I'd thought about things like I should have done, I don't know how I'd have coped. I remember thinking, What happens when I have to come off the drugs? I knew already that they were what fuelled me and took away the stress. You couldn't stop the bands from making you stressed, but you could always buy another gram.

We'd also signed another of our biggest bands by then, Teenage Fanclub. Again, it's Bobby Gillespie I have to thank for that – he was instrumental in persuading them to change labels for Creation. I'd known them for a few years as they were from Glasgow. When they started to get a name for themselves in 1990 I used to run into them in Euston station, me jumping a train to Birmingham to see Belinda and them getting off from Glasgow to play some gigs in London. They had a deal already with Matador and another album contracted to give to them. There was some legal wrangling before they could sign to us as Matador didn't want to accept the instrumental album that was offered to them to complete the deal. Matador thought I was behind that. People are always ascribing Machiavellian manoeuvres to me, and I find that quite flattering, but they're normally incorrect. It was all the band's doing. They wanted to be on Creation and set out to try to fulfil their contract to Matador. Once that was sorted they headed off to the studio.

I wasn't involved at all in the recording of *Bandwagonesque*. I went up to the studio in Parr Street in June expecting to hear an indie album that would sell a maximum of 30,000 copies and heard hit after hit instead. Don Fleming had done a brilliant job producing it. It was really melodic and influenced by Big Star, who I adored. And mixed in with those tracks were harder grungier tracks that would appeal to Nirvana fans. Suddenly we had another big record to add to the year's schedule next to *Loveless* and *Screamadelica*.

Midway through 1991 Dick and I realized how truly and absolutely fucked we were for money. We needed three-quarters of a million quid to survive. My Bloody Valentine had fucked us. We had a killer schedule ahead of us – we'd just added Saint Etienne (who I'd started managing and who we were joint releasing as a one-off with Jeff Barrett's new label Heavenly) – but none of the money was in yet. We needed records out quickly to pay the bills that were coming in and so we tried to double our output to get the cashflow going. We'd put out pretty much anything in those days – we released four Ed Ball albums. He'd do them for hardly any money and we'd get them out as quick as possible.

It was a good job then that the big deals I'd negotiated in the US weren't as lucrative for the labels there as I'd claimed they were going to be, or I'd suddenly be having to pay the artists a shitload of royalties. If Swervedriver had done what I'd hoped, it would have bankrupted us. We were terrible at planning for the future. We just winged it, day after day.

We owed money to Ride and they could have walked – they were very loyal to us.

The scariest thing was whether we would even have the money to put out *Screamadelica*. Scary because it was such a masterpiece. It had been a slow process getting it out of them because the band were quite messy by this point. They were available for work two days a week basically, Wednesday and Thursday. They'd be partying Thursday night through to Sunday, then need two days to recover. Two-day weeks! They did not suffer from the Calvinist work ethic, that is for certain. And *Screamadelica* got made this way, while other bands were nicking our space.

After 'Come Together' we considered releasing 'Don't Fight It, Feel It', which is a terrific song, a total house classic, a floor filler. But I was convinced the singles needed to keep having Bobby on them or we'd lose his power as a figurehead. So we picked 'Higher Than the Sun', perhaps my favourite single we ever released on Creation, a collaboration with the Orb. It's not an obvious single in many ways – you'd never have a major label release it. I always tell people I was more about the money than the music, and I still think that's true, but – make your mind up when you listen to this. You don't know what you're hearing to start with, there's no beat, just weird organs and long sliding whale groans before Bobby comes in and sings. The beat comes in with the chorus and the whole thing is so euphoric and psychedelic, just beautiful. It's basically a hymn to drugs, a celebration of where they can take you creatively, spiritually. It's the music I'd like to have played at my funeral.

We put that out in June but it only charted at 40. The whole office was mad about that single, and it was disappointing. But we knew they'd made something more important than that, something that would last the test of time.

The album wouldn't be out till September but they were starting to do gigs and had recruited Denise Johnson to tour with them for the rest of the year. They were going to be very different shows to the ones they'd toured *Primal Scream* with.

My Bloody Valentine finally recorded the vocals for *Loveless* during May and June in 1991. The end was in sight. We found Shields yet another studio where he thought he could finish the album. Dick Green was in a bad way, so stressed about the numbers that were about to doom us. I thought maybe there was light at the end of the tunnel. Then Shields decided the studio wasn't working after all. That was when I started to weep down the phone line again at him. It was September or something when he finally finished. It takes a day or two to master an album. Shields took thirteen. But after those thirteen days, it was done.

We rushed out 'Don't Fight It, Feel It' in August, and it failed to go Top 40. Each single had done worse than the last and so it was a frightening time leading up to the release of *Screamadelica*. We'd already released half the album as singles. It wasn't new to us, more like a compilation album of singles and extra tracks. Would people feel they were being cheated?

We hoped not. We were happy with the way the new tracks had gone. I'd suggested we bring in Jimmy Miller as a producer for some tracks, the legendary producer of some of the Rolling Stones' best albums, from *Beggars Banquet* to *Goats Head Soup*. I'd met him at New Music Seminar in New York in 1989. He had a bright red face and, Okay, I thought, he's a fucking alcoholic. Like I could care less. He played me a track he'd been working on with another band and it sounded exactly like it could have come from *Exile on Main St*. I realized immediately this is his sound – and the next thought was, I can apply this to Primal Scream. They learned a lot from Jimmy Miller. He taught them how to get the groove that the Stones had. It was about using cowbells on the off-beats, hand claps and different percussion. Call and response with the vocals and the guitars.

The Scream anyway have always been the world's biggest Rolling Stones fans, and what's brilliant about that band is that they don't see any contradiction in starting their acid house album with a Jimmy Miller-produced song that wouldn't seem out of place on a Stones album. 'Movin' On Up' is a perfect start to the album. It's an acoustic guitar riff you hear first that Innes made up, then Duffy's classic piano, Miller's touch bringing in the congas and shakers, Bobby calling and a gospel choir and Throb's guitar solos responding. The whole band's happy. It's the start of a weekend, the start of a bender!

The tour to accompany the album would be ferociously hedonistic. It wasn't all about ecstasy any more. The irony was that the Es started getting shit just as Primal Scream released their perfect ecstasy album. You still got good ones occasionally but more and more they were cut with smack, and that gave you such a different buzz – it erected boundaries between you and other people rather than broke them down. I'd switched more or less completely to coke by then and there was a lot of coke on the Primals' tour too. Not that I ever saw myself as a cocaine addict. I was an everythingist. Whatever was going, I'd have some of it.

But the spirit of collaboration on *Screamadelica* was something very in keeping with the way ecstasy and the acid house scene broke down boundaries. It had changed the way Primal Scream made music forever.

We thought we had recorded one of the best albums of all time, but we thought it would remain a cult classic, maybe sell 50,000 copies if we were lucky. Fuck were we wrong.

We'd sold all 50,000 of those by the Thursday of the week it came out. We'd never done anything like it.

The tour that accompanied it was Rolling Stones madness, *Cocksucker Blues*-style. Heroin had made an appearance and some of them had started freebasing cocaine too, which was a horrible thing. They loved it and I tried it with them a couple of times. There'd be about six of us round a table, smoking cocaine through a pipe made out of a water bottle and tinfoil, and by the time two people had had their turn after you, you wanted to kill them, because you were so desperate again for a hit. They called it 'going on the pipe'. It was always, I remember, a Vittel bottle. It was their Brighton version of crack.

I really hated it. It was so dark. It brought out the snidey snidey versions of us all. What I loved about E was it brought out the good versions of us all. But the Primals, they were obsessed with the dark side of life. And they loved it because it brought out the worst sides of their character.

As I've got older I've got more interested in the dark sides of our natures, but then I wanted to be happy. I wasn't happy a lot of the time, but I was trying! They were almost trying for the opposite. Out of curiosity I guess. It was such a dark phase. It was antisocial. I hated it.

We had to kick the reporters out of the dressing rooms when they started reporting what was going on in there. It was fun to start with, but it quickly got frightening.

During all this time I became very glad I'd moved to Pinnacle because Rough Trade distribution completely collapsed. For a while it took out Rough Trade records, Mute, 4AD, and pretty much everyone bar Factory, us, and One Little Indian. We were probably the eighth or ninth biggest independent label before it went down, and afterwards we were number two. I felt bad for a lot of the labels, some of whom never recovered from it. But I didn't feel sad for Rough Trade. They'd taken the piss for ages with the percentage they charged us and always treated me like I was an oik, even when I was making them a lot of money. Me and Joe Foster partied like we'd never before. We danced on their graves. It was a glorious week. For us it was like the death of Thatcher.

I did my best to forget it but the House of Love still existed and I was their manager. My relationship with them was awful now. I couldn't really hide that I thought they were all such babies, and I was still furious that they'd thrown out Bickers. They invited me along to the studio one day and Chadwick tried to bollock me for not being interested enough. When I said I didn't want to manage them any more he begged me to stay. I did, but I should have quit straight away.

The album actually wasn't doing that badly by then. It sold about 500,000 copies worldwide in the end so it wasn't as big a disaster as it's made out. It did really well in France, though we nearly didn't notice. A woman rang me up from Phonogram in Paris. 'Do you have any idea what's going on in France?' she asked me. We'd put the record out there about nine months ago and sold about 10,000 copies.

'What've you done, about 20,000 copies?' I asked, feeling optimistic.

'Alan, we've done 100,000 copies,' she said. 'I need you to tour over here immediately.'

And House of Love were suddenly massive pop stars in France. They played two nights at the Olympia, where the

Rolling Stones play if they come to Paris, and then we did a sold-out regional tour to at least 2,000 people a night. You can never predict what the French will like. Pete Astor was really big there. Pete Doherty is massive there now. Once they've decided they like something, they just don't take it off the radio.

But I was much more interested in the success of Creation by then. So when Guy finally sacked me I wasn't at all surprised. I hadn't called him for five weeks, I didn't really give him any option. He expected me to be gutted and was annoyed at how well I took the news.

I look back on the early days with House of Love as being great times. We were good mates. Then the money corrupted everything. Guy nearly got himself a butler, for Christ's sake. He thought he was royalty. Suddenly I was managing Mick Jagger. He was known as a lunatic in the Creation offices. He'd ring from a tour in America, out of his mind, at what was eleven in the morning for us and three in the morning for him, just to flirt with the receptionist. I should feel guilty, I guess, for getting them that big deal. But I would much rather have kept them on Creation: I just did what they'd hired me to do.

One thing was for sure: I was glad not to be involved in the recording of the next record, *Babe Rainbow*. It was enough to have My Bloody Valentine and Primal Scream on my hands.

Ride spent the summer of 1991 doing European festivals and preparing their new album which was to come out in 1992. Andy Bell met his wife Idha while he was in Sweden.

They were changing their sound then. All the sixties

records I'd played them had made their mark. They were more distinctive at the start but they wanted to try a cleaner, less effects-driven sound, without the quiet bit then loud bit structure that worked well for them on *Nowhere*.

Their first single from the new album was amazing – an eight-minute powerhouse called 'Leave Them All Behind' which was easy to mistake for an instrumental as the vocals didn't come in for a good two minutes. It was a statement of intent I guess – they didn't want to be part of any 'shoegazing' scene. It was an ambitious record. When you have a young band delivering you something that shows they're wanting to stretch themselves – you'd be dead if you didn't get excited. I suppose there were poppier choices of singles we could have chosen. But we were Creation, we were pioneers – we loved bands who pushed things forward. And so did record buyers – the single went straight in at number 9.

The year 1991 ended with us releasing two masterpieces in the same month.

Loveless by My Bloody Valentine was an incredible album, no way of disputing it. It arrived on 11 November in the shops, more than two years late. It did well, and we reached 50,000 sales quite quickly. It's sold steadily ever since and I still make money from publishing it today. But back then I couldn't really listen to it, it had been too hard an experience, it wasn't something I wanted to think about. Dick Green never played it. We'd been smashed by the whole experience. We were proud that it existed, but we were never going to do it again. You can only do so much crying on the phone. It wouldn't have worked a third time.

The third masterpiece of the year after *Screamadelica* and *Loveless* was *Bandwagonesque* by Teenage Fanclub. It was a brilliant record, a lovely pop record, with great harmonies.

This was the biggest surprise because when I signed the band I never thought they'd ever be more than 'indie big'. Their last single 'God Knows It's True', released by Paperhouse in the UK, had been indie big, played on the radio in the evenings. I thought we'd sell 30,000 copies of an album.

They sold 400,000 copies of *Bandwagonesque* worldwide. Half of those were sold by Creation in the UK and Europe: the other half by Geffen in America. America got them straight away – it was their classic rock sound, with the heavy guitars of grunge. Kurt Cobain was a fan. They did great live shows, full of banter and charisma.

I always thought they didn't become as big in America as they could have. They could have been massive. The reason why they weren't bigger is actually quite simple: they just didn't want to be.

Teenage Fanclub didn't want to play the game. It's not for everyone. There were people jumping out of the cupboards who they didn't want to know. The real music business in America took interest, and these people are different to the guys you find on indie labels. They're not cool. They're corporate as fuck.

In the end Teenage Fanclub were happier being the big group in Glasgow, a big group on Creation, than in smashing America with Geffen. Success isn't just about talent, it's about aspiration. Noel Gallagher wanted more than anything to be in the biggest band in the world, and he wouldn't stop believing that. I wouldn't stop believing it for him either. It wasn't plain sailing for them – Liam and Noel were walking off US tours to start with, but when they realized what they had to do, they did it. With Teenage Fanclub, there was an element of self-sabotage in the way they went about their next album. It's a Glasgow thing, of wanting to be cool rather than big. It's why I offend the Glasgow music scene so much – because I've never hidden that I'd rather be big than cool. It sounds crass to go on about wanting success, but there's nothing wrong with ambition. It was why I loved it in America and they loved me. It was so refreshing. In Britain you have to be embarrassed about any success you're having. Americans loved me because I didn't have any of this embarrassment. I'd say it straight: I want to make loads of money, how do I do it? What do I have to do to become successful? Someone would tell me who to talk to, and I'd knock on their door and talk to them.

I was flying to America at least twice a month by 1991. I loved it. But I was flying on seriously heavy fuel by now and, high as I was, I wondered sometimes how long it would be until I crashed. There would be a big explosion if I ever did.

10: MILLIONAIRE

By 1992 I was flagging. The pressure hadn't let up for a second. Dick didn't want me to be crazy Alan McGee all the time in the office but he needed me to be that with the Americans, to turn up mouthing off about having found the biggest bands in the world. He'd try to make me look at the figures and take his advice but I wasn't willing to listen to him most of the time. I'd decided I was going to do it my way. My energy came from booze and pills and lines and whatever else might give me a bump. It was a lonely lifestyle sometimes. That's why meeting Tim Abbott was such a relief for me. It didn't make me any less tired, high or deranged, but at least I had some company.

I first met him in Birmingham. I'd gone up one night with Bobby in 1991 when 'Come Together' was in the charts. We were there for a Heavenly gig, Saint Etienne and the Manic Street Preachers, which Tim was promoting. Nicky Wire had a dig at Bobby Gillespie during 'We Love Us', shouting, 'Yeah, let's all come together!' before going into one of their mad punk songs. Bobby didn't care one bit. We went back to Tim's gaff for an afterparty, whereupon he produced ten more Es. I liked his style immediately. He was working as a management consultant and running a club called The Better Way at weekends. He knew where to get brilliant pills and was one of the few people who still could in 1991 and 1992. Anyway, I invited him to the office in Hackney to do an audit of something or other. Not the type of thing we had spent a great deal of time worrying about in the past, hence the financial disarray we were often in. I ended up offering him a job and he moved down to London.

He had some good ideas that saved us money – like stopping outsourcing the artwork and getting our own art director. He definitely saved us money there. He was good at his job, though a lot of people in the office hated him. He was an unknown quantity. He'd arrived from nowhere and started doing time and effectiveness studies on them. Nothing of the kind had ever been attempted in the Creation offices. They were thinking, Who the fuck are you? The fact was, he was my mate and I was in charge, so I could bring him in if I wanted. And I wanted to. They didn't have to like it and they didn't. I think they all thought I'd given him a job just because he loved drugs and bad behaviour as much as me.

Well, if that was true to begin with, what was wrong with that? People not liking what I was doing was often what most firmly convinced me to do it.

For two years we ran riot together. I moved him into 'the Bunker': the office Dick and I occupied in the basement. It was a bit of a boys' club in there. My wall was covered in pictures of Helena Christensen and Kate Moss and other supermodels. *It's just totally sexist!* said Belinda, whenever she came into the office. Yeah, she was probably right.

Abbott's wall was worse though: pictures of prison riots and mutilated people, people shot to bits in America, sick stuff like that. And there was a big homage to Chris Eubank there too. Abbott and me loved his fuck-you attitude to the world.

Dick's wall was a bit more practical. Some charts. Release dates. You'd look at Dick's side of the room occasionally and surprise yourself by remembering you worked for a record label.

Sex on my wall, death on Abbott's, flowcharts on Dick's.

I wonder sometimes if we pretty much invented *Loaded* magazine's idea of lad culture down there. This was January 1992, before that kind of lad iconography was fashionable. We were the trailblazers. I think James Brown might have copied that from us when he launched his magazine a year later. He must have been down to the Bunker. And he did call his magazine *Loaded*. And he did become addicted to drugs.

It wasn't unusual that Abbott would rack out a line of coke at two in the afternoon. And if he did one, I'd do one. And then I'd pick up the phone and rattle off whatever abuse came to mind at whoever came to mind. That was when Creation was fucking great fun. We spent a couple of years on the absolute razzle dazzle.

Poor Dick. He must have been thinking, How have I got myself into this situation with this pair of loonies? I wouldn't have liked to meet myself in those days if I wasn't on drugs. I don't know how he coped with the pair of us. I think he had enough of me then to last him a lifetime. I love the man very much, but it's probably not a coincidence we've only seen each other three times in the last thirteen years. Having to cope with my behaviour on a long-term basis might have had an adverse effect on the friendship.

Having said that, I don't want to make out that Dick was boring. Far from it. He'd come out and enjoy himself too. But not like us. He had a family back home. We didn't and we were extreme. Abbott was single (he normally was). Belinda and I had moved in together that year to a flat in Rotherhithe but she would always be leaving and going to stay with her parents in Sheffield. In the end I moved out of the flat we shared and into a penthouse flat in the same block with Grant Fleming and Karen Parker. I loved Belinda, don't get me wrong. I did. But we were on and off. She'd come and stay with me in the penthouse for a while but she was always leaving me. I was too much for her. She couldn't keep up with the lifestyle. I'm not proud of that. No one could keep up apart from Abbott. We were running riot together.

These days, we ring up and moan to each other about our backs. How the train to London hurts mine, how his bag hurts his – and he tells me we're like two characters from *Last of the Summer Wine*. But in those days we lived it large.

But as well as being my drug buddy, Abbott really was good for Creation. He was a fresh pair of eyes and could look at problems coldly. For example, the rest of the company were caught up in the church of My Bloody Valentine – no one would have thought about dropping them. He listened to the stories, looked at the figures and laid it on the line: They're causing you nothing but problems, get rid of them, McGee. Which was exactly what I wanted to do, and I needed someone at that point who could see things clearly from a financial rather than emotional perspective. He was right. As soon as you took the cult of Kevin out of the company, the figures began to make more sense.

I rang up Kevin Shields on 6 January 1992 and told him we were dropping him. I wasn't trying to be horrible but I said it straight: 'It's over. I can't be doing more records with you.' He was completely shocked. He didn't realize what he was doing to me when he was having his shouting fit in Church Studios, paid for by my mum's cancer money, whereas I'd known in my heart from that day it was over. The next day there were ten record labels battling to sign him. Island paid something around half a million for an album that they never saw.

After Creation dropped them, I fell out with Kevin for years. Then we buried the hatchet, watching Oasis in Dublin in the late 1990s. And then we fell out again when I read this interview in a magazine where he was calling me names, saying I hadn't supported him. When someone slags me off in public, I keep coming back at them. So I was busy giving him stick for a while. What stopped a lot of my bitterness was the film *Upside Down* they made about Creation in 2010. Watching that made me remember that, actually, it was good, and everyone involved tried their best. No one was doing anything to hurt each other. We just had incompatible needs a lot of the time. I ran into Kevin soon after seeing the film and realized I really liked him, that all the grievances had been petty.

I hope we're friends again. When he signed for Creation, I promised that I would stay out of his way and let him make his records, and within reason, that's exactly what I did. He was a genius and bringing out his records made me look great. And for that, I'm grateful.

His new album came out in February 2013, only twenty-one years and three months after the one I put out. I suspect that's about how long *Loveless* might have taken if I hadn't had that sense of urgency in 1991. It was never going to come from Kevin. But the new album *m b v* is superb and I'm really impressed with the way he's released it. You can only get it off their website, nowhere else; I love that. Well done, Kevin, you took out the record companies and did it yourself. You have to admire his courage.

Back in 1992, dropping My Bloody Valentine caused some problems in the office. Laurence wouldn't stop trying to drag me down to see them, to get me back into the project. But at that stage I was never going to back down. There was nothing to suggest he wouldn't do it again. He did do it again! He did it ten times worse! I've got nothing but love and respect for Kevin for making those two albums and letting me release them, but I've never regretted not being involved in the third.

Despite the regime of drug madness Abbott and I operated under, we were getting more and more professional as we attempted to sort out our finances. I was under pressure from James Kyllo to change the share we'd always agreed with our bands. It wasn't standard any more, if it ever was – certainly you didn't get that with the majors. I'd copied this model from Factory and always believed in it: a fifty-fifty profit share with the bands. I tell people these days that I was always in it for the money, but I was never in it to rip off the bands. So we'd always given them a good deal, a fair deal. It nearly made us bankrupt a few times but it also showed the bands we cared about them.

Bands would sign to us because they understood me. We were honest and we were generous. We were always *late* paying the bands, I acknowledge that, we were late for years, but we always paid them. No one ever got ripped off. Our reputation was always great in that respect.

It was quite an indie thing, being fair to the bands. Rough Trade were always fifty-fifty profit share with their bands too, and everyone's always known they're fair. I might think they're all fucking hippies but they're financially honest hippies at least.

One of the frustrations I had in those days was with international distribution and how we could improve sales in Europe. This is when selling a share to a major became very interesting to me – I thought it could take us to a new level internationally. Take *Screamadelica* for example: we were on about 11,000 in Germany and it was 180,000 in Britain, and I couldn't understand how there could be such a disparity. I was tired of the indie structure, of alliances with other indies in Europe, and I was curious about what a big player could do to change the situation.

I bumped into Paul Russell, the chairman of Sony, early that year at Heathrow airport. It was a bad week: neither of the singles we had out that week – Primal Scream's *Dixie-Narco* EP (which was number 12 but we needed Top 10) and Teenage Fanclub's 'What You Do to Me' – had done as well as we'd hoped, or needed.

I wanted to know whether he thought Sony's sales teams could have given them the positions I thought they deserved. He wanted to talk more about it, tell me what he thought Sony could do that Pinnacle couldn't.

I was always being approached by the majors and up till then I'd always told them to fuck off. I remembered what an awful time I'd had with Elevation at Warners. It was only through me being able to do my own thing that we'd succeeded with the bands everyone else had written off. But I was at the point now where I knew I had records that should be selling more than they were, and I wanted to do whatever we had to do to sell those copies.

It never occurred to me that any of this might be due to a recession, that sales were down everywhere. I was so off my tits that the fact that there was a recession never penetrated once into my consciousness. For us it had always seemed like a shit climate so we were just getting on with business as usual. It wasn't a new thing, we'd been going broke for years! The way I dealt with it was always by not dealing with it, with another pill or another line. As crass as it sounds, I just don't remember the recessions. The price of bread might've been going up but a gram of coke was still fifty quid and a pill was always a tenner. Some things are reliable, even when the economy's falling apart!

As I didn't even know there was a recession it was easy to buck against the recessionary trends. I decided to launch three new labels. I'd been partying with Chris Abbott, Tim's brother, for a while, and he started a Techno imprint for us called Infonet. He knew his techno, and no one else did, so he was the man for the job. And we hired Dave Barker, who was the first guy to sign Teenage Fanclub, to run a guitar label called August. And the third label saw the return of one of the early heroes (anti-heroes) of Creation, Joe Foster, who launched a reissues label called Rev-Ola.

Joe Foster's music knowledge had always been incredible. I credit him with being a bigger influence than anyone on my music taste. He was an encyclopedia of the 1960s. You could never catch him out. He could tell you the name of every single member of the Artwoods. You could ask him what the B-side was on a German-only single by the Creation and he'd know instantly. He got me into the Velvets, got me into the Byrds, taught me that David Crosby was an amazing song-writer. You know how you have one swotty mate, who knows everything about everything? Well, Joe Foster was that mate. He was perfect for the reissues label, as you can imagine.

He put out weird sixties records, knew exactly what they'd sell. William Shatner and Leonard Nimoy – each of their records sold 10,000 each and made £50,000, and Joe would buy them for about a grand. We got great reviews, a steady income stream. We didn't make loads of money from it, but he knew what he was doing, knew his market, what they'd sell.

Of course, he was also completely vociferous and absolutely mental. You couldn't invent Joe Foster. His sense of humour was so wrong. He's probably the most politically incorrect person who's ever walked the earth. For example, he found this album he wanted to bring out by Peter Wyngarde, an old TV actor who'd played detective Jason King in the 1970s: Joe loved records by weird actors. He had a thousand copies of *When Sex Leers Its Inquisitive Head* pressed up and ready to go. This is later, at the height of Oasis, the time I'm working for a government committee, taking Margaret McDonagh out for dinner. Someone in the office said to me at the time, 'Have you heard that record?' I was thinking, No, I never listen to Joe's records. They were always very strange.

And they told me to listen to track 3.

'Okay, what's it called?'

'"Rape".'

Oh . . . I put it on and it's this guy taking the piss out of a rape – talking about the Italian rape, the Chinese rape, the German rape, as if he was taking the piss out of going fishing. It was probably very ironic, but it was so ironic I didn't get the joke. I'm thinking: a) I don't agree with it; b) the *Daily Mail* are going to have my balls! Oasis guru advocates rape.

So I pulled it. Joe wasn't happy. I had Peter Wyngarde ringing me up roaring down the phone, *It's Not About Rape!*

Well, you took the rough with the smooth with Foster, and actually he did a great job with Rev-Ola. And in one respect he did come back to Creation a changed man: he had stopped punching people. In all other respects, he was exactly the same.

The week after Primal Scream didn't make the Top 10, Ride flew straight in at number 9 with 'Leave Them All Behind'. Number 10 in the charts was 'Reverence' by the Jesus and Mary Chain. Primal Scream number 11. I had a royal flush of bands I'd signed! Tim and I celebrated with a four-day party.

In the excitement we pressed too many of Ride's new album *Going Blank Again*. The manager was talking about them playing Wembley. We sold 45,000 in the first week and it went gold eventually, but we'd pressed up far too many.

Meanwhile, the Screamadelica tour rolled on. It was great fun to start with. They'd gone from a tiny punk band to a huge live acid house explosion. But when they took the tour to America in February they started to come apart from all the drugs they were doing. It was serious now. Heroin had really set in among the band. I had some strange times out there with them. Completely deranged, being driven around by Kim Fowley, not knowing how I'd got there.

I was never officially Primal Scream's manager, but I *was* the manager, from about 1985 to 1992. It really was a conflict of interests after a while. I wasn't taking a percentage for managing their band and Bobby was ringing me up, screaming because a monitor engineer hadn't been paid on time. That was the last straw. He was screaming at me as if I was his employee even though he wasn't paying me a penny for managing them. If he'd paid me 20 per cent to be the manager I'd have put up with him screaming at me. (Guy Chadwick, he used to do that to me all the time on the phone. He'd be screaming and so I'd put the phone down on the side, go for a walk, get a beer out of the fridge, open it, come back, pick up the phone and say, *Yes, I agree.* I'd never know what I'd agreed to.) But I'd supported Primal Scream from the time they were nothing and taken no percentage for managing. I couldn't do it any more. They were becoming an international act and they needed someone dedicated.

We brought in Alex Nightingale, their live agent, as manager.

I remember when I first met Alex. He'd been trying to get involved in the music business for years, but he couldn't get a foothold because everyone knew he was Annie Nightingale's son. We all looked down our noses at him at the time too – because he was Annie Nightingale's son. No one would give the poor bastard a chance because they felt he wasn't there on merit, just on nepotism. He lived in Brighton so we'd bump into him a bit, and one night I invited him to come back with us. I think it was me, my friend James Williamson and Alex. I was jumping around on an E and decided to test out his personality. So I started firing CDs at him, slinging them at him hard like little mirrored

Frisbees. James joined in too. Both of us jumping on armchairs and hurling CDs at him all night, hundreds of CDs. *What the fuck are they into?* he must have been thinking, but he didn't get the hump so I began to feel a bit of respect for him. That was his initiation and he passed. No one painted his balls; he was quite lucky really. In the morning, he told me he was going for an interview with Mike Hinc at a booking agency. Mike was one of my best mates in the industry from when he'd used to work at Rough Trade. I told him this and he asked if I could put a word in for him so I phoned up Mike and told him Alex was my pal, because I'd just fired two hundred CDs at him and he never attacked me – well, of course, I didn't actually say that – and Mike gave him a chance and gave him a job.

That was how he got into the music industry and since then he's been the agent for the Chemical Brothers and Lily Allen, and you've got to respect him for making a career for himself.

He was a good choice for Primal Scream at the time. You had to be mad to take on a job with those lunatics, had to be awake with them every night at 5 a.m. Towards the end of 1992, I think I had an inkling that I was coming out of that style of living. It took longer than I expected, and it was more dramatic than I expected, but I think I'd already begun to make the decision to change my life.

I quite liked Alex. The last I saw of him was on TV, a classic albums programme, about *Screamadelica*. He was weirder than me on it! That takes some doing. He's obviously still into the idea of the music and the madness, and that's fine, I'm sure he enjoys it and I'm not knocking it.

There was an election in 1992. I was too high to notice. I believe the Tories won. I'd play a much bigger part in the next one.

Dick Green had started to make plans for life after Creation. Although we'd had some good successes we still weren't selling enough to justify what we were spending on recording and promoting the albums. We didn't handle the money with any discipline and we were so far in the red it looked like it was over. I'd probably have come to the same conclusion without the regular cocktail of reality avoiders, but they gave me a bit more hope. That's not to say I wasn't desperate at times though. Quite a lot of times. There was only one thing that would save us – we had to sell a share of the company.

The first people who showed interest were China Records. Derek Green had set China up around the same time as Creation, but distributed through the majors until very recently when he switched to Pinnacle. He was very ambitious, wanting to expand quickly, and one way you do that is by taking over other companies, like us.

It's always good to have someone interested when you're trying to get a good deal with someone else. Now was the time to follow up on that conversation I'd had with Sony's Paul Russell at Heathrow earlier in the year.

I met with him and his colleague Jeremy Pearce and listened

to what they had to say. It sounded good. They'd throw a lot of money in, take care of international distribution but – they claimed – leave me with creative freedom as to who I signed.

I still liked Derek Green too. But I couldn't believe what he told me over dinner one night – he was the managing director at A&M when they dropped the Sex Pistols in 1977! How could I go into business with someone like that? Of course, I look back at the age of fifty-two and think, Really? You didn't sign because of that? But at thirty-two you see things differently, especially if you're a drug addict.

Perhaps there were other reasons the offer from China was less appealing than the Sony one. I suspect that in the end they would have raped Creation, sacked almost everyone but me, left me as head of A&R . . . It would have been terrible for the company. I'd have still got handsomely paid, but it would have bored me silly.

By July both China and Sony were offering around £2.5 million for half the company. Whatever the reasons, I decided fairly early on that it was Sony I was likely to do business with.

Word must have got out that we were in trouble and thinking of selling. In the middle of our talks with Sony, when they were offering two million and we were negotiating upwards, Derek Birkett from One Little Indian requested a meeting to discuss making an offer to buy us.

At the time I was fucking angry at the cheek of him, but I wouldn't be surprised if he was put up to it by Brian Bonnar, who as well as owning more than half of One Little Indian was also the managing director of Mayking. We owed Mayking about £200,000 for pressing our records and they had just put our account on stop so we couldn't make any more. Perhaps Bonnar thought we'd be glad of any buyer.

Derek Birkett came down to the Bunker and offered £400,000, told me what a reasonable offer it was. He had no idea that Sony had just offered £2.5 million and that I was hopeful of getting more out of them. I listened to him trying to hustle me while I kept calm. You should have seen Abbott's face when they started talking. He didn't know if I was going to whack them with a chair. I kept calm, let Birkett say his piece. And then I told him he was an *absolute* piece of work, told him to get the fuck out of my office, that he should be embarrassed. I laughed at him. *You're a corporate whore.* Told him to fuck off.

Everybody thinks you're mad anyway, he said, and rushed out. We sent the little Indian packing.

There was quite a few of those type of scenes in the Bunker. I enjoyed them. People would come down and demand things of us and I'd just listen calmly for a while. And then I'd inform them, in great detail, why they could go and fuck themselves and in how many different ways they could go and fuck themselves and how they should get the fuck out of my office or I would demonstrate the ways in which the fucking fuckers could fuck themselves. Unbelievably, I kept my teeth. Somebody should by rights have come in with a metal bar one day and whacked me in the face with it.

After we did the Sony deal, just to properly torture Brian Bonnar we took all our business away from him apart from the Ed Ball records. He would get about a thousand pounds a month from us, where he had been having sixty or seventy grand a month. And of course, when Oasis happened he missed out on millions of pounds of work. It might have bankrupted him, poor man.

The deal with Sony took a lot of negotiation. We had a great lawyer in John Kennedy. I'd met him when we were doing the Mary Chain record deal. He was the guy who got the Stone Roses out of their madly exploitative deal with Silvertone.

We had to keep talking to both China and Sony in case one of the deals fell through. There was a lot of debt we needed to resolve. On paper, we were absolutely fucked. The figures did not add up! But Sony and China thought I had some kind of vision, and that Primal Scream had the potential to be international superstars. They thought I had the vision to find a band that would become massive.

If the deal had collapsed, then that would have been the end of Creation. I remember our press officer Andy Saunders leaving to go on his summer holiday. 'Call me if we go bust or if we do the deal,' he said on the way out. There wasn't a middle option.

We survived. Sony bought 49 per cent of the company for £2.5 million in September 1992. The deal included an extra million to Creation to stop us from going bust immediately.

Our keeping 51 per cent was a clever way of slanting the

publicity but it made fuck all difference to how much control we really had. It sounded like I was still in control but, contractually, they had huge power to influence what I did. To seal the deal I had to commit to give them the option to buy my 51 per cent of the company at market value in four years' time. That was a worrying detail I tried not to think about. I wouldn't have to think about it for four years but in 1996 I might have a problem. What they didn't reckon with is what a stubborn cunt I am and what little respect I have for contracts.

I certainly wasn't worrying about that at the time, anyway. I was a millionaire! I'd always said I was going to be a millionaire but I'd said a lot of things in my life that hadn't come to pass.

Surprisingly, one of the first things I felt was sadness. I wanted to tell my mum. I wanted to tell her I could give her whatever she wanted, that she could be proud of me.

The next thing I felt was a burning urge to call my drug dealer.

11: GIVE OUT BUT DON'T GIVE UP

Doing the deal with Sony mostly made us feel triumphant. We'd got through a situation that looked certain to crush us and we'd survived. But it was also the moment that Creation began to die. It's almost unheard of for an indie label to have had our kind of success and not buckle under the changes selling to a major forces on them. The only one I can think of is Beggars Banquet and XL with the success they've had with Adele. Success can be as dangerous as failure. Going to the top of the ladder gives you much further to drop.

We had surrendered some of our independence but we handled the presentation of the deal perfectly and managed to avoid any negative press at the time for selling out. The press, I think, were just pleased we hadn't gone under, like Factory did that November.

I was gutted for Tony Wilson when that happened. I loved Factory because it had a spirit of independence but also ambition. They weren't aiming low. It wasn't a moral cause. They just wanted to release the best music they could and do it in style. I thought it was crazy that with his bands he wasn't doing better. (Though did he not spend a million pounds on a table Peter Saville had designed that hung down from the ceiling? Cocaine's a wonderful drug.) It was hard for Tony after Factory went down, and probably hard, over the next few years, to see me do so well out of a Manchester band he turned down.

Oddly enough, the negativity we got for selling Creation all came later, and it would arrive in bizarre places you weren't expecting it, for example from some Icelander in Reykjavik who'd bound up to me and shout, *You have sold out ze culture!* (Everyone in Iceland I've found wants to either fuck you or batter you. And it was normally battering me. For selling out ze culture.)

I had changed my drug habits in response to my windfall. Overnight I went from buying one gram at a time to buying seven. It was the inaugural year of the Mercury Prize and Primal Scream were shortlisted for *Screamadelica*. We were one of the favourites but didn't know in advance if we'd won. The band didn't even want to go to the event, but I was playing the game for Sony just then, and I hired them a limo to get them there on 8 September 1992. They got in the limo but Bobby refused to get out when they arrived. Instead, he spent almost the whole night driving around in it – god knows what he was on, he always took the strangest drugs of anyone – and then he walked in at the last minute to the Savoy Hotel to hear the announcement. Saint Etienne were on the list too, who Jeff Barrett had put out as a Heavenly release using Creation's distribution, and my old mates the Jesus and Mary Chain were there too with *Honey's Dead*. I didn't nominate

Loveless because I thought Kevin Shields would win it and he'd annoyed me too much at the time. Petty? Yes.

And the prize goes to . . . *Screamadelica*! Everyone from the label was overjoyed. The band didn't seem to care less and ran away from all the publicity that had been arranged.

Jeremy Pearce from Sony came along to the afterparty with us, and I think that was when he first understood what absolute drug addicts we were. We went back to Tim Abbott's weird turreted house in Highgate. There was a pyramid of cocaine the size of a sandcastle on the table and everyone was just digging into to it with teaspoons and throwing it up their noses. Everyone had told Jeremy I had some issues with drugs but I'd managed to keep him uncertain of the extent until then.

That night Alex Nightingale managed to lose both the award and the cheque for £25,000 and had to ring up the Mercury Prize the next day to ask them to write him a new one. They must have really wished they'd given the prize to someone else.

If Primal Scream were getting all the critical acclaim, Teenage Fanclub were quietly doing the business in America. They did *Saturday Night Live*. Kurt Cobain and Courtney Love turned up to see them in LA and I got to meet them. Cobain was incredibly quiet, really softly spoken, whispering. Courtney Love sounded like a bomb going off, 'Hey, yeah, mother-fucker!' That wasn't the last I'd hear from her.

I remember *Thirteen*, the follow-up to *Bandwagonesque*,

as a bad record, but in retrospect it probably wasn't. They took over a year to make it in Manchester, staying in a Jurys Inn, which would have depressed the hell out of anyone. The thing about music is you have a window, a moment, and you have to take it. Bands make the mistake of thinking they've all the time in the world. They might only have a month, and if they don't do what they need to do in that month to sell the records they need to, they might never have the chance again. What people want to hear at a certain time, there's no way of predicting how that will change. In 1991 Teenage Fanclub had the world at their feet; by 1993 it was a different story. The world heard *Bandwagonesque* and in the time it took for *Thirteen* to come out it had moved on and it was ready for Oasis.

All the cocaine I was doing in those days made me pretty unpredictable. It was a way of ignoring my unease about the Sony deal. I kind of knew I'd given up a lot of my power then, and I resented it. I've read about how I'd shout down other people like our press officer Andy Saunders, like Tim Abbott – *this is not a democracy, this is a dictatorship*, all that. Well, yeah, but it was.

And yeah, we bored a lot of people with all the drugs we did, but we also gave people the perspective that Creation was a rock and roll label. Tim was another rock and roll obsessive, like me, like Bobby and the Scream. There was a lot of people before Tim who were steeped in the indie thing. I was never interested in indie. It was rock and roll we were interested in. This was in 1992, when it was quite unfashionable to say this. The indie thing was just a term to me. Rock and roll was about the Stones, it was the same spirit that the Jesus and Mary Chain had which attracted me. It was bad behaviour, it was fuck you. Tim Abbott backed that up. If we were an 'indie' label to begin with in the 1980s, by the start of the 1990s we were in my mind a full-throttle rock and roll label. There were a lot of people in the company who thought that Tim was arrogant, that I was a lunatic, but we had a spirit that took things to the edge.

Primal Scream were doing their best to take over from My Bloody Valentine's role as the biggest threat to my sanity. *Loveless* is legendary as the album that nearly bankrupted us, so what a lot of people don't realize is that *Give Out But Don't Give Up* took just as long to make and cost far more. £420,000 in the end! We spent the first £48,000 demoing new songs in the Roundhouse in Camden with Jimmy Miller. This was September and October 1992. Unfortunately I was right about Jimmy Miller's excessive lifestyle. It was very bad for his health to introduce him to Primal Scream and he died soon after those sessions from liver failure. He was dabbling again during the recordings. It wasn't actually the Scream that killed him, but it can't have helped. He was a great guy, a genius producer, but as reckless as the rest of us, and much older. He was always phoning me up saying, 'Alan, I want you to buy my points [royalties] off me' – for *Screamadelica* – and I'd say, 'Jimmy, I don't want to buy your points off you; one day they'll be worth money for you.'

We call the two months they spent at the Roundhouse together the Brownhouse sessions. All they did was smoke heroin, watch *The Simpsons* and record cover versions. Sony have about sixty different versions of 'On the Dark End of the Street' covered by Primal Scream, produced by Jimmy Miller. It's an okay cover, but fuck me. They never even came out as B-sides. That was the Brownhouse sessions. The producer was addicted to heroin and three of the band were. And then there was the entourage. Brighton is full of smack. Camden is full of smack. They were practically falling over it.

I couldn't believe we'd just come through *Loveless* and it looked like it was going to happen again. Why were all my bands so dysfunctional? Probably because I signed them. Later on, I just gave up trying to get bands to deliver albums. Just come and see me when you've got one finished was my new philosophy.

Primal Scream were never going to do any work in Camden, that was for sure. So we had the bright idea of sending them to record in America, in Memphis. And, actually, they did find it harder to get heroin there, but of course – and this is what always happens with bands – the first guy they met was a cocaine dealer driving a taxi. By the time I got there they were on the strongest coke I'd ever tried, perhaps the strongest coke known to mankind. I had one or two lines of it and had to stand against a wall in Memphis for three days to make sure there was no one creeping up behind me.

My relationship with Bobby went through one of its rockier times then. But I didn't give up. It was all about loyalty with

Primal Scream. I'd given everything to the Mary Chain and I'd got fucked. William Reid told me in Times Square I was the fifth member of the Mary Chain and then it felt like he betrayed me. I knew Bobby wouldn't fuck me. And that's why I went to the wall for them. I just believed in them. It wasn't about music at first. It was about people. I knew they had talent. I knew they were rock stars. I believed in their attitude, in Bobby and Andrew and Throb.

So I wasn't too annoyed with how irresponsible they were being. It wasn't personal. They were just like that. They'd thought they were superstars when they lived in Brighton with fuck all, when no one knew who they were. And now they'd had a massive album. They had always been obsessed with the mythology of rock and roll and now they'd tasted success they had the drugs to finish off the obsession. But I wasn't going to give up on more Primal Scream albums.

So in early February 1993 we had to have a crisis meeting to address the fact that half the people there were addicted to heroin. This was eighteen months after *Screamadelica* had come out and they had no new tracks we could use. The message was, clean up or ship out. It was the lowest point in their history, but they acknowledged it and wanted to move on. So they gave up heroin and became alcoholics.

Thankfully, not everything was as difficult and dark as it was with Primal Scream. I'd signed one of my favourite musicians in the world, Bob Mould, with his new band Sugar. I'd always loved Hüsker Dü but after they'd disbanded Bob Mould's two solo albums had completely bombed. He came to the office and told me they'd sold 80,000 copies but I checked and they'd actually sold 7,000 – we had to lower his advance quite a bit after we found that out.

We put out two records by him. The first, *Copper Blue*, was released on 4 September 1992 and became an absolutely massive record. We had world rights and he sold 400,000 copies internationally. His second, a mini album called *Beaster*, went in at number 3 a year later and sold really well too.

He'd come out as being gay at this point. I was in New York with him, in Queens, in a studio. He was sitting in front of a huge mixing desk. Swervedriver were playing round the corner and I asked him, 'Do you want tae head?'

Here was another man who couldn't understand my Scottish accent: he thought I'd asked him, 'Do you want some head?'

He sat bolt upright and turned around. 'What!'

I probably should have been offended. I slowed down and said, very slowly, 'Would you like to go to the Swervedriver concert now?'

Bob Mould was looking at me thinking, You weird little fucker.

It shocked us all how well we did with Sugar. It made me really happy because Bob's a great guy and so talented; he deserved everything he got. It was significant for me because *Copper Blue* was the first record we released after the Sony deal. We put it in the chart and watched it explode. There seemed to be no reason for it – his solo albums hadn't done

172 / ALAN McGEE

anything. Again, it was about timing. Nirvana had opened up people for that sound – even though it was Bob Mould and the Pixies and Dinosaur Jnr who'd invented it. Suddenly it was trendy to be Bob Mould.

I was glad to have had my judgement vindicated again too, just when Sony were realizing what a dangerous investment they'd made in Primal Scream. The way they were going, *Screamadelica* looked like it might be their masterpiece, and their swansong.

12: OASIS

Debbie Turner had been one of my very best friends since we met in the Hacienda days, and I did my best to keep in touch. On 31 May 1993 her band were playing her first ever gig, at King Tut's in Glasgow, third on the bill, supporting a Creation band, 18 Wheeler, and another band called Boyfriend. Debbie's band were called Sister Lovers – after the Big Star album; we all loved Big Star. I thought it would be really funny to turn up unannounced at Debbie Turner's first gig and wave at her from the crowd when she came onstage.

She shared a rehearsal room with another Manchester band but I didn't know she was bringing them down with her. People don't like to believe in luck: they assume it's too much of a coincidence, that Sony sent me to the gig on a tip, but I really thought I was just going to surprise my mate. I'd planned to see my sisters, hang out, go to an Italian house night at Sub Club, have a nice time, a holiday.

I thought I'd be arriving just in time to see Debbie's band but I hadn't been out in Glasgow for a while and didn't realize the licensing laws had changed. They'd decided now that people could drink, in Glasgow of all places, till half past six in the morning. And then they'd open again three hours later.

Somehow, that was supposed to cut down on alcoholism. Anyway, the change to the licensing laws meant that the first band wasn't going on till half ten or something. So I was really early when I got there and had to get pissed. Debbie was shocked to see me. It didn't help her nerves at all. I gradually became aware that there was all this drama going on with the bouncers and another Manchester band who had come down for an away day and demanding to play even though they weren't on the bill. I could hear all these Manc accents arguing. I looked over and saw Liam Gallagher for the first time. He looked amazing. A proper, Adidassed-up mod. He had hair like a young Paul Weller. And I thought: He's got to be the drug dealer. Because nobody in a band looks that good. So that's what I thought.

I said to the promoter, 'Why don't you let them go on and play four songs?' It was going to turn into a fight otherwise. They'd brought a proper little crew up. And when the good-looking drug dealer walked on stage and picked up the microphone, I thought, Okay, this is interesting now.

The first song they played was 'Bring It On Down'. It was amazing. I'd had about four or five drinks so I thought, Hang on, Alan, maybe you're wrong. Then they played the next song, 'Up In the Sky'. It was unbelievably good. Liam could sing – he had the attitude – he was a natural star. And Noel was a hell of a guitar player – he really stood out over the rest of the musicians in the band. I was with my sister Susan, and I said to her, I think I'm going to sign them. Still, I was quite pissed. *Hang on, Alan.* And then they played 'I Am the

Walrus', which is one of the most occult songs ever. It was that song that made me absolutely certain I wanted to sign them, and I don't think it's a coincidence because years later I became fascinated by occult writing. At the time I just put it down to the fact that they were Beatles fans too, that they might have the same way with a melody – that was enough for me.

While they were playing I found out who was in charge from Mark Coyle, who'd recently been sacked by Teenage Fanclub for taking coke and being a bad influence. (It was ironic that their manager thought *Mark* was a bad drugs influence on the band when they were signed to *my* record label.) Mark was doing the sound for the gig and I went over and asked him what the band were called.

'Oasis,' he said.

'Have they got a deal?' I asked.

'No.'

'Have they got a manager?'

'No.'

I was getting excited now. 'So who's in charge?' I asked, and he turned and pointed at the guitarist, Noel Gallagher. As soon as they'd finished playing I ran over and introduced myself.

'That was great,' I said. 'Do you want a deal?'

'Who with?' he asked.

'Creation.'

'Yes,' he said.

I liked him immediately, he was together, intelligent, a proper little Manc: *aright, aright, fookin' right.* We talked bollocks for a while. I caught him looking with slight fascination at my shoes – I had a pair of bright red Gucci loafers on.

'Do you want a tape?' he asked.

I didn't. I knew already.

'I don't want your tape – I want to *sign* you.'

He gave me one anyway. The tape was good, not as good as the live thing, but still really exciting.

I phoned Dick Green the next morning and told him that I'd found a band, *the* band, the one to take us stratospheric. I don't think Dick opened the champagne straight away though. He'd heard that one before.

Liam, Noel and Bonehead came to see us at the office in Hackney on the next Friday. It made a good impression. We had a wall of heroes in the Bunker as well as the supermodels and atrocities: Rod Stewart, Paul Simonon, Alex Chilton. Noel was checking them out and nodding approvingly. The one thing that office made clear was that we fucking loved music. Liam was rolling his shoulders, giving everyone the eye. I'd told all the women in the office they were going to fancy him, so they were all determined to pretend they didn't. You had the sense that Liam felt himself totally entitled to be there, that it was his destiny. Noel, who'd been burned before, was a bit more wary, not wanting to get too far ahead of himself in case it didn't happen. (Tony Wilson had turned Oasis down for Factory in 1992, saying they were 'too baggy'.) Bonehead was there to stop Liam and Noel from killing each other.

Abbott understood what was great about them straight away. We were chopping out lines for Noel and Liam before too long. And they went away with a firm offer to come to Creation and we had their firm offer to come to us. A shake of the hand.

As soon as I'd said I was interested, Mother (U2's label) offered to double the deal, and Go! Discs were in too. They were serious contenders. That used to happen – record labels would get interested in a band because they heard I was interested in them. But Noel had given me his word and I knew he wanted to go with me. He is a very loyal guy and I believed he wanted to sign with us.

Signing Oasis came a bit close to the bone. There were lots of suitors. They'd found a manager quickly – Noel had told me Johnny Marr and Bernard Sumner's manager Marcus Russell was interested, and I thought that sounded like a good fit and told him so. They took on Marcus and his company Ignition Management straight away. I liked Marcus and he had respect for Creation, could see we were a good bet to break the band in the UK.

I had to talk them up in LA to get Sony to come in internationally. Marcus Russell and Noel believed in me, but getting the wheels in motion for Sony was a reminder of how much autonomy I'd lost in the partnership. But we got them on board eventually and Marcus was more impressed with them than any of the other American labels who wanted them. Sony's label Epic signed them for the world, we signed them for the UK. Marcus trusted me to do the business for them in Britain and I was determined not to let him or the band down.

I chose Johnny Hopkins for their publicist. He was new to the company but had loved them from the moment he saw them. Laurence was disappointed not to do it. She hadn't seemed very happy over the last year at Creation, ever since I'd dropped My Bloody Valentine. She thought Tim Abbott was arrogant. Well, yes, but he was more than that too. She was supposed to report to him while I was abroad – I was always abroad – but she refused to. Then I found out she was slagging off Oasis. It had come to the end and Andy Saunders took over her job eventually.

There was some organization amid the chaos. I kept track of what I did each day with a list, which I've heard Tim Abbott describe as a stroke of management genius in interviews. A list, written on a piece of paper. The fact that this gets celebrated might give you some idea of how organized the place really was. On this list would be the phone calls I had to make and I'd go through them, score them off until they were all done. This was before anyone had computers in offices. Well, Dick Green had one, a little green-screened Amstrad. I don't know what he did on it. I just had my list.

I was still taking way too many drugs. Cocaine all the time, and I'd get hold of legal speed in diet pills from America. My life had become very strange. I was always on planes. Flying to Los Angeles every couple of weeks – that's no way to treat your body. Anyone who does that is going to start to lose it a bit with the time differences and those twelve-hour flights. I didn't keep normal hours anyway, even without that jetlag.

I remember Sony insisting that I met Michael Jackson. This was in Japan. I was out there with Primal Scream. They love Primal Scream in Japan, still do. They go wild for Bobby. I was out there watching their gig when I heard I was to be honoured by getting to meet Michael Jackson. Sony really wanted me to meet him. I was thinking, That's a bit weird, what am I going to say to him? Bobby got wind of this and demanded he got to meet Michael Jackson too. Sony were like: No fucking way are *you* meeting Michael Jackson. Bobby had something of a rock and roll reputation. They hadn't figured out yet that I was much *worse* than Bobby at this stage. They still thought I was the guy in charge. They didn't know yet that no one was in charge.

I didn't even want to meet him, that's the joke. But anyway, I went through three security checks to get to a room of fifty people. There was a screen at one end of it, surrounded by security, and only five of us fifty people were going to be lucky enough to meet Michael Jackson. They pulled our names out of a hat, and it must have been set up, because the first out was Alan McGee. I was like, *For fuck's sake*. I was with Luc Vergier, my pal from Sony, he's a good guy. Me and Luc went behind a screen and Michael Jackson was there. We'd been given our instructions carefully. I had to introduce myself and say: *Alan McGee, Creation Records*. Now when I get nervous I get really Scottish, super Scottish. So I just growled at him. *Aran McGree, Creashrecads*. He looked at me shaking his head with this expression on his face, like I was from outer space. He was really tall too, six foot two, looking down on me. Really thin. Must have been on that drug. He was so, so thin. OxyContined off his fucking tits, I expect, even then.

So he didn't even say a word to me before I was ushered away. Sony dragged me to his show in the evening and I'm glad they did. It was unbelievable. Hit after hit after hit. Mind-blowingly good. This was just before all the allegations about abusing children came out.

I had my first big scare around that time. It was on a plane. Always on a plane. I was going up to Glasgow again. I thought I was having a heart attack. If you're always taking coke and speed, it's easy to think that. You put your hand to your heart, and surprise, surprise, it's hammering. So you panic and that raises your blood pressure further. And then it's a full-blown panic attack and you have to get off the plane before it's taken off. Andy Saunders gets a bit flowery in David Cavanagh's book about Creation, has me checking in to a hotel and holding a bellboy's hand and weeping. Well, that never happened, but it was pretty terrifying.

What I found out later was that it wasn't just me suffering these panic attacks. Dick Green had one too, in the middle of Morrisons supermarket. It was the speed we were buying. And it wasn't just me and Dick – loads of other people nearly had heart attacks. One of the Creation staff, who in this case shall remain nameless, was knocking out the stuff, left, right and centre, and it had crazy effects. God knows what he was cutting it with. Imagine the most insane person you can think of.

Imagine how insane you'd have to be to buy the stuff off him. We all did. We all went back for more. We all nearly died.

I was in a terrible state, I realize now. Belinda was sick of me – I was never straight. I was incapable of reflecting properly on anything. I was really unhappy and I couldn't face confronting that unhappiness so I just numbed it instead of dealing with it.

I was still working hard though. I was actually very good at working the day after a night out. Primal Scream couldn't believe I could do it. For seven years I ran on rocket fuel.

In July 1993 I won the Weber Prize for excellence in business and music at the New Music Seminar in New York. I took my dad with me. We were trying to get on at that point. He was quite proud of me then. I had given him 5 per cent of shares when they were worth nothing and so he had been paid £100,000 when we sold the company. It was enough for him to retire from the panel-beaters – I gave him a nominal job on the company and a salary too. I felt sorry for him, on his own now he'd lost his wife.

It was a strange do. I was seated next to Boy George, who I think was flirting with me. 'Ooh, you've got Irish blood in you,' was the first thing he said. A black female record president won the main award, which was announced before my award, and she did a ten-minute speech during which she was crying in true American Oscar-night style. There was about nine minutes crying and one minute's speaking. I see now what an achievement it was for a black woman to have succeeded in the music industry then, but at the time I remember thinking, Typical Americans. It was both theatrical and sincere at the same time, which only Americans can do.

I was announced afterwards and walked up to collect my award. But how do you follow a Whitney Houston-style performance like that? So I just said thank you and walked off. For a minute there was a shocked silence, before everyone started laughing.

I gave the award that night to my dad, who might still have it on his mantelpiece. Primal Scream were in New York that night to play a gig, and later we all ended up chasing Boy George around a night club, asking him for drugs. 'I'm clean, get away from me,' he kept saying as we ran after him.

Whatever state I was in, I knew with Oasis we had something with potential to be really big. It was my big remaining ambition. I wanted to break a band on a massive, international stage. I'd always thought this would have been Primal Scream, but we'd been stalled by the band's drugs problems and the effect they'd had on recording.

And to start with we had similar recording problems with Oasis. We tried with Dave Bachelor, with Anjali Dutt, with Mark Coyle. It wasn't working – the demos Noel had given me were better than the studio recordings. They were trying to record the instruments separately, something that never works for our bands. It was another of our links to the 1960s; our bands worked best when recorded live.

Noel was innocent at the time and said, 'Oh, we'll get it

right by the second album.' There was no way I was going to take that risk – most of the time you only ever get one chance. It was their time – they had to do it properly. We did keep 'Slide Away' from those sessions.

So much hope was beginning to be pinned on this album. Our sales were down in 1993 from 1992. Our biggest album, *Giant Steps* by the Boo Radleys (a great album), had only done 60,000 in the UK despite ten out of ten reviews everywhere and the full page adverts we'd taken out. Sony were pressuring us to rein in the expenses, to cut back on releases, on new signings.

Ride were hoping to do their third album with George Drakoulias, who produced the Black Crowes and the Jayhawks – hoping he'd help them in their new American rock direction. Drakoulias had rehearsed them but then decided he couldn't do it, so they were suddenly aimless and lost after their incredible beginning. They did the album in the end with John Leckie, who'd produced the Stone Roses, but the mood of the band was really bad. Andy Bell had never recovered from feeling he wasn't getting the credit he deserved. When I'd met them, they'd been as tight a unit as you'd find – they shared songwriting credits, stuck up for each other, had complete artistic control of what they did and a manager who wasn't going to let that end. Now Andy Bell was dictating what the bassist and drummer played, very possessive about who owned the songs – it was a battle for control. One side of the album would be written by Mark, the other by Andy, and unlike the early days there was no cross-current of ideas on each other's songs.

Ride had wanted Drakoulias, but I'd always wanted him to work on the Primal Scream album and been ignored. Instead Primal Scream were working with another legend, Tom Dowd, who was about sixty-six by then. He was one of the few people they'd respect enough to get some work done, who Bobby would listen to when he told him not to take cocaine before he was recording vocals. But when Dowd sent me the tapes, I couldn't find one hit on it. There was something weird about all the recordings, they sounded flat. Dowd's hearing was shot by then. He couldn't hear high frequencies and the high end of the record was all missing. In the end Innes flew out to LA to work on new mixes with Drakoulias, and they ended up mixing all the singles there. Drakoulias put the incredible drums on 'Rocks', and suddenly we had a big single. Drakoulias saved *Give Out But Don't Give Up* in the end.

I probably sound like a cunt when I say running a label is like a dictatorship, but you've got to remember how few people at Creation at that time liked Oasis. James Kyllo didn't rate them. Laurence hadn't. Andy Saunders didn't think they'd work. If I hadn't seen the business as a dictatorship, if I hadn't had absolute faith in my judgement, Creation would not have put out the records of the band who became the biggest in the world.

A lot of what was so good about them was Liam and Noel's charisma. There was a whole generation of music listeners who had come through Acid House, which was phenomenal, a new form of music, a new culture – but there had been no personalities in the scene to inspire people. I mean, Paul Oakenfold, you know what I mean? With Liam and Noel we had two enormous personalities. We thought it could be like the Beatles again, who'd had real personalities, like the Stones. We thought people were going to love them.

Marcus Russell was very patient about releasing an Oasis single. He didn't want to move too quickly. We put out a white label demo of 'Columbia' at the end of the year, and Radio 1 played it twenty times in two weeks. Just for a demo that wasn't on sale. We knew then that the band were going to be massive. More than anything now it was going to be a matter of not fucking things up, of not missing an open goal.

13: BREAKDOWN

Hanging out with Oasis was exhausting. I'd go from one night out with Liam and Noel – Noel could really put it away – to a night out with Primal Scream. I'd be down in Wales with Oasis recording the album, doing drugs every night. They'd arrive in London and I'd go on another two-dayer with them. Then on to hang out with Throb Young. I was just waiting to snap.

I was supposed to be in LA over Christmas 1993 but I took a bad overdose of MDMA powder. I was in the penthouse in Rotherhithe with Grant Fleming, his girlfriend Jenny and Alex Nightingale. It sent me to bed for days. I didn't realize how strong it was and took big lines, like it was cocaine. I snorted what I think must have been the equivalent of thirty-six Es. I thought I was having a heart attack. I was psychotic. I went over the edge and had to claw myself back up the cliff. Grant Fleming was trying to give me a pull on a spliff, thinking it might calm me down. I was in bed for nearly two weeks with him looking after me and perhaps I never really got over it.

Any sane person would have stopped at that point, and I made a vow that I was going to, but I didn't know how to live without drugs. I was on them again by mid-January and flew out to Los Angeles, where Abbott had been waiting for me for weeks. I wasn't allowed to stop. Creation was getting bigger. Primal Scream were getting bigger. Oasis had just been signed. It was coming up to the Creation tenth anniversary. The pressure was on me to be the larger-than-life Alan McGee, no matter how bored I'd become with the performance.

When I made it to Los Angeles in mid-January I hooked up with Abbott and we went at it again. When you're a drug addict every town in the world is the same, and there isn't such a thing as jet lag. You get off the plane, get drugs, get pissed, and the same party continues. I got back to my room at four in the morning, and that's when the earthquake hit. It was serious. The lights went out. The whole room was shaking. That's what it felt like in my head too. The whole building felt like it was about to topple to the ground.

Back in London I got back to the penthouse. I'd hoped I might see Belinda, that she might have come back, but there was no sign of her stuff. It was six or seven in the morning. The phone rang almost immediately. It was Noel, to tell me that all of his band mates had been arrested for brawling with Chelsea fans on a ferry to Amsterdam and sent back without playing a note – every one of them apart from Noel, who'd been in bed.

This was the first trouble we'd really had with the law. Primals were outrageously out of order at times, but incredibly had never been arrested. Abbott and I had never been arrested either, which is also quite amazing.

The arrest was brilliant publicity for the band in the end. It made them stand out from a lot of the other contenders. There weren't many dangerous bands left, and people wanted to hear one. Jonny Hopkins did a great job of blowing that up in the press and it made the band immediately notorious.

I didn't have any time to rest. Next up were some serious sessions with Primal Scream, who were rehearsing in Waterloo. I had the flu. I should have been in bed. But I was taking coke with Throb Young. This was Throb after Memphis. He racked them out nearly as long as your arm. I made the mistake of taking one of those lines, and that was that, a night of madness began. All back to mine, to the penthouse. I didn't get to sleep before it was time to get another flight to Los Angeles. Another line from Throb before I left.

My sister Susan was with me. I was supposed to be showing her a good time in Los Angeles. She fell asleep, but there was no chance of that for me.

I was on the plane, with no downers, no Valium, no Temazepam, my heart pounding away, just in hell, really. The panic came on as soon as we took off. There are eleven hours before I can get off the plane. I could lose my mind before then. Eleven hours is eternity. I felt like I was on a bad acid trip. There were voices in my head. I thought I could hear the conversations of people at the far end of the plane talking about me. The stewardess was asking me if I'd taken acid. 'I've taken a line of cocaine the size and width of Robert Young's forearm,' I wanted to say, but I didn't. I was trying not to scream. Just get me off this fucking plane. It lasted the whole trip. My poor little sister next to me, who I'm supposed to be showing a good time in LA.

The stewards telephoned ahead for an ambulance. I thought I was dying. I was met by paramedics who diagnosed me with 'nervous exhaustion'. It's an American code-phrase, 'nervous exhaustion'. It means: go and check into rehab immediately. I didn't go to hospital because they thought I just needed to dry out. But I still hadn't learned. I went to bed that morning but got up in the evening to go and see Swervedriver at the Whisky a Go Go. I'd have felt guilty otherwise for not showing Susan around – that's how crazy my thought processes were at the time. I was doing a lot more than that to feel guilty about.

That night was the final straw. I drank a bottle of Jack Daniel's and downed a load of diet pills when Susan started pleading with me to take it easy. I was totally addicted. I just couldn't control myself.

When I went to Warners the next day I was hallucinating. The walls were literally moving in on me. I thought I might be going mad permanently – it was terrifying. I still don't really understand what happened to me. It's hard for me to remember the days leading up to the breakdown. I've no idea how much sleep I was getting.

I got out of that meeting fast but in the taxi back to the Mondrian Hotel things weren't any better. I felt like I had a steel rod in my back, like I was on fire. I got back to my room and had a shower, hoping it would calm me down, but

I started panicking again. My bones felt so hard, like steel, like I was turning into metal. I had hypertension, that's what it feels like. It was really painful. I thought it was a heart attack. I told reception to call an ambulance. They asked me what the problem was. I didn't want to admit to being a drug addict so I just said I'd had some diet pills and a bit to drink.

I knew when the guys in orange jumpsuits were putting the oxygen mask on me and carrying me out that I'd fucked up. It was like a bad American soap, except this time I was the fucking main character. They measured my blood pressure and decided my life was at risk. Thought I might have a blood clot or be having a heart attack. They were really worried that I was going to die before they could get me to hospital. I don't know if they were overreacting or if I was under-reacting. I was conscious throughout all of it.

In the hospital they sedated me. My sister had been out at the zoo all day, came back and couldn't find me. She rang my mobile, 'Where are you, Alan?' I was in hospital with wires coming out of me. When she turned up and saw that she started crying and I felt awful for putting her through that. 'What's Dad going to say?' she was asking. Of course, I didn't want him to know.

I left the hospital after a couple of days and went back to the hotel. They had a doctor who used to come round every day and give me a painful shot of sedatives in my arse cheek. Fuck knows why he had to do it that way. Maybe it's an American thing. I stayed there for a couple of weeks, feeling pretty insane. I couldn't access the energy in my body – my brain had shut down my body completely: 'You've had enough, you need a rest.' I had my own private nurse, who I proposed marriage to at one point. She'd told me earlier that she was a virgin. When my Gran Barr called up, I announced I was going to be married.

'She's a virgin,' I told her.

'What, verging on the ridiculous?' she asked.

I wasn't talking to anyone from Creation on the phone by then. The phone was off. I couldn't face the idea of a plane home, but I couldn't stay in America either. Two weeks in my room and Susan stayed with me. At one point I got driven to see the Jesus and Mary Chain record a video with Hope Sandoval. 'I'd heard you were dead,' said Jim when I arrived.

I ended up calling Ed Ball, who was in Japan playing keyboards for the Boo Radleys, and asking him to come and help me get back. I flew back with him and my sister. I was too weak to even hold my bags when we got the plane back. Ed had to carry everything for me.

14: RECOVERY

Back in London, I stayed in bed every day. I didn't realize that I'd had a breakdown or how serious it was. I was waiting for it to finish so I could get back on with my life as usual.

But it was hard for me to even get up and go to the toilet. My brain couldn't access the energy in my body. It was pretty wild. I was totally fucked. All I could do was lie there.

I asked my dad to come and look after me. I don't think he wanted to, but he came. I'd run out of anyone else to ask. Belinda had dumped me and no wonder. Who would want to go out with a guy who's had a breakdown, who can't face the world? Maybe someone who'd been married to you for years, but not a girl nine years younger than you, a twenty-four-year-old. I don't blame her at all. In fact it's too cruel to say she left me. Cruel to her. She'd put up with enough from me. Although we'd split up all the time, I knew that this time it was for good.

There was nothing to be done about it though; I needed all my energy just to concentrate on staying alive. I went to the doctor and he didn't know what was wrong with me. I went to see another doctor after that and he referred me to Dr Colin Brewer, a psychiatrist, and that was the very first step of recovery. I would see Colin Brewer for the next two years.

For the first two months I kept wanting to get back on the Primal Scream bus and have a party. It wasn't so much the drugs I was craving but the excitement of the lifestyle. Without the excitement I had to think about all the things I didn't want to, the huge amount I had to regret. I wanted to throw myself back into my old lifestyle and for things to be normal again, and at the same time I knew for a fact that my body and my mind couldn't take it. I began to realize I wasn't going to work for a while. I couldn't give a fuck about Creation at that point. I was just trying to survive. And I had this epiphany then: I don't want to do this any more, I want to get better. I don't have to be in the music industry any more. I don't have to be larger than life. I don't have to take twenty-five calls every hour and shout at people. I can stay in bed.

Susan would come down to stay and Ed Ball would always come round, but for a while it was just me and my dad. He didn't have to work any more because of me; so he didn't have any excuse as to why he couldn't help out. And he took keeping me off the booze and drugs seriously, which I suppose I should be grateful for.

Noel came round to see me with Marcus. I wasn't able to keep a close track of what was going on with the business but I was still interested in Oasis. They played me new songs they'd recorded. After trying three different producers hadn't worked out Marcus Russell had recommended Owen Morris.

I thought that was a weird call. Johnny Marr's engineer – who the fuck was he? He had no reputation at all. He was the guy who mixed Electronic. But Owen had got it bang on. He'd Phil Spectored it, a big wall of sound, a wall of guitars.

My dad kept a close eye on us all. He'd be peering round the corner of doors at us. Noel went to get himself a Jack Daniel's at one point and found my dad had replaced all the bourbon in the bottle with cold tea! Noel loved it! It cracked him up.

My dad suggested I move back to Glasgow for a while. I was hating living in the penthouse by now – it looked like a big, empty party venue, the kind of place where a man like me would do damage to himself. I ended up staying there for six months, renting a little house in Renfrew. I couldn't explain what was happening to me, to myself or to Dick Green. It was unquantifiable. I cut myself off from everyone – only Dick Green had my number, and I'd told him not to call under any circumstances. Jeremy Pearce sent me a text at one point asking if I wanted to come to Creation's tenth anniversary (which by then was actually our eleventh anniversary; we were slow in getting organized). I went mental at him, told him to never speak to me again. I was convinced by then that I was never going anywhere near the music industry again. I just stayed in and watched football on Sky. I would literally watch any game at all, St Mirren v. Kilmarnock, anything. What got me through those days was the gradual realization that no one could stop me doing this, that I was a millionaire and instead of taking thirty phone calls an hour from loonies, musicians and managers, I could hide out on my own if I wanted to. I realized I could run at my own pace instead of at everybody else's.

Around August I went for about six weeks to rehab in Charter Nightingale, Lissom Grove. By then getting me off drugs in the short term wasn't the issue, because I hadn't taken any for months. They were looking long term, trying to recalibrate the way I saw the world.

Rehab isn't like the telly. Rehab is pretty fucking boring to describe. It takes you a long time to come round and start seeing the world normally. I had Colin Brewer, my psychiatrist, in the morning and Keith Stoll in the afternoon, and I was really getting into the therapy. Keith Stoll was brilliant, a psychotherapist who every day made me think hard about myself in a way I hadn't done before. I'd always run away from anything painful. Now he was encouraging me to ask questions of myself and I was willing to do it.

I kept myself to myself there. I refused to do Twelve Steps, knew immediately that it wasn't for me. Surrendering to a higher authority? Me? Fuck *off*. I wasn't going to remove my entire personality.

I remember reading a lot. *Head-On* by Julian Cope, his autobiography, and thinking it was brilliant.

I started to get my energy back. I'd go for long walks in the afternoon, down to Harley Street and back to Lissom Grove. The parts of London where you don't see one indie person! It was amazing, I never saw one person I knew out on those walks. No one was looking for me. I loved it. I'd put on a lot of weight by doing nothing and being in Scotland and eating too much, but I lost two stone on these long walks.

I wasn't trying to follow everything that Oasis were up to, but I knew the singles had done well and that the anticipation for the album *Definitely Maybe*, which came out on 30 August 1994, was massive. Liam and Noel's charisma – and dangerousness – was winning everyone over. They'd have fights during interviews for the *NME*. There was a legendary one with John Harris, the tape of which was later released on vinyl, called 'Wibbling Rivalry'. It will be on YouTube now, everything is. They had a huge argument, with Noel taking Liam to task for being arrested on the ferry to Amsterdam. It was the first time in years there'd been such an outspoken band, the first time in ages there'd been two huge personalities who weren't scared to say what they thought. They didn't watch what they said and they weren't scared of anything. I think that's why I liked them so much.

When I finished rehab I went back to Glasgow, and it was a shock to be away from the routine and be confronted again with my loneliness. I didn't know what I was supposed to do with my life. One morning I even went to church. That's how desperate I was. I came out of church knowing it wasn't the answer, got back into my house and there was a voice message waiting for me from Dick Green. 'Hey, we're number one with *Definitely Maybe*!' I just wiped the message, didn't even smile. It meant nothing to me, in fact it annoyed me. I felt like I'd paid the price for everyone else to have a good time. I know it was no one's fault but my own but I felt incredibly bitter that I'd been destroyed while they were all still having a party.

But I'd had enough of Glasgow by then too. The walks around London while I was in rehab had got my strength back up and I thought I could go back and see if I could stick it. But when I got back to Rotherhithe I couldn't stand it. I remember sitting in my massive penthouse with Joe Foster, looking around it, thinking, Is this it? It felt so lonely, so empty. It was a different man's idea of where a man should live, a man who I'd only ever pretended to be. Pretending to be that man had almost killed me, and I worried that it still might do, and I couldn't stay there any more.

I never went back. I moved straight out and booked into the Landmark Hotel, just round the corner from where I'd been in rehab. I'd walked past the hotel a few times and thought it looked a nice place to stay. I felt safe in this part of London, safe from the music industry. I ended up staying there for two months. Andy Saunders would come round to visit me and we'd stay up till one in the morning watching Spanish football matches. The rest of 1994 disappeared this way. I wanted nothing to do with Creation Records; I couldn't bear to even think about the place.

By coincidence, Noel Gallagher was staying there a lot of the time too, and we'd bump into each other occasionally. He'd worked really hard that year, touring constantly. Abbott had saved Oasis on one occasion, after Noel had left the band and gone missing in America. He'd flown out and tracked him down at a girl's in San Francisco and talked him out of it. I remember the night when Noel was going off to the Q Awards and he came and knocked on my door. I think he was a bit taken aback at how out of it I still was. It must have been a shock to him – he'd known me for only nine months before I changed so drastically. He was just getting started with the rock and roll lifestyle, but I felt like I was finished with it forever.

He'd give me reports on what had been happening. *Fucking hell, I met Bono! He knows who I am!* At this point, we were both still blown away by things like that. We didn't feel famous yet, we felt like we had gatecrashed a famous person's party.

He'd always ask me if I wanted to come to the parties in his room. I never once went and had to beg him not to tell anyone I was there. The last thing I wanted was people knocking on my door asking me round. And I have to thank Noel, because he never told anyone. He's a man of his word, a great guy.

I was angry at the people who hadn't come to see me. I tried to contact Primal Scream a few times during their tour of America with Depeche Mode, when they were really coming apart at the seams. They didn't get back until months later, by which time I was too offended to take their calls. I'd been having a nervous breakdown and I'd needed to talk to them then. I realize now that they needed me as much as I needed them and they were feeling abandoned. They were as lost as me and having their own crises, just a little more privately. (Bobby Gillespie got sober, I think, in 2008. Toby Toman can't even set foot in London, to this day.)

I was only thirty-four years old at this point. It was a bit early to be feeling like I was finished. My energy was beginning to return and I took longer and longer walks and became a member of the Landmark's gym and swimming pool. I remember walking in at eight one morning in my Adidas to the Landmark just as Patsy Kensit and Liam Gallagher were driving off in a taxi after having been up all night drinking in the bar, Liam leaning out of the window shouting, 'McGeeeee!'

I began to get curious again about Creation at the start of 1995. I began to think about going over to Hackney to see what was happening. I'd built the ark, and I wasn't ready to completely give up the chance of sailing it again. But I knew the office in Westgate Street was the absolutely worst place for me to be around. There wasn't a room there I hadn't taken drugs in. The place was inseparable from the crazy times that had nearly killed me.

So I approached slowly. I would walk all the way to Hackney from Marylebone, a good two-hour walk, at least five miles, I reckon. I'd do it twice a week and as soon as I arrived I'd look at everybody and think, What the fuck am I doing here? I'd only last half an hour before I'd have to get a taxi back to my nice hotel! I was behaving like Syd Barrett. I made everyone feel really awkward. They'd tell me stuff which wouldn't compute, that I'd just have no interest in. I was a completely different Alan to the one they were used to. They didn't know what to say to me any more. They'd tell me about a great party they'd been to and it would engage me as much as if they were reading out a shopping list. More than anything it was the memories

Westgate Street inspired that I couldn't cope with. It brought all the monsters back, all the ghosts. It felt like I was being pulled back to the life I'd left behind. It made me scared that it wasn't behind me at all. Everything associated with my past brought the nightmares up. I couldn't imagine how I was ever going to come back properly again. Everyone was basking in the glory of the success and the man who'd signed all the bands was too ill to join in. I didn't mind them enjoying the success, but I couldn't see how there was a place for me there any more. I was depressed and it was hard not to be bitter sometimes.

Once the contract had run out at the penthouse I rented a tiny little flat around the corner from the Landmark and moved in. I know it sounds berserk, but living close to the place where I'd done my rehab was very calming; it made me think help was on hand if I needed it.

I should have been in therapy a long time before then, really. I'm very grateful for what that did for me. I'm still friends with Colin Brewer. He's in his seventies now and we meet for lunch occasionally. We saw each other professionally for a couple of years and I feel like in doing this we really got to the bottom of me. We spoke a lot about my past, my childhood. The violence and the fear and the powerlessness had fucked me up, there's no doubt about that. Big deal: everyone's childhood fucks them up. But it had fucked me up in a big way. Once we worked that out it was a lot easier for me to go on. I could never work it out: what is this fucking thing going on in my head? Why am I so miserable? They worked out all the things that had fractured me. We worked out I'd had some sort of breakdown when I was fifteen and never really recovered. I've only just finally begun to close it all. I can control my reactions to things these days, whereas before, because I wasn't facing up to what was bothering me, I'd fly off the handle whenever someone or something tried to make me confront it.

One day, when I was on one of my walks I ran into Laurence Verfaillie. We were pleased to see each other, and she told me she was going to see Slowdive that night with her friend Kate. 'Kate from Frazier Chorus?' I asked.

She'd introduced me to Kate Holmes before. I'd first seen her on TV when I was going out with Belinda. She'd been dressed as an angel, in a TV appearance for her band at that time. Frazier Chorus was a bit like Britpop before Britpop, like Pulp at the wrong time. They were a whimsical indie-pop band from Brighton, signed to 4AD, ended up on Virgin, never made it. After that she fell in with Youth and his Butterfly records label. I thought she was very cool.

I'd mentioned to Belinda at the time that I thought Kate was attractive, and Belinda had told me, like she always did about other women, that she was disgustingly ugly.

Then Laurence had introduced me to her in person a couple of years earlier, in 1992 around the time I moved into the penthouse with Grant and Karen. I was moderately sober that night (for me, that is) and Kate was wasted – one of the few occasions ever when she was out of control while I was in control. Because I fancied her I told her to come and play me her new stuff. She never did, because she couldn't remember having had the conversation.

It took a long time for me to be able to enjoy gigs after my breakdown, so it was a big thing when Laurence invited me to the gig that night and I said I would. There's no way I would have gone if Kate hadn't been going.

After the gig we ended up in Blacks, a private members' club in Soho. I was supposed to call her in two days but I messed up by calling her after two weeks, thinking that's what she asked. (I actually think I've got that right rather than her, because I'm really good with dates. To this day, she claims she's said things that are completely different from what she actually said when she's drunk.) When I finally called her she was annoyed because she'd been waiting for me to phone her for a week and a half. She thought I'd been playing a game but I hadn't at all. We sorted out that misunderstanding and started to hang out. We'd go to art galleries, to gigs. She realized quite soon that I was in recovery, that I wasn't all there yet. It wasn't until the end of that year that I began to start feeling a lot better. Her mother was a bit freaked out for Kate that she was going out with this guy with issues. I'm not surprised she was worried.

We moved the Creation office to Primrose Hill in April 1995. The Hackney premises were getting broken into all the time and we needed to change the office lifestyle. Until I'd had the breakdown, the office had been the world of Alan and Tim.

Cocaine at the desk. Parties still going on when people were arriving for work in the morning. We'd set a bad example for the younger members.

When we moved to Primrose Hill it felt like the start of a new day. I was beginning to come clean to everyone about what had happened to me – before I'd just said I 'was ill'. That was true, of course, but it wasn't the half of it.

We couldn't be a drug label any more. The office in Hackney was the office of a drug addict. When I got straight, Creation had to straighten out too. Sony wanted me back and I couldn't go back to that environment. People couldn't get fucked up in the office in front of me – I would have run a mile and never come back. Dick Green was a true friend and wasn't going to put me into a situation like that. He had always hated the McGee and Abbott brand of madness in the office anyway, and he was glad to enforce a new regime for me.

I'd missed a lot during 1994. Ride's new album *Carnival of Light* had come and gone, sold 10,000 copies and wouldn't nearly recoup the recording costs. As I've said, Primal Scream were touring America with Depeche Mode and coming apart at the seams. Sony forced Dick to drop loads of bands: Adorable, the Telescopes, Dreadzone . . . They nearly pulled the plug on the whole company and if Oasis hadn't gone to number one when they did, they probably would have done.

Definitely Maybe had come out and smashed it. The fastest selling British debut ever, by a band I'd signed, and I hadn't cared.

What made me care again was hearing the new tracks for *(What's the Story) Morning Glory?*. I remember the first time I heard them. Around June 1995, I was on one of my long walks when I ran into Noel on Marylebone High Street. Noel claims now that when he saw me then was the first time he knew I was getting better, when he'd seen me without glazed eyes.

They'd recently played their biggest gig at Sheffield Arena and I'd still felt too fragile to go. All I did in those days was go from the new offices to the flat, the flat to Kate's house, Kate's house to the offices. It was always one step at a time. Kate was helping me a lot. I was in the office but not with nearly the same presence or involvement as I had been. I was coasting, to be honest. It was all I could do.

Noel told me he'd finished the album and Marcus had a tape. I called up Marcus and he sent it round.

He put three songs on the tape: 'Wonderwall', 'Morning Glory', 'Don't Look Back in Anger'. Within about eight seconds of hearing 'Wonderwall' I had shivers down my spine. It was quite humbling. I knew they'd done it. Exactly what they said they were going to do. It was a song the whole country was going to love. I knew then that we could sell 20 million albums. And I wanted to be there when they did. I wanted to come back.

15: BACK IN THE OFFICE

When I started coming in to the Primrose Hill office, Abbott had gone to work with Oasis as a freelance managing consultant. It was for the best. Everything I'd loved about the way he worked was now the reason we were completely incompatible colleagues. I look back on the two years we had before my breakdown as having been really fun. He was a brilliant friend and colleague, and you have to hand it to him for the way he managed the *Definitely Maybe* campaign when I was out of the office. He was very likeable. The bands loved him because he was rock and roll. We were all on our way up. Good times. But once I'd cleaned up, it was never going to be possible for us to remain friends in the same way we had been. He was still on the same wagon. It wasn't for me any more.

Abbott cleaned up in the end, in 2003. He studied to be a cognitive therapist and, bizarrely, he qualified. Long live the Abbott. He still heads out to parties, even though he's given up the drugs. He rings me up at one in the morning telling me Grace Jones is trying to get off with him. Good on him. It's not for me.

*

When I came back to work, two things were happening at once. I was sober and people found that very strange. I don't know if they'd ever seen me sober. But the change was more profound than that. My whole personality was different. That's what happens after a nervous breakdown. Now, I was much less aggressive, more considerate. People wanted to see me more than once.

The other thing that was happening was that Oasis were becoming the biggest group in the world. So the atmosphere was euphoric. How could they let it out? Well, not like they used to in Hackney. My new team, Jon Andrews, Andy Saunders, they were all pretty clean, or they were in front of me, at least. Everyone still on the drug train realized they couldn't do it in front of me any more.

The ones who couldn't stop were taken out by Sony to encourage me to come back. It all came from Sony really. It had taken me a long time to be convinced to return. It was my A&R judgement that they had paid so much money for – and so they had to make it a safe place for me to return.

It wasn't the only part of the office culture that had changed while I'd been away. We had never had a marketing department before my breakdown but when I came back there was one firmly in place and I hated it. These people were probably only a reflection of what the music business had become. Or had always been, apart from us and a few other indies. It wasn't that these people were bad people – I liked them all as individuals – but they didn't have the energy and maverick spirit of the old Creation. And it zapped the mood of the office for me, and for the older members who remembered how it had been. But it was bigger than Creation – the independent music scene was dying, and this was just a reflection of that. Guitar music becoming popular in the way it did was one of the things that killed guitar music.

There was a lot for me to get my teeth into. Ride were straight back in the studio, and I wanted to play a bigger role in their fourth album. They'd started off so promisingly, with two gold albums, but they were in danger of disappearing after the disaster of their third. But in the end there was nothing I could do. Andy said he'd let Mark sing the songs, and then when they got into the studio he wouldn't let Mark sing at all. Andy's not that great a singer, so it was a bad move, and now there was an album with no songs by Mark and no singing by him, what else could Mark do but quit the band? Andy had taken over as the main songwriter but would only work on his own now. I didn't blame Mark for his decision. It was a sad early end to a band who for a couple of years looked like they could have had it all. Andy formed a new band, Hurricane #1, influenced a lot by Oasis, with singer Alex Lowe's harder-edged voice. Andy had realized – too late – that he couldn't sing. I'd always loved Andy, and when I met Alex he was a ball of fire and I took to him instantly. There was never any doubt we would offer the new band a contract; we signed them immediately.

*

We expected success after Oasis. With a big success you need to hire more people to deal with it and so you need to have more big successes to justify your wage bill. We'd hit the heyday of Britpop now, with massive sales for Blur, Oasis and Pulp meaning loads of imitators were being signed by the competition. At the time Marcus Russell was keen that Oasis weren't too associated with it. He insisted we pull them from a big 'Britpop' promotion, even though it was 20,000 orders. They refused to appear in a Britpop special on TV which Damon Albarn hosted. At the time, Britpop was a big deal; as a significant musical movement, was it fuck. Oasis were a rock and roll band: they never saw themselves as a Britpop band and Marcus thought that by standing outside of a hyped movement, they'd survive the end of it. The music press were always inventing scenes – they might be useful in the short term but they could kill a band's long-term prospects.

We went all out, however, to take advantage of Britpop to promote the Boo Radleys, who had followed *Giant Steps* with an intentionally poppier follow up *Wake Up!* in March 1995. 'Wake Up Boo!', the lead single, was a massive chart hit. Radio 1 played it all summer and the album flew in at number one. We had indie bands doing stuff that wasn't indie at all – the Boo Radleys being interviewed by Richard and Judy, doing children's programmes.

The Boo Radleys became much bigger than I ever thought they would. In 1993, before I'd had my breakdown, they were supporting Sugar in America. Sugar did everything in a white Transit van, but the Boo Radleys had the Cult's tour bus on loan. Sugar, the headliners, were selling out venues across America while travelling in a white Transit van; the Boo Radleys were in the Cult's tour bus, losing $70,000 a week. How not to tour America if you want to make any money.

I think Martin Carr would laugh looking back at that. I hope. I didn't rate their management. When *Wake Up!* took off, they were still coming to us asking for us to pay for tour support. If you've got a number one album, you shouldn't be asking for tour support. They were another of the Creation bands that in the end cared more about being cool than about being successful. They tried being successful as an experiment and once it had worked they went straight back to strange, experimental records that were never going to have the same appeal to a wide audience. They did incredibly well for a band that didn't have one good-looking member.

We had our first number one single in May, when Oasis released 'Some Might Say'. I was the only person in the office who was stupid/bold enough to suggest to Noel the B-side 'Acquiesce' should have been the A-side. I thought it would have been a brilliant number one. We believe in each other – what a revolutionary message. But by that point Noel was definitely not taking requests. When I suggested it people were looking at me, panicked: 'Don't annoy him!' written all over their faces. I hadn't got with the programme yet: whatever Noel says goes.

When it got to number one I remember being quite miserable about it when I saw Keith Stoll for my therapy the next morning. 'I never asked for all this success!' I said to him. I was still feeling quite depressed, still a long way from being better.

But I was trying to play a part in things now. It was at the party to celebrate being number one when the Blur v. Oasis rivalry first started and it was all my fault. There'd been a lot of testosterone flying around at the Brits earlier that year, when Blur had won Best Band and Oasis Best Newcomer. Liam and Noel are as bad as each other in that respect, both as stubborn in their animosities. Liam's more direct; Noel's more barbed. They'd been jeering and shouting at Blur all the way through the ceremony.

I'd always liked Damon Albarn and Blur, and Andy Saunders and I knew them socially – I even went down to the studio when they were making *The Great Escape*. So when we threw a big party in Covent Garden to celebrate Oasis getting to number one I invited them along. Noel and Liam were furious when they heard Blur were coming, but because I was paying for the party no one could take them off the guest list. I should have realized it would cause trouble. To be honest, I knew it would cause trouble. I wasn't *completely* reformed.

As soon as Damon walked in Liam strode straight up to him. *We're number one, you're not, you're not*. There was another reason why Liam hated Damon too, but I can't tell you that. For the rest of the night he kept winding Damon up.

By now there was real animosity from Oasis towards Blur. I don't think Blur understood how serious it was. Damon thought it was a funny game to wind up kids from a council estate in

Burnage, but they wanted to batter him. They were both about to release new albums that summer, Blur with *The Great Escape* and Oasis with *(What's the Story) Morning Glory?*. Both bands had singles scheduled for August that would be dead cert number ones. Oasis were due to release 'Roll With It' on 14 August while Blur's 'Country House' was lined up for 21 August. But Liam had really got under Damon's skin, so Damon moved the date forward by a week so it would be a head-to-head battle for the top spot. I wasn't surprised when Damon did that: in those days his ego really was in charge of the band. I suggested to Oasis they could move theirs back a week and was told to shut up immediately. So it became a battle of independent v. major label – I made sure of that when I spoke to the press. We were still distributed independently, whereas Blur were EMI, so it wasn't a lie: we were at a disadvantage.

We lost. There were problems with a barcode that wouldn't register. They spent more money, gave more singles away free to the shops and multiformatted the CD so people would buy two copies. We did what we'd always done. But who knows, we might have lost anyway, even if all things had been equal.

But if Damon had thought that would settle who was the bigger band between Oasis and Blur he made the biggest mistake he could have done. Blur were four times bigger than Oasis at the time. We lost the singles battle but it helped us sell a lot of records. Then we put out *Morning Glory* and suddenly we were the biggest band in the world.

They let us into their party by moving their release date. We were top of the second division at that point and they

were in the premier league, up there with Eric Clapton. They
let us in! They let us into the boxing ring! Everyone in the
country knew who Oasis were now. They might never have
had that exposure if Blur hadn't given it to them.

It was then that Noel Gallagher was quoted as saying he
wished Damon Albarn and Alex James would both die of
AIDS. It was an off the cuff comment in an interview, comic
exaggeration gone wrong, not meant at all seriously, but
journalist Miranda Sawyer ran it – she hated Oasis. It sounded
much nastier than it was, and I don't know if you'd get away
with it these days. But the fuss soon blew over. It shows you
what you can get away with when the wind is with you. Noel
talked his way out of it as usual. It was supposed to be comic
exaggeration, he didn't mean it.

Morning Glory sold over 350,000 copies in the first week. It
was selling to people who would never have bought a Blur
album. People who'd never heard of Primal Scream and never
ever would do. We more than doubled the numbers of
Definitely Maybe too, and I knew I was getting better and
better because I could really take pleasure in the success with
this album. I went to their biggest gig so far at Earls Court
in November and heard the band drowned out by tens of
thousands of people singing their songs back at them.

I still wasn't completely recovered though – not by a long
way. That Christmas Kate flew off on holiday to Jamaica. I
stayed at home, too scared to fly, thinking, Fuck, I can't even
go on holiday with my girlfriend.

We bought Noel a chocolate-brown Rolls-Royce to congratulate him on Oasis's success. His girlfriend Meg Matthews left me with no option. We were in a marketing meeting at Sony. We'd employed Meg to run our 'artists liaison' and she was brilliant at it. She made us sexy in a way we'd never been before. We'd always been a party label, but before it had always been about drugs more than anything. Meg made us glamorous – we had the sexiest parties in town, Kate Moss and her friends showing up. Anyway, in this marketing meeting she reminded me that I'd said I'd buy Noel a Rolls-Royce if he sold, I don't know, a million copies. I didn't remember saying anything of the sort but before I could object she'd pulled out a brochure and was pointing at the one we should buy. Well, when Noel's girlfriend tells you to buy him a Roller, that's what you do. He certainly deserved it.

The success hammered the final nail in the coffin of the old Creation. It led to an Oasis/Creation split in the office, as more and more people were brought in just to work on Oasis. That was inevitable. And it must have been hard to have been Primal Scream or Teenage Fanclub. Sony would only want to concentrate their energies on one band, and that band was always going to be Oasis now.

Suddenly I had the biggest band in the world. Or did I? The four-year option for Sony to buy the rest of the shares in Creation would be arriving in 1996, and now it looked like it was going to be in their interest to exercise it. I was back working, I had achieved my biggest ambition, and now I could lose it all again. It was time to go back into battle.

16: FIGHT TO KEEP CREATION

Jeremy Pearce at Sony was my main contact. Paul Russell was his boss. Jeremy had done some good work, backing us up at the right times, and though in an ideal world I'd rather not have worked with him at all, he'd shown belief in Creation and without him Sony might have pulled the plug while I was recovering from the breakdown.

We'd rewarded their trust by breaking the biggest band in the world. The year started with solid proof of how big Oasis were. At the Brits in February 1996 they won Best Band, Best Album, Best Video. That was great fun. We won three Brits, Oasis insulted everyone and Jarvis showed his arse during Michael Jackson's performance of 'Earth Song' and completely stole our thunder. My dad had a great time there too. It was the last good year of the Brits before the Spice Girls won everything; I've never been back since. A year earlier Blur had been wound up when Oasis won Best Newcomer. Oasis were now in a different league now. Now, after all the talk, the competition really was U2.

By this point the tabloids were obsessed with Oasis. It was at this point that *Mirror* editor Piers Morgan sat Andy Saunders and me down and told us the *Mirror* was going to support us, that he was planning to put us in the newspaper more, and could we help him out? I was like, Fantastic, we've sold 22 million albums, are you seriously suggesting *you* can do something for *us*?

We didn't want any more tabloid attention. I was there when the *News of the World* pulled a stunt in Dublin and brought Noel and Liam's estranged father, Tommy Gallagher, into the hotel they were staying at. It was another thing the Gallaghers and I had in common: a difficult relationship with their father. Bringing him to the hotel really shocked me – it was horrible, cheap as fuck. Liam was threatening him down the telephone. Overnight they changed the level of security in place for the band. Before that, it had been very easy to get close to them. That there was no wall separating them from journalists played to their strengths, because Noel and Liam were very charismatic and outspoken men. Journalists saw them as down to earth and liked them. From that point on there was a barrier and their press began to change for the worse.

With the great success we'd had with Oasis I should have been in a strong position but I was getting worried about Sony. I couldn't understand why Jeremy Pearce didn't want to talk more about the future of Creation. When I spoke to him about selling my shares, he was always saying, 'Let's talk about it later, there's no rush.' I thought Paul Russell and he were trying to fob me off before they forced me to sell my company to them when the crunch came. They were legally entitled to do just that. But I wasn't going to let that be the deciding issue.

What I hadn't realized is that Jeremy Pearce had been talking to Richard Branson who was keen to set up a new record label, called V2 (he'd sold Virgin to EMI for £500 million in 1992). Branson wanted me to run it. It was a really ambitious plan: they offered me a lot of money to go and work for them and bring whichever bands I wanted. And they thought maybe we could get Oasis to come along too, at least in the UK.

I was very tempted. Dick too. We went to meet Branson, who I liked. He was wearing a big cream Arran-knit jumper and looked like the Queen Mum.

But I knew Oasis. They were loyal but they were deeply practical too. Sony worked for everyone. They'd had two massive albums with them. Oasis weren't going to mess around with a situation that was working wonderfully for them.

I spoke to Paul Russell and accused him of not really wanting us to stay, of trying to show us the door. He denied it.

All I'd wanted from Sony was some recognition for what I'd done, for signing Oasis and bringing them all this success even while I was busy getting off drugs. I wanted them to offer me a decent wage and another four-year contract but Jeremy wasn't closing the deal. They could have had us much cheaper if they'd done it earlier.

By the time we were talking properly about renegotiating

the contract I was furious and defensive. I felt we weren't getting enough respect. It felt to me like they were about to fuck us.

I often wonder if I should have taken the new challenge and gone to V2. I could have been a whore. I think we'd have succeeded in bringing everyone bar Oasis, and we might even have been able to buy the name Creation off Sony, who only really cared about Oasis, if they were honest.

But when you've spent twelve years trying to find the biggest band in the world and you finally get there, it's too hard to turn your back. Financially, I should have done it – I was offered millions of pounds as a signing-on fee. They had a fund of a few hundred million, which we could have had a lot of fun with. I would have stuck it for the five years of the contract and made a lot of money. But Creation was mine, I'd built it, and I wanted to stay with it. We were at the top of the world, and we wanted to stay at the party a wee bit longer, even if it was a party where I drank Diet Coke instead of champagne.

The offer from V2 certainly helped the nerves though, when I went into the negotiations to claw on to my company. Jeremy jumped and went with Branson. When he'd gone, I found myself missing him a lot. It was the beginning of the end of our relationship with Sony. He'd been integral to the deal from the start, the first real enthusiast at Sony for Creation. It was he who had the vision and made it work.

Now Jeremy was gone I was convinced Sony were about to usher us out of the door. I was prepared to fight dirty the only way I could. Andy Saunders and I invited an *NME* journalist to the pub for an interview. I read a prepared statement out and Andy taped it so I couldn't be misquoted. 'Creation is an A&R company,' they quoted me saying. 'The moment I let some fucking corporate arsehole in New York run the record company, I will resign. [But] it seems as if they are refusing to negotiate, and it seems to be saying that they don't want me and Dick at Creation. We are Creation. If we go, I believe most of the artists and senior staff at the company will want to leave.' And I mentioned Primal Scream, the Boo Radleys and *Oasis*.

Sony did their own bit of boxing in the press then, releasing a story that they were buying us out for 12 million quid. A total bollocks story that made it seem like we were desperate to sell.

Well, if they equalize, you can't stop playing, can you? So we got in touch with a journalist at the *Financial Times* and prepared to make more trouble. We managed to get them to print a story about troubles at Creation and anxiety from the bands and whether Sony could afford another PR disaster after their recent court case with George Michael. This was when Sony started to negotiate properly and we sat down with Paul Russell. Dick Green was worried Paul Russell would have read the articles. John Kennedy was reassuring him: Don't worry, he won't. The first thing Paul Russell said when he walked in was, 'Who's your fucking press officer?' Dick pointed to me.

'Right, I'll get us some coffees,' Paul said, smiling briefly.

He was amazed that I was that ballsy and I think he quite admired it.

I nudged John under the table. 'He read it,' I said.

It was only because I was such an unreasonable human being that we managed to avoid selling to Sony in 1996. By law, they had every right to buy us. And they wanted to. But I was so unreasonable and loud and was going to make such a fuss that they didn't dare to exercise their right to buy. They worried it would be the end of any credibility they had, the end of their involvement in new music forever in Britain. Everyone would have thought they were a bunch of fucking cunts. They knew I would have made sure of it.

It was the type of brinkmanship that many others might not have tried. They were threatening me, and I learned from my dad not to listen too hard to threats. I felt pretty confident in those negotiations, even though the contract should have nailed me.

My position of strength was complete bullshit – there was no way on earth Oasis were going to walk away from the label that had made them rich, just to please me. But they couldn't know that for sure.

Marcus wasn't over-impressed by me using Oasis as currency in the negotiations. Noel, however, thought it was funny. There's always been an evil genius streak to Noel; he enjoys a bit of machination.

In the end they paid Dick and me an eight-figure sum to keep the terms basically as they were for another five years. I celebrated becoming a multimillionaire in a very different way to becoming a millionaire. No booze, no drugs. I'd moved to a bigger, much nicer flat in Bickenhall Street by now, still not too far from Charter Nightingale. My next door neighbour was Michael Buerk who read the news on BBC. I went back home and put some records on. I think I must have played them pretty loud.

Now we could really go back to work. We had bands to find, records to release.

Dick Green had brought in an A&R man called Mark Bowen while I was sick. Big Mark was a total Creation believer. I never really dug him myself, but he wasn't offensive, just a big guy who Dick liked. The one brilliant band he did bring us was the Super Furry Animals – perhaps the last great Creation band. They came out of the Cardiff music scene, and their lead singer Gruff Rhys was really charismatic. The rest of the band were Huw Bunford on guitar, Guto Pryce on bass, Cian Ciaran on keyboards and Dafydd Ieuan on drums. Big Mark took me to see them in the Camden Falcon at the end of 1995, where they were supporting Pearl Lowe's terrible band Powder.

The sound through the PA was that bad I thought Gruff Rhys was singing in Welsh. I told him afterwards it would help sales if he'd sing in English, and he said, 'I was!'

We put them in a studio and recorded a demo with them and they did 'Something 4 the Weekend'. They reminded me of Blur, raucous, quirky pop, and I was really happy to sign them.

I didn't play a huge part in their development. My only real interference with them was when Dick and Mark were going to put 'The Man Don't Give a Fuck' out as a B-side, and I insisted they bring it out as an A-side. They nearly missed that chance, and it became the band's best known single. It could have been written for me, you know, there was no way that wasn't going to be a single on my label!

We had fun marketing the band. We were going to give them a full page in the *NME*, and they said, 'We don't want that, we want a tank. We want to deliver the single to Radio 1 in a tank.'

That kind of logic wouldn't have appealed to every label boss, but it seemed perfectly reasonable to me and I happily handed over the money. It probably got loads more press attention than an advert would have done, but that wasn't the thinking behind it. It just appealed to my sense of mischief. I wonder if my sense of mischief, whatever trouble it's got me into, has also led to some of my greatest successes.

I was starting to hang around with Oasis again around that time. I found it much easier to resume contact with them than with Primal Scream. It hadn't been such an intense personal relationship and so it was easier to come back and be a different person to the one I was in the beginning, when I was off my face all the time.

Liam was really lovely to me, really kind. There're a lot of different versions of Liam. People focus too much on his aggression. Overall, my relationship with him has been great.

There have been some tense moments when he's coated me off, and maybe I've deserved those. But he's a warm guy. Great fun to be around. He has the best one-liners out of anyone I know. In 1997, when I'd started flying again, he decided that he wanted me to take him to India. 'But none of that Brian Epstein stuff,' he warned me. Now, I'm guilty of many things but not of repressing a secret bisexuality, despite any early confusion about David Bowie. 'None of that funny stuff,' he said, and I assured him there would be no problem about that. We went as far as booking tickets.

Just before we went I was beginning to have serious reservations about my ability to cope with Liam Gallagher on this kind of trip, so I rang up Marcus: 'Marcus, he wants me to take him to India – to meet the Dalai Lama.' Marcus couldn't stop laughing.

Kate really didn't want me to go either, but not because of Liam. She didn't want me to get the anti-malaria tablets, which can send some people mad. 'You're mad enough, Alan, already,' she kept saying.

But I didn't want to let Liam down. And then, on the day I was about to take the first pills, Liam phoned me up.

'Al,' he says, 'we can't go to India. I've only got a week off. Patsy won't let me.'

My biggest breakthrough in terms of getting back to fitness came when Oasis played Maine Road in April 1996. It was the biggest gig they'd done, 20,000 people, and they were doing two nights. I went up with Kate and her mates. My family came from Glasgow and had a great time. Perhaps it helped that it was in Manchester, which had always had good associations for me. The whole stadium singing every word of every song – it was wonderful. I felt flooded with energy. And after that each day was better than the next. It was like I'd had a shot of speed. I really wanted to work again then.

I'd never seen the Sex Pistols first time around, and I was suspicious of going when they reformed in 1996. But Noel reckoned they were good, and dragged me along to see them in Shepherd's Bush one night. They were brilliant. I spoke to Andy Saunders in the morning and told him I wanted to review them for the *NME*. So I rang Steve Sutherland and he told me to send it to the letters page. Because my ego was so enormous at the time, and my bands were selling so many copies of his newspaper, that was not enough for me. Tell you what, then, I said, I'll buy the back page. That really upset Sutherland, that I could do that. Bobby Gillespie loved it, kept calling me Citizen Kane for a while.

I did it because I was so pissed off that all these journalists were saying how rubbish they were. They're a bunch of cunts. So predictable. It wasn't true! The band were all better musicians and they were only in their late forties, and they were fucking great. Lydon got in touch afterwards: he loved it.

And then people started saying, oh, genius *branding*. Fuck off! That's not how I thought. I might have a lot more money if I thought that way. Except I don't think the people who go on about what genius branding it was are millionaires.

Knebworth would have made a brilliant end to Creation records. In 1983 Joe Foster and I had dreamed of a psychedelic punk label to refresh the British music scene – and now thirteen years later, on 11 August 1996, we had a psychedelic punk band playing to 300,000 people, with millions having applied for tickets. We'd done exactly what we'd set out to do.

The actual concert wasn't much fun. It was overblown. Too big. The bouncers wouldn't even let me in my own fucking hospitality tent at times, there were so many liggers there. It wasn't my thing. It was an Oasis thing. It wasn't even their thing. They just wanted to push it as far as they could, just like I would have done if I had been them. If I'd had the balls, I would have chucked it in right after Knebworth. It would have been a glorious, poetic exit. I could still have all I have now. I'd made all the money I ever needed to make. It would have been a better ending, that's for sure. But it was too hard to walk away from the success of it. Everybody wanted us. We'd never had it like that. So we carried on.

17: 10 DOWNING STREET

One of the things I really enjoyed about being sober was that people would invite me back again to parties or to dinner. When I was still drinking, I'd never get invited back to anything, ever. I could never see what a nightmare I was being. I thought I was being funny but I was just rude, embarrassing. I thought to be accepted you had to be mental, so I'd been acting up for years.

Now I was sober people would invite me and Kate to parties, and not just once. People started to like me. I thought everyone had wanted Alan the whirlwind, Alan the car crash, but they didn't: they liked sober Alan who'd listen to what they were saying and think before he spoke. And being this way was taking me to places I never would have thought possible.

I wasn't really famous at this point. Okay, so *NME* readers knew who I was, and some Oasis fans. But the average person who sung along to 'Wonderwall' had never heard of me, never would. In the end it was through politics that I got the most attention.

Now I was sober I was paying a lot more notice to what was going on around me, to what was happening in society.

I'd barely even noticed the last election, except that Kinnock fell in the sea at the party conference. Now I could see the country was fucked up. You saw that at the Maine Road gig – so many people going to that gig got mugged in Manchester. What kind of society is that where all those kids feel that's their only option?

I'd decided to join the Labour Party in 1995 but they never even sent me the little card to say I was a member.

A year later, just after Knebworth, Margaret McDonagh, the general secretary of the Labour Party, rang me up. 'Are you Alan McGee, who runs Creation Records?'

'Yes, I am,' I said. 'Where's my membership card? You've cashed my fifteen pounds' cheque.'

'We'll be right round with it,' she said.

Within ninety minutes Margaret McDonagh and two others were at my flat and they stayed for three hours to talk about politics. She was trying to work out if I was sincere, or a fascist – and I was sincere, and I wasn't a fascist. She asked me if I'd like to help get the Tories out, and I said I would. So the first thing they asked me to do was to come to the Labour Party conference in Blackpool, and to give Tony Blair a platinum disc on stage. They wanted me to bring Noel, but he was just back from tour and knackered, so he suggested we give them his platinum disc for *Morning Glory* instead.

I went up with Ed Ball and Andy Saunders. It was a special event at Norbreck Castle Hotel, a party for young Labour members. We arranged for one of our bands – 18 Wheeler, who Dave Barker had found – to come down and play a gig there. They were a good band from Aberdeen, and had been the headliners on the famous night at King Tut's when Oasis had blagged their way on to the bill. I didn't know who all the Labour dudes were at that point, not really. There were only ten of us when I arrived and Peter Mandelson was dancing next to me, shuffling around. There were some cool people there. Waheed Ali, Steve Coogan. Me and Ed Ball were immaculately suited, done up in Paul Smith. *Loaded* journalists queuing for the bathroom. Andy Saunders was walking around trying to boss everyone about, like he normally did. 'Andy,' I had to tell him at one point, 'you're not in charge of the Labour Party.'

Tony Blair came in and walked through the crowd, shaking everyone's hands, smiling wider than I knew was possible. He gave a speech on stage and I came up with him, shook his hand and gave him Noel's platinum disc for *(What's the Story) Morning Glory?*.

Then Blair introduced the band and got their name wrong, calling them 'Wheeler 18'. He'd never heard of them, of course he hadn't. The party was pretty boring afterwards. There were no women around, just lots of teenagers coming up, saying, 'Hey, how are you?' and telling me how good their bands were. So I went to my hotel room early and turned on the TV. And it blew my mind. I was on the TV, shaking hands with Tony Blair. I stayed up till six in the morning watching the news channel. I was on it every hour.

That was the start. They began to invite me in for more

meetings. Alastair Campbell would be there. I liked him. I know it's not cool to say but I have to be honest, I liked Blair too. It's hard to justify the way they took us to war in Iraq but at that point it hadn't happened. My experience of the party then was positive. I believed in Blair's good intentions, like he might have done himself then. Andy Saunders did too, and so we did everything we could to help him.

A little digression here, because I haven't introduced Andy Saunders properly yet, and he was very important for Creation.

Andy had come in just before the Sony deal in 1992. He was seven years younger than me. He came to Creation to do press after a stint at Roadrunner records and it was me who hired him.

We're very different but he's like me in one way: he just says what he thinks. He would offend everyone in the office; those types of employee would always be the ones who ended up being my best friends.

This is a typical story. He brought me over a letter in the office one day, an official complaint to me from the editor of a London paper, telling me Andy is a liar and a cunt and implying that unless he's sacked the paper is never going to give any more coverage to Creation bands. Andy knew I'd like this letter. I took the letter, took a big felt pen and wrote FUCK OFF on it. You know what to do with that, I said, and Andy went away with a smile on his face, wiped his arse on it, and sent it straight back. How are you not going to love a man like that? We had Oasis: how are they not going to mention them in the paper? What are you going to do, not write about Oasis? – go fuck yourself. We could behave as badly as possible and no one could stop us.

By 1997 there weren't many men like Andy left at Creation. Sony's influence was everywhere and the place was full of people who had to deal with them all the time, who felt they had to play Sony's game. Whether Sony had brought them in, or Oasis's management had brought them in – they were loyal to Creation, but they played the corporate game. Saunders was old school and refused to go along with that.

For four years running we won the *Music Week* award for being the best independent label, 1995–1998. On one of these occasions we were sitting at a table, surrounded by suits, and Andy Saunders goes to me, 'This is fucking rubbish.' I agreed with him, it *was* fucking rubbish. Rob Dickins from Warners had already picked up an award. We knew we'd won and were waiting for it to be announced. Andy leaned over and said to me, 'I'm going to shout out, "You're all a bunch of corporate cocksuckers" when we collect the award.' Everyone at the table heard this and started saying, 'Don't say that, Andy, you can't say that.'

I looked at him and said, 'You can say that if you want.'

So when they picked up the award, there's Andy on stage: 'You're all a bunch of corporate cocksuckers!'

This did not go down well. The whole room began to shout abuse at our table, about what hypocrites we were and how we're owned by Sony – fair enough, we are! 'Sony, Sony,

Sony!' the whole room is screaming their piece at Andy, and we're flicking the Vs back. It was top. Just madness.

I knew Saunders was out of control at that point. He had to sober up after that. Moira Bellas, who was high up in Warners then, told him he was never going to work in the industry again if he carried on like he was, and I think that made him sit up and think about where he was going. He cleaned up then. I think it was me who sent him to the drug doctor. They got him sober and then he was depressed so they put him on speed. So then we had Andy Saunders charging around on speed. He's a big guy and doesn't need to be any more aggressive than he is. The only way he could get away with his behaviour was that we had the biggest group in the country and he was my personal PR guy. He was unsackable, or he definitely would have been sacked by Sony.

And I thought he was brilliant at his job. He made me famous for five minutes in the 1990s and I'm still reaping the benefits – people calling me up to play DJ sets in Brazil for £7,000 a time – that only happened because of the mid-1990s.

You need people in a company who don't give a fuck, who are outspoken and brave. It was being fearless that was the key to my success, I've always believed that. The punk spirit. There were still people in the office who had it but they were being more and more outnumbered by the week.

By the end of 1996 I stopped going in. I didn't know who anyone was any more. There were about forty people in the office and I only liked a handful of them. I bought an office

House of Love
1989, all set
to become the
new British band
and under too
much pressure.
Left to right:
Chris Groothuizen,
Terry Bickers,
Guy Chadwick
and Pete Evans.

In 1990 Ride had the world at their feet. From left to right:
Loz Colbert, Steve Querait, Mark Gardener and Andy Bell.

Above: With Bobby in Birmingham, reading *The Face* on the Screamadelica tour 1991.

Below: A Boo Radleys radio session in 1994. From left to right: Martin Carr, Sice and Timothy Brown.

Above: Oasis in 1994 on a tour of the Netherlands. From left to right: Tony McCarroll, Bonehead, Noel, Liam and Paul McGuigan. I was in no state to keep track of the business but was still interested in Oasis.

Below: Re-signing Teenage Fanclub in 1995, with Dick Green on the left, Gerard Love, Norman Blake and Raymond McGinley. I was starting to involve myself with Creation again after my breakdown.

Above: Winning Independent Label of the Year at the Music Week Awards, 1995.

Left: With Tim Abbott the same evening. I loved his attitude to the world.

On stage with Oasis at the Brits in February 1996 where they won Best Band, Best Album, Best Single – solid proof of how big they were.

Above: Oasis in performance, Maine Road 28 April 1996. I felt flooded with energy – and finally wanted to go back to work again.

Below: Super Furry Animals in 1996 – perhaps the last great Creation band. From left to right: Gruff Rhys, Guto Pryce, Dafydd Ieuan, Cian Ciaran, Huw Bunford.

Above: Helping get the Tories out! I was asked to give Tony Blair a platinum disk of *What's the Story Morning Glory?* at the Labour conference in September 1996.

Below: When Noel's girlfriend tells you to buy him a Rolls, that's what you do!

Left: I love Courtney Love – like me, she's a square peg in a round hole.

Right: With Kate Moss in New York 2004.

Left: Pete Doherty and Carl Barât, best friends and worst enemies, at the NME Awards February 2004 where the Libertines won best UK Band.

Right: My cool wife Kate in her band Client in 2009.

Above: With Kate and our daughter Charlie in Spain, 2005.

Right: At my gaff in Wales in 2008. I love the place.

Below: Dean Cavanagh's logo for my new indie label, 359 Music.

359 MUSIC

BANG YER OWN DRUM

EST. NEVER

block round the corner so I wouldn't have to see anyone if I didn't want to. I had it done up and rented half the space to Meg Matthews' promotion company. She was good fun to have about if I wanted to talk to someone. The only person who was allowed in my half was Bobby! Sometimes Dick Green. But if anyone wanted to give me a message, the easiest way was to go and give it to Bobby.

No wonder politics became so interesting at the time. I was beginning to hang out with Margaret McDonagh more and more. We'd go for dinner a lot. I'd started going to Stamford Bridge to watch Chelsea with Ed Ball and Andy Saunders, and we'd hired our own box now. So I took Margaret to Chelsea too.

Creation, Oasis and McGee gave Labour 'a sense of now', that's what she told me. I gave them some money too. I gave £15,000 in early 1997 to the Scottish Labour Party. I did it on the condition that it was all spent in Scotland. Because I don't like living in Scotland doesn't mean I don't still care about the place and want it to be better than it is for the people who live there. (Of course they probably took my money for Scotland and spent it on whatever they wanted; how could I know otherwise?)

Peter Mandelson and Margaret McDonagh then took me on a tour of Millbank, showed me the campaign videos they were preparing leading up to the 1997 general election – 'Things Can Only Get Better'. I said they should choose a better song. 'Wake Up Boo!' would have been brilliant. They kept with fucking D.Ream.

As I was getting into politics, I was aware of how Paul Weller had been damaged by his involvement with the Labour Party through Red Wedge. But I hated the Tories and I thought I could help. I never imagined to what extent they'd involve me. That wasn't why I was doing it. I just thought I could help. I gave them another, bigger donation then.

If I don't remember there having been an election in 1992, I definitely remember there being one in 1997.

I was at the Royal Festival Hall in May when the election results came through. I've never heard a louder cheer than when Portillo lost his seat, even at Oasis gigs! Everybody hated him and the whole place went off.

There wasn't much suspense about the result. It was obvious Labour were going to win. Branson was working the crowd, and when you see him hanging out with the Labour Party you know the tide has turned.

I went up with Kate. We were having a great time. Then Margaret McDonagh asked me to look after Mick Hucknall, who was making a nuisance of himself with the blondes, and I had to stand beside him to distract him. We've said some pretty snide things about each other actually, but you have to hand it to him, he's a hell of a singer.

Blair and New Labour threw a party at 10 Downing Street to thank those who'd supported them during the campaign. Noel and I were invited. I was in the Landmark gym that afternoon on the running machine and watching Sky News. The newsreader was telling everyone that *Alan McGee is going to be asking Tony Blair some awkward questions tonight.* Is he? It took me a few seconds to realize it was me they were talking about. *What's Alan McGee going to say?* They were having a discussion about it. Fucking hell!

That evening Kate and I went round to Noel's, got in the Roller with him and Meg. It was madness when we arrived; cameras were going off everywhere. It suddenly occurred to me that this was going to be a part of history, like when Harold Wilson met the Beatles. There will be a picture of Noel meeting Tony and I'll be in the background with Kate and Meg, and we'll probably see this picture being used in twenty years' time. It was an incredibly optimistic time. Princess Di was still alive. *Be Here Now* hadn't come out. Labour were just in. We all believed in them.

Sure enough, Blair shook Noel's hand and the cameras went mental. The Pet Shop Boys were there, Kevin Spacey, everyone. We spoke to Blair for five minutes and then Alastair Campbell kept on our case for the rest of the night, a big Scottish hoolie assigned to make sure we behaved. There were some really funny moments. Kate gets pissed pretty easily. Jack Straw had me cornered at one point, asking me why I liked cocaine, a question I did not begin to know how to answer for him, and Kate used that as an opportunity to run off and explore. I looked across the room and saw she had Tony Blair trapped against a wall and was giving him a Grooverider remix of her band on CD. She'd drunk a whole bottle of champagne by then. You could see him looking at her with a fixed grin on his face, slowly trying to back away.

The funniest bit was when we were leaving. The Rolls-Royce was right outside, where there were 200 cameras. Noel and Meg went first and walked through the Downing Street gates and then they shut behind them, leaving me and Kate trapped. I saw Noel suddenly stop and realize he'd lost me, all the cameras going crazy. Where's Alan? I'm banging on the bars, shouting, 'I'm here! I'm here!' He had to shove all the journalists out of the way to let me out.

We went back to theirs afterwards and watched the news all night. That *was* the news, us four walking down the street. It was surreal.

After the election victory I was invited to be a captain of industry to assist Chris Smith, who was the new government's secretary for culture, media and sport. There were six of us: Paul Smith, Waheed Ali, Richard Branson, Gail Rebuck and Lord Puttnam: the Creative Industries Task Force. I'm still proud of the work I did to try to get musicians a fair deal. I thought they should be exempt from the forced employment training scheme the government were planning for eighteen- to twenty-four-year-olds, the New Deal for the unemployed. I wanted to create a New Deal for musicians that recognized they needed time to develop their music. This wouldn't even have been discussed without me speaking up against the plans, and Labour didn't like me for doing it, but my attitude was, if you ask me to the party, you've got to listen to what I have to say.

Everybody else in the music industry, George Martin, Rob Dickins, was dead against the New Deal for musicians. Their argument was that it *should* be hard for musicians. You won't find the next Rod Stewart unless he's been through the mill. It was a rubbish argument. It seemed to me they were just Tories who didn't believe in welfare and wanted to pretend that it wasn't just because of their selfishness. We were in a position to help people and I thought it was our duty to do so. I worked with John Glover and Stuart Worthington to propose the idea that musicians could be given time to develop while claiming benefits and not being forced to look for other jobs, and after some consideration Chris Smith passed it: the New Deal for musicians.

It really wound up everyone else in the music industry that I was in this position of influence even though they worked for much bigger companies. They couldn't get nearly the same access to politicians. These were the people who *actually* ran the music industry. And there was me, walking round the corridors of power!

Say what you like about Thatcher, may she rot in hell, but her enterprise allowance scheme helped me and Tracey Emin, for example, and a lot of others who probably wouldn't want to put their hand up to it. It's what funded most people at Creation Records to begin with, including Jeff Barrett. I just wanted kids to have the same chances that I had.

I don't know how successful the New Deal for musicians was, but we did it in good faith. I never wanted a medal for it; it just seemed like a good idea, and something I could do.

I got a load of stick for doing it at the time. Bill Drummond took me to task on the *Today* programme about working too closely with the government. I didn't even want to go on but reluctantly agreed. It was one of those things where you get surprised and don't turn it down quickly enough: *okay*. So I went on, really early in the morning, said my piece, and then they announced that of all the people you want to argue with at quarter to eight and half asleep, they're about to go over to Bill Drummond. That woke me up. *No fucking way!* He took me to pieces. There was only one person who'd have been worse to have to talk to then, and that would be Malcolm McLaren. Drummond absolutely *lambasted* me. I tried to give it back but my heart wasn't in it. What a disaster.

18: BE HERE NOW

By the end of 1996 we'd sold millions and millions of *Morning Glory* across the world. The third Oasis album had started recording at Abbey Road. There was a media scrum around the place, and in the middle of it Liam got arrested for possessing coke. So they moved studios to Ridge Farm in Surrey. These days people see *Be Here Now* as the thing that stopped Oasis' momentum, and I guess that's true. But there are some great songs on that album. Songs that don't go away are amazing songs. 'All Around the World' is an amazing song, for instance. That will stand the test of time.

The thing that let that album down was the production and having too many drugs in the studio. You could hear the coke in the production, all top-endy and no bass. It seemed to me that more than anyone else Owen Morris lost the plot producing that record. Noel was adding guitar part after guitar part and all I could think when I went down to the studio was, This is *loud*. Owen had taken all those overdubs off the first album, but now he'd lost control. I remember hearing 'It's Gettin' Better (Man!!)' and hearing Liam singing those words for the forty-seventh time in a chorus – and I knew it was too long. But the band were a runaway train by then.

It was hard to say who was in control. I had to hope I was wrong.

At the start of 1997 I hadn't been on a plane for nearly three years, not since Ed Ball took me back to Heathrow after my breakdown in LA. There were people at Sony America who had never seen me. After we'd renegotiated the contract with them they'd begun to realize that, for four more years at least, I could still write cheques, and I imagine this was quite worrying for them. I wasn't quiet about what I felt was my worth to them – Oasis were their biggest sellers. I'd therefore decided to reward myself by commandeering the Sony limousine.

I was going to a lot of football games then. I had a box at Chelsea and I was mates with Walter Smith, who was managing Everton. I'd ring Walter and ask who he was playing. Man U, he'd say. Right, I'll get the limo, I'm coming up. So I'd fill my limo – I'd decided it was my limo by then – with my mates and off we'd go.

For four years, with Oasis, we were pretty much paying the rent for Sony so I thought it was quite reasonable that I should have the limo. Of course, it pissed a lot of people off that I was being driven around in the company limo all the time. But I quite enjoyed that.

At Chelsea I knew Ruud Gullit, Gianluca Vialli, Ally McCoist, Pat Nevin. I was mates with most of them. I had the biggest band and I liked football and I was clean and I had a limo to drive people around to wherever they wanted to go – no wonder I had loads of friends then! I'd take them to whatever club they wanted to go to and sit there in the corner with my Diet Coke while they drank champagne. I had a good four years just coasting around in the limo. Who wouldn't take advantage of that situation? Can we ask Sony to get us a helicopter to take us to the Isle of Wight? Can we? Of course we can! So that's what we did. Should we get a helicopter over to Ireland? Of course we should.

Did we lose the plot? Gloriously! But I'm not apologizing for that. I just wanted to see how much I could get away with. I was waiting for Sony to say no, and they never did. I think it was easier for them just to say yes than to risk me being a cunt and threatening them with taking Oasis away. I couldn't really have done that, but they were making so much money no one wanted to risk rocking the boat. They thought I was a fucking loony, to be honest. But I was a loony who sold a lot of records. They don't care what you do as long as you sell. They hated me, but I didn't mind. They should have hated me by rights, I acted like a cunt. I stole the boss's limo for four years.

So it was no wonder Sony in America were getting concerned. They were hearing reports of this madman in London. Some of them had never met me and the ones who had hadn't seen me for years. They'd delegated this young woman, Rachel Felder, the junior A&R person, to deal with me. She'd fly over from New York every couple of weeks to find out what the hell I was up to. I'd be swimming in the Landmark's pool over the road from my flat and I'd hear a piercing American voice, *Hi, Alan!*, and look up to see her waving at me. I'm great friends with her to this day.

I realized I had to show the Sony people in America that I was still alive. And for myself, I needed to get over my fear of planes. I didn't want to be stuck in Britain forever, watching Kate leave the front door with her suitcase packed for a holiday. It would be nice to see the sun again one day.

Who do you want with you when you're facing a frightening flight? Ed Ball, of course. So we set off on Concorde to see Tommy Motola, the head of Sony. It was scary, I admit. A white knuckle ride. But once you're up in the air, what can you do? They were very thin planes, Concordes, quite cramped. They really rattled. Three and a half grand a pop, and it was quick, four hours to New York, but it was also quite easy to believe the plane was going to suddenly shake itself apart.

But we got there okay, and I was pleased to have jumped that hurdle. The next day we met Tommy Mottola. He's quite an intimidating character. His office – I've never seen an office like it – is painted all over in dark mud brown. He opens his door with a remote control like a TV zapper. There he is sat behind a massive desk. There was nothing to worry about – I was responsible for him having just sold 20 million records. It must have been weird for Ed Ball, being wheeled in to meet him with me. Mottola was looking at him curiously and saying, 'And you are?' Ed was actually Creation's most prolific recording artist. I just loved having him there with me. 'Don't shut the door!' Mottola shouted as we left the office, and lifted up his remote controller to do it for us. He obviously enjoyed doing that. It's a shame he never got to see the Bunker – I wonder what he would have made of that.

There were some funny moments on that trip. Ed and I were sitting in a restaurant with Joe McEwen, Seymour Stein's A&R man. The whole music industry used to eat in the same restaurant in those days. Tommy Mottola was in there and bowled over, grabbed me and dragged me off to his table. 'Alan, Alan, I want you to meet Daryl Hall and John Oates.' And there they were, Hall and Oates, looking twenty years older, both eating huge plates of spaghetti bolognese. 'You've got to manage them,' he says to me. And then he turns to them and says, 'Alan's from the street! He'll get you back on track.' Just when you thought life couldn't get any more surreal. I quite like Hall and Oates. But I couldn't go for that.

And then, on the plane back, we met Michael Jackson for the second time. He was sat at the front surrounded by security guards and started laughing his head off when he saw us, like he'd never seen two bald guys before! Ed Ball wanted to go up and have it out with him. I had to stop him. Jackson was sitting there with a face mask on, giggling away. I was thinking, You're a cunt, but you've got four security guards.

'Calm down, Ed. What can we do?' I said.

'I'm not having it, I'm going to go up,' Ed's insisting.

I had to hold on to him to stop him. They'd have probably shot him dead. Tasered him at least.

You run into all sorts of people if you're always getting planes. I was met once at the gate by a man with a machine gun. 'Show me your passport!' I didn't argue. Even Michael Jackson didn't have security this intense. And when I got on the plane, who was there, sitting in seat 1A?

Margaret Thatcher.

It was a good job I was off the drugs by then or who knows what I would have said.

Even as we were enjoying Oasis' heyday, I could see the music business was changing, becoming even more commercial. Supermarkets were selling records, demanding massive discounts. It was getting harder and harder to compete on a level playing field. Guitar bands were going out of fashion again. Britpop was dying and the Spice Girls were coming through and another wave of dance music.

We were trying to break Hurricane #1 in this new market. We tried all the commercial tricks, multi-formatting, etc. It started off well. We had a bit of momentum beforehand. Oakenfold had done a really good mix of 'Step Into My World' and that had gone in at 19 in May 1997. Their first album went to number 11 in the charts and sold something like 100,000 copies.

But the next year I made a big mistake advising them to let their song 'Only the Strongest Will Survive' feature on a *Sun* advert. At the time, I thought it made sense because the money on offer would pay for their next album. But I think this killed their careers and lost them any credibility. If you played the corporate game too much, you alienated the indie fans. Having an edge had to be a big part of the appeal and we blunted any chance of them having this edge with that advert.

They were up against it anyway because they weren't Oasis and they sounded like Oasis. They probably arrived about nine months too late to really capitalize on the Britpop fad. Cast sold a million albums and that could have been Hurricane #1 if they'd got there first. All those Oasis fans, like Andy Bell, wanted something else to listen to. After Andy gave up on Hurricane #1, he was about to become a student again when he got the phone call after Bonehead left the band: would you like to be in Oasis? Yes, he would. And now of course he's in Beady Eye with Liam.

Be Here Now destroyed a lot of the affection people had for Oasis, for Noel and Liam. They'd been a refreshing change before when they'd first arrived, down to earth and laddish in a way the average guy from Salford understood.

The campaign for the album was all wrong and left a bad taste in everyone's mouths. It made them seem aloof, like they thought they were above everyone else. Ignition management took control of it and insisted we embargo it heavily and not allow it to be played on the radio before release. In one fell swoop, we managed to turn all the journalists off Oasis. Ignition insisted on everyone signing non-disclosure agreements, stuff that wasn't necessary. There was a real paranoia to it. And Ignition used us as patsies – it was our name at the top of all these agreements and so everyone thought it was us getting too big for our boots.

Jonny Hopkins was caught between a rock and a hard place. He was employed by Creation handling Oasis' press, trying to please both us and Ignition. But we had no real power against Ignition – 90 per cent of our sales were Oasis and so we had to do whatever their management said. The risk of upsetting them was far too great.

But while Ignition were busy alienating the press, Verve got hold of the football and ran with it and became the biggest band of the moment with *Urban Hymns*.

I don't think Ignition understood what they were doing. They decided they had to clamp everybody's mouths shut and didn't really understand how the internet was making it impossible to stop any leaks. It worked against the band and made them look as if they were prima donnas, as if they thought they were U2. Whereas in fact, the reason people loved Oasis, which I'd always understood, is that they were the people's band. There wasn't this big separation: this 'I'm a rock star, I'm untouchable' attitude. And now there was this big wall protecting the band, and it turned off a lot of journalists and people in the record shops. By this point, to be honest, it was Ignition who were in charge of Creation in a lot of ways. They had their people in the building and they were using us as the proxy Stasi. The waiver forms were issued from us but they came from Ignition management.

I remember the *Sunday Times* reporting that I was a Svengali controlling the press. It wasn't true. I thought the way the press was being managed for that record was going to lose people. And it did. We let the Verve in. We blew it.

We blew it and we sold 11 million copies in the process. Now that's a sentence you don't hear said very often. That's how big Oasis were at the time. But they'd never be as big again.

Be Here Now seemed to signal the end of Britpop, the end of the success guitar bands could have making pop music. The other big 'Britpop' bands moved on and became less poppy to reject the label – Blur's new album was in a harder, more American direction, and Pulp's was much darker and without obvious hits.

Success is a really weird thing, a paradox. The environment that made Creation so great, so different, was failure! So when we succeeded, we started to destroy the environment of adversity that made us so great.

Vanishing Point by Primal Scream had come out on 7 July 1997 and was an incredible record. The record did well, 300,000 copies, something like that. It went in at number 2. I thought it should have been bigger, but it was becoming harder and harder again to make ambitious music work commercially.

At the time it came out, things weren't good between me and Bobby. I didn't A&R the record, that was Jeff Barrett, and he was back doing their press too. Bobby and I were quite estranged, quite distant. I look back at that album and see there are some amazing songs on it. 'Burning Wheel' might even be their best. But at the time I was indifferent.

The flashpoint for us falling out was the gig they played

in Liverpool, a benefit gig for the dockers. Bobby had really put the pressure on me to come and see them. I'd been wary of it. I knew they were still a drug band and I was fearful that contact with them might undo all the work I'd put in to my recovery. I hadn't been in their dressing room for years. There was no attempt to hide anything from me. Bobby necked a couple of Es right in front of me. I thought, Dude, I've come all this way, can't you have some consideration? There wasn't one ounce of malice in him doing it but it still really hurt me that he couldn't imagine what it would be like for me to see that. It wasn't that it made me want to take them myself, but at the same time it freaked me out to see it, for me to know how close I was again to the lifestyle that had nearly killed me. *How hard do you want to make this for me?* I was thinking. I'm here, I live miles away, just give me an inch. I didn't see them live again for years after that gig.

As the years went on I became able to watch people take drugs and not feel weird. (It's basically impossible to work in the music industry and not be surrounded by people on drugs.) But then it was hard – and doubly hard because Primal Scream were my crowd, from when I was a child. Being with them was like being back in my old body, and I couldn't block out what had happened to me, what I was recovering from.

They couldn't understand where I was at, because they were still out of their minds. It's hard to make thoughtful decisions when you're in that state. And it's probably unfair of me to have expected it. There're no badges when you get clean or sober. They were probably looking at me and pitying me, thinking what a better time they were having than me. It's fair enough if they did – you've got to decide how to live your own life. I needed to have a break from the band so we could get on again, so we could remember we were friends first and foremost and not business colleagues. Any problems we had we kept strictly between ourselves and out of the public domain, and I think this is why we've managed to stay friends.

Occasionally Bobby would still call me up to battle for him. He wanted to release 'Kowalski' as a single and the rest of Creation were telling him he couldn't. That's not how it works in my company, especially not with Primal Scream, so I overrode everyone and told them we were releasing it as a single. We still had the same gang ethos, even if we were keeping our distance temporarily. Let's be honest, we both didn't like each other much at the time. They were out on their own in many ways.

There was a clear line from the Jesus and Mary Chain to Oasis. It was there in the sense of danger, the classic melodies and the fuck-you attitude. Bobby Gillespie arrived in my office one day in 1997 and told me I had to re-sign the Mary Chain. No one else would have put the record out. Their sales had been on the slide for a few years now and Geoff Travis had turned it down. I listened to the demos and knew it wouldn't be an amazing Mary Chain album but I knew it would be a good one. I really liked the Mary Chain but Bobby *loved* the Mary Chain. I didn't think much about the financial repercussions of decisions in those days. I thought I'd earned that right. So I just said: 'Let's do it.' It was an attempt to try and reclaim our past and get back to the early days; and it was a naive ambition, because we'd gone beyond the point where that was possible.

We offered them a reasonable deal, they agreed and then on the day they were supposed to be signing the contract they rang to ask for a load more money! We'd offered them a £60,000 advance to include the cost of recording, and they'd thought we meant £60,000 plus the cost of recording. No one else in the industry would give them a deal and they were still demanding last-minute improvements. But because it was the Mary Chain Dick and I just went, Oh, yeah, give it to them. It wasn't worth the hassle. They were the same old band.

It was only at that point that William Reid and I ever got close. He'd decided he wanted to get to know me. Perhaps because I was so friendly with Jim. So we were walking down Charlotte Street near Soho. He isn't very worldly at all, William.

'What is this, Alan?' he's asking me. 'Who lives round here?'

'Malcolm McLaren,' I said.

'Can we go and see him?' he asked.

Er, if you like. So we called for Malcolm McLaren at his flat but he wasn't in. Still, just ringing the bell had made William quite excited. 'What shall we do now?' he asked me.

At the time I was a member of the Groucho Club and that was round the corner, so I mentioned that – not very enthusiastically. If there's one place I'm certain I'll never set foot in again these days, it's the Groucho. I don't think I'd be comfortable even walking past it.

William, however, was amazed by the idea. 'The Groucho Club! The Groucho Club!' he starts repeating in glee.

I know the place is a fucking pit but he hasn't been there. 'Yeah, it could be . . . okay?' I said.

'The Groucho! Do girls go there?'

'A few,' I said.

'The Groucho! Can we go?'

So off we went and the minute we got there I saw seven or eight girls in their mid-twenties I knew, good pals. So I introduced them to William and they were all going, 'The Mary Chain! You were my hero!'

This was about thirteen years after we'd released 'Upside Down'. They must have been about twelve then and they were telling him, 'You were my fucking hero!'

Anyway, we hung out with them for a while. William was having the time of his life. I was a bit bored. The next thing I know, Will Self comes up and calls me a cunt. No reason. Just comes over and informs me I'm a cunt. Then he's off.

'What did he call you?' asked William.

'Ah, he just called me a cunt, don't worry about it.'

I didn't give a fuck. This was when Will Self was an alcoholic, a junkie. I just thought, Go off and take some more smack, overdose and die, do us a favour.

The next thing though William has gone up to him: 'You, you cunt, outside!' He was trying to drag him outside and batter him. Will Self was holding on to the bar, smacked off his tits, as William was trying to drag him outside and give him a doing. That was the day I decided I quite liked William sometimes.

And it was great to have the Jesus and Mary Chain back on the label again. I'd always loved the band. It was a link with the time of Creation when it had been really exciting. It just wasn't like that on a day-to-day basis any more.

I proposed to Kate that year and she accepted. I was a bit nervous about getting married again, not because I had any reservations about Kate, who I knew I loved and wanted to be with. But I dreaded all the fuss. We'd talk about a wedding and who we had to invite and, before you knew it, it was Knebworth all over again.

We had a holiday planned that Christmas in Nevis. I'd hired a huge house with ten bedrooms and we'd invited lots of our friends to stay with us. Three days before we flew, I had the idea that it was probably the kind of place where you could organize a marriage quickly. I mentioned it to Kate and she was into the idea, though she didn't believe I'd go through with it and manage to get it organized in time. Go on, I *dare* you, was her attitude. When we were out there, on New Year's Day 1998, I got in touch with a local judge and priest called Cecil Byron – he could have people married or executed – and he agreed to execute, no, marry us the next day in the porch of the house we were all staying in.

So that night Kate had a hen do and I had a lads do – me

sipping Diet Cokes while Paul Gallagher (Noel and Liam's brother who worked in A&R for Creation) made everyone cry with laughter.

The next day we were married. The moment they said, *Do you take this woman*, I flashed back all those years ago to Yvonne and thought of the mistake we'd made. But I knew that I wasn't making a mistake with Kate.

I stopped going to the political dos after a while. I remember sitting at the high table next to the American ambassador at a dinner at the Labour conference in Bournemouth. He asked me what I did, and I was always quite modest about it in that company: Oh, you know, I do music. He'd heard of Oasis so we had something to chat about. Campbell was walking Blair about to say hello to different people. The minute he saw the American ambassador, he went into overdrive, really turned on the charm. You got the real sense that Blair had to snap to attention for him, that it was the American who was really in charge.

In the end I became disappointed. I realized they weren't listening to me. They had their own agenda, and if I said anything that fitted in with that, that was fine, but otherwise they were ignoring me.

The whole idea of it being a glorious time to be British, the whole Cool Britannia thing, that was made up by the press. But Oasis' support of the Labour Party, and their huge success at the time, did give Blair a sense of being the man of the moment. They used us and got what they wanted from us. I don't feel bitter about it. The New Deal for musicians did something good for bands trying to make it, and I'm glad I could make that difference.

Doors were opening up now everywhere I looked. The royals were courting me for a while. Charles invited me for 'supper' three times at Buckingham Palace. Perhaps Blair had told him what fun I was. Kate's always been mad that I never accepted the invite. I can't stand the royals, fucking can't stand them, and once I said that in the papers the invitations stopped.

Now I sort of wish we'd gone. My new philosophy is, if you don't go, you don't know. I don't know what Prince Charles is about and if I had gone I'd know now. But I had and have no respect for them. I was more principled then: I didn't believe in the monarchy so I couldn't bring myself to go. The invitation was up on the mantelpiece for about a week and Kate was getting excited, and I just told her, I can't go. I can't.

Perhaps they were sounding me out about giving me an honour. They can stick their honours up their arse, I'd never take one.

It was sometimes a bit rocky between us and the Blairs. Cherie always liked me and seemed to think I was the kind of guy she should be hanging around with. She once asked me and Paul Smith to take her to London Fashion Week. I've really got no interest in fashion, not much then and less now.

(I dress for the country these days, tweeds and dark greens.

I saw Lee Mavers in Leeds recently, when I was dressed head to foot in Barbour and wearing a tweed hat. 'Why are you wearing that?' he asked. 'It's my image,' I said, straight-faced. He walked away, shaking his head. Apparently it *is* becoming fashionable now. But I don't see Bobby Gillespie turning up on stage in plus fours any time soon.)

Anyway, Kate loves fashion and runs her own label, Client, so she really wanted to go. But when I asked if she could come along I was told no. Not famous enough, I guess, not enough of a photo opportunity to help advertise Cherie's 'sense of now'. The next day Kate called up New Labour and told them never to ask me for another donation again. (I'd given them another £20,000 recently.) They really didn't understand the dynamic going on in my family. It's Kate who's in charge.

Two weeks later, to make amends, an invitation arrived to spend a night with the Blairs at Chequers. This was on 23 October 1999. We were driven down there by a West Ham football hooligan in the Sony limo I had been stealing very frequently, and we arrived at half seven. There were full SWAT teams over the lawn to greet us. I got out, Paul Smith-suited-up, Kate wearing Prada, and we walked on in. And there was Blair, scruffy bastard in his Gap jeans: *Hello!* Tony and I had a ten-minute discussion about music, about Oasis and Blur, and just as that finished we turned round and *Now then, now then, now then*, Jimmy Savile walked in the room with a security guy. We both stood there looking at this 1980s TV star, with a cigar and a mad fucking rock and roll jacket on. *Now then, now then, now then.*

'This can't get any more bizarre,' I said to Tony, and he burst out laughing.

At the table, it was Tony and Cherie, me and Kate, John O'Farrell and his missus, Judi Dench and her husband Michael Williams, Admiral Boyce (the guy who presses the nuclear button), John Reid (the home secretary, a Scottish guy who did well for himself and later had a spell as chairman of Celtic FC), and a couple of others. And Jimmy Savile. Kate was placed right between Jimmy Savile and Judi Dench. And he immediately started to hit on her (Kate, not Judi). He was kissing his way right up her arms, kissing her fingers. Kate wasn't too happy about this. I was thinking, What a dirty old man. I had no idea he was a nonce, just thought he was a dirty old fucker. And a cheeky cunt to boot. His security guard looked tasty so it would have been a bad idea to put an elbow in his face, much as it was tempting. When at Chequers, it's not the done thing to break Jimmy Savile's nose. The fact that I was in a position to even consider it was mindblowing enough in itself.

Eventually, the dinner was over. Kate came over and said, 'He's a dirty old pervert,' and I said, 'I know!' He left her alone once she was next to me at least.

I'll tell you something about Jimmy Savile though. I couldn't tell he was a paedophile, all that's just the benefit of hindsight. But I knew straight away there was something sinister about him. This hasn't come out yet, but I'm sure at some point it will. He was a gangster, I'm convinced of it. I've dealt with people like that. There was an edge to him, a quiet menace, the threat of violence. I come from Glasgow, I can tell when someone's dangerous. I could tell he was connected. He was perhaps seventy at this moment but I knew he was a gangster.

In fact everyone was trying to avoid Jimmy Savile. Why he was invited, I don't know. It was as if he was the host of the party rather than Tony. He was speaking to the whole table apart from when he was trying to suck Kate's fingers. He'd stand up and walk around too. It really shows the strange power and connection to the establishment he had. I don't think we've heard the half of what he got up to yet, and we probably never will.

What really drove a wedge between me and the Labour Party was when I backed Malcolm McLaren for London mayor ahead of Frank Dobson at the end of 1999. I'd always loved Malcolm. I'd even tried to *be* him for a while when I was managing the Jesus and Mary Chain. We'd met first in 1996 when we'd done an interview together for *Punch* and I pulverized him in it. I was a right cunt. I said if I'd had the Sex Pistols they'd still be going, I'd have sold 60 million records. He couldn't really answer back about that, because I had the biggest group in the world by then in Oasis.

Of course, to be fair, with the Sex Pistols he changed culture and I never did. Unless you count inventing Shoegazing.

We became pals afterwards. I used to go and see him in his office on Denmark Street. He'd phone me up regularly and we'd go for four-hour dinners, during which he'd order the two most expensive bottles of wine on the menu and proceed to talk for three hours and forty-five minutes. Then for fifteen minutes he'd want a rest and to eat his dinner, during which time I would be allowed to talk. I must have bought him dinner twelve times. He never paid once. But it was an education, worth every penny

I'll tell you what – he was genius. This was in the mid-1990s and he was going on about China, how they were going to become the world's biggest economy, about the internet and MP3s and how that was going to transform the music industry. It's all come true. (It was listening to him that gave me the ambition for my next label Poptones, and the problem with listening to a man so far ahead of his time is that the idea for my label was ahead of its time too.)

Malcolm was always doing speaking tours. He bragged to me once about one talk he gave to an audience in Norway for eleven hours! He waited till they were all asleep before he stopped! Malcolm, you've got to love him!

Particularly for the way he got me to put him up for Mayor of London. I had absolutely no say in the matter. In fact, I was in the Caribbean when I heard I was putting him up. I was with Kate and my sister Susan and her husband at the time, Louis, and her fantastic daughter Jade who's the only one in my family who likes the music I released. (Everyone else thinks it's fucking rubbish.) Anyway, so we're there on holiday and we started getting calls because it had been announced that I am putting Malcolm up for Mayor of London.

This wasn't the first I'd heard of his plans to run for mayor. He'd told me all about it over dinner the week before and asked me to put him up. And I *hadn't* agreed. I clearly remember *not* agreeing to put him up for the Mayor of London. So, he just announced it anyway!

I was impressed by that. See, it was an education hanging around with Malcolm. I sounded vaguely intelligent in those days. The biggest problem Malcolm had was how to connect his ideas with making money. His ideas were miles better than mine – he just didn't know how to make money out of them. That was my skill. That was why I was in a position to help. So I went back to Sony and asked them to write a cheque to Malcolm for £20,000.

'Why are we doing this, Alan?'

'It's an art project,' I said.

Creation's accountant was looking at me thinking, *This man should not be in charge of the company.* I've always been pleased I got Sony to pay for that. And I'm glad Malcolm tricked me into supporting him for mayor. It was time to end that link with New Labour.

We ran the campaign for a few months but then Malcolm withdrew when Ken Livingstone stood as an independent, as we both liked him. And of course Ken Livingstone beat the Labour candidate Frank Dobson. I felt bad for Margaret McDonagh then. She took the blame for that and finished as Labour Party general secretary soon after that, but I don't think Malcolm McLaren had much to do with it.

I was gutted when Malcolm died. I'd had no indication

at all that was going to happen. He was always so full of life.

The last time I saw him was in LA, maybe a year before he died. He had a laugh unlike anyone else's in the world. I didn't see him first, I heard him. From a table on the complete opposite side of the room. There's only one guy who laughs like that. It was a delight to hear. I'll always remember that laugh.

There's nothing that could make me get involved in party politics again. I no longer believe in the political system we live in. I like individuals in the system who try to sort out people's problems, like our local MP. But I've come to realize, no matter what, Labour, Tory or Lib Dem, they're all puppets for the shadow government above it, business, America, the people who really run the world.

19: THE END

In those days I had never ever used a computer. I didn't have one in my office. I couldn't understand what I would do on one if I did. It was Kate who turned me on to the internet. Predictably, I wasn't interested at first. Fuck all that internet rubbish, etc. But she knew how to get me into it: type a band that you're interested in here. So I typed in Oasis, and a whole list of stuff came up, and about an hour later I was, *wow*, I want one! How do I get an internet?

Straight away I saw the implications of it. It was obvious. That's how people were going to get their music. So I wrote an article predicting the end of the music industry as we knew it, that people would stop buying CDs. Malcolm McLaren had helped me see that was going to be the case, but it was completely obvious as soon as you thought about it. But most people in the industry didn't want to see the obvious, because of how disastrous the implications were for them. So my article pissed a lot of people off, particularly Rob Dickins and the BPI. They said I was insane.

I don't want to say I told you so but . . .

*

Guitar bands were on the slide so we had a go at branching out in a different direction at Creation. We wanted to see if we could compete with the majors by doing what they did – moving away from white boys and guitars and focusing on pop acts. It was a sign of how far we'd come from when we started – it had been a passion to begin with; now we were making business decisions. But it was interesting too, or I wouldn't have done it. You've got to push yourself out of your comfort zone sometimes.

I'd put out an ambient record *Underwater Symphonies* with Kate first when she was recording under the name Scuba. I started seeing her just around that time. She was on Sony as part of a pop duo called Sirenes and they tried to screw her. Sony were trying to throw Kate out and release the tapes as though the singer was a solo artist, even though they were Kate's songs that had been recorded. So I went in to get Kate's tapes back. I was earning most of Sony's money at the time through Oasis so I was never going to stand for them messing my girlfriend around like that. I went in and the boss said, 'How can I make you happy?' The tapes were delivered to mine later that night.

Kate had never seen anyone beat a corporation before. She thought it beat you every time. 'No, it doesn't,' I said. It didn't beat me, anyway. She became very confident after that in her dealings with the music industry.

She should be because she's a very talented songwriter. We signed her new band Technique and tried to break them as a commercial pop act, but the singles stalled at about 64 and 56 in April and August 1999. The interesting thing is that her songs made her quite a lot of money. In 2001 we got an email from a star in Asia called Coco Lee who'd heard Technique's second single 'You and Me' and was going to do a cover of it. It was number one for six months in the whole of Indonesia! So Kate had a number one. She made a decent amount of money out of writing songs. The first song 'Sun is Shining' was used in a major video game. Years later her next band Client put out four or five records with Depeche Mode's label. They were a modest hit in England in 2005, but they'd play to big audiences in Germany and Hungary. They had a strong visual sense and all wore uniforms and Kate took this for the starting point for her fashion label Client, which she now runs from the house in Wales.

I didn't just come back from my honeymoon with a new wife, I'd found a new act there too, Mishka, and we released his debut album a year later. He's a white reggae singer and I'm supposed to feel embarrassed about that. Bollocks. That's like saying black guys can't play rock music. And I found out recently that in May 2013, he was America's number one selling reggae artist that month with a record he put out on Jimmy Buffett's label. *Mishka*, the album Creation put out in 1999, sold about 100,000 copies worldwide and went Top 10 in Japan – for a failure, that's not too bad!

He probably would have worked better on another label without our reputation for white boy guitar rock. He would have been taken seriously then, but with us, people were jealous of Oasis's success and would decide in advance that any attempt to try something different was bound to be ridiculous. We thought naively we could break out of our genre. But we couldn't.

This is why I still think about what would have happened if I'd gone to V2 with Richard Branson and Jeremy Pearce in 1996. It would have been a fresh chance. I might have been able to break out of my mould there.

My final, glorious failure at Creation is the one I'm most proud of, the one that showed that the Creation spirit still lived, even if only in my head and a couple of other people's. That was when I signed Kevin Rowland as a solo artist. He'd released one solo album in 1988 after Dexys Midnight Runners had split up, but no one had heard of him for the last ten years.

I'd always loved Dexys Midnight Runners but I'd been warned in advance that Kevin Rowland could be hard work. I'd heard a story that Martin from Heavenly had offered an opinion about his demo in a meeting they'd had; Kevin had told him to shut his fucking mouth, he only wanted to talk to Jeff Barrett. Of course, this just made me more interested.

When I met him, he was lovely to me. He had strange clothes on that day. He looked like a dethroned king. Like Henry VIII without the crown.

Anyway, he sang 'Manhood' to us. Just a capella. It was beautiful. He finished and I said straight away, 'I'll sign you.'

He was, like, what?

Everyone else he was talking to was umming and ahing, adding conditions. None of that with me: I just trusted my instincts, like I always had done.

So he signed and we got on with doing the album. He'd ask my opinion about certain things. I never sugarcoated anything, so I'd tell him, no, that's shit.

That approach didn't work. He was twitchy. He'd just got clean, and he was pretty raw. He couldn't handle my directness then, not at that time. We agreed at a certain point that the record was never going to get made with me A&Ring it. So Mark Bowen babysat that record.

It's funny that Kevin Rowland couldn't cope with me. I was the one being warned in advance from other labels that I wouldn't be able to cope with Kevin, and he couldn't cope with me!

I give Mark Bowen his due, it's a great record. Kevin wanted to reinterpret records that had got him through his depression, and it was a brilliant concept.

Andy Saunders was really upset he wasn't going to work on the publicity campaign. He was a big Dexys fan, but Kevin wanted a woman. Saunders thought I'd betrayed him. So, I said, 'Look mate, you don't want to do the publicity on this, trust me. Wait till you see the cover. It will blow your mind.'

The truth of the matter is the record was brilliant. The thing that stopped people liking the record was the cover: Kevin in a black velvet dress, pulled down to show his nipples, pulled up to show his silky black knickers, stockings and suspenders.

264 / ALAN McGEE

It's Kevin Rowland, you let him do what he wants. You've got two choices: you do what he wants to do, or you don't do the record. It was eleven years since his last record. It could be eleven more. Why would he listen to Alan McGee about his image?

The choice was to try and influence him and fail, or just to put the record out.

There was a naughtiness to my decision too. I knew Creation was likely to end soon. And I knew that this was a great record. Once I saw the cover the first thing I did was order 10,000 posters printed and put them up all over the country in accident black spots trying to cause a car crash. I imagined these commuters, barely having woken up, at eight in the morning being confronted by Kevin Rowland's big balls in black knickers and driving straight off the road.

I liked the sleeve a lot. We both did. He thought it was a work of art. I thought it was bonkers.

Going ahead with it was old school Creation, not giving a fuck about what anyone thought. And all the corporate people at Creation, the people who worked on Oasis records, thought it was outrageous, that it was ruining the name of the label. They thought the label stood for corporate indie, but I thought the label stood for bonkers brave fuck-you creativity. For provocation. Independence wasn't a fucking musical genre. A lot of the staff couldn't take it and were bitter that I was still allowed to make decisions they thought were crazily uncommercial.

Their animosity was symptomatic of the new music

business landscape. The independent music scene was dying, and this was just a reflection of that.

We sold 500 copies of the first single, 700 copies of the album in the UK. It was a shame the cover put everyone off because otherwise, as an album of respectable covers of pop standards, it was perfect Radio 2 music, like a good Robson and Jerome. But you'd never see that pair wearing women's knickers in public, and therein lay the problem. How much of a disaster the record was is always exaggerated. We ended up selling 20,000 copies of the album worldwide: not bad.

And that was one of the last things we did. There was an incredible Primal Scream album due for release at the end of 1999, *XTRMNTR*. They had their own studio by now, could move at their own pace and we never had any troubles again like we did with recording *Give Out But Don't Give Up*. By that time the band had become a Bobby and Andrew creative partnership. Throb had been missing in action for a while.

In the first words Bobby sings on the album he accuses a money man of losing his soul. I had the money now. But I wasn't ready to say goodbye to my soul yet. And every day in the office felt like it was killing it. There were fifty people in the office and I only really talked to half a dozen of them. Joe, Ed, Dick, Jon Andrews, Andy Saunders – after that I was struggling to find anyone I had any affinity with.

Dick and I were hardly going in any more. I remember one particularly bleak February morning in 1999 I phoned him up.

'This is rubbish. I hate it.'

'I fucking hate it too.'

'Do you want to carry it on?' I asked.

'I haven't wanted to carry it for four or five years now.'

'Why didn't you say?' I asked.

'I thought you wanted to carry on.'

He'd wanted to go from the beginning of Britpop!

Well, that was that then. It felt like a huge relief.

Sony weren't happy that I was quitting. Paul Russell would have liked to keep me on and strip the company right back, make three-quarters of the staff redundant, drop all the acts apart from the big four: Oasis, Primal Scream, Teenage Fanclub, Super Furry Animals.

But I just wanted out, to quit while we were ahead. Bobby was upset – he'd been involved since day one and believed in what we were doing and he was about to release what he thought was Primal Scream's best album. We told Oasis in November. Liam was disappointed too. He thought I was abandoning him to the tabloids. There was quite a gap in our ages and perhaps he found it helpful to have me around as a sort of father figure. Noel was much more cool about it. 'We won,' he said. 'They didn't.'

We were going to shut up shop after the fourth Oasis album in 2000, but Oasis decided to start their own label, Big Brother, and license it to Sony. The Sony accountants looked at the huge operating costs we had and decided to pull the plug earlier than we'd intended. They were going to take the big four successful bands, Oasis, Primal Scream, Teenage Fanclub, Super Furry Animals, and let everyone else go. I felt sad for artists like Ed Ball, who lost their musical outlet.

The staff took it badly when we told them we were closing. They hated me for my decision, saw it as a betrayal. I understood that. A lot of people had their dream job at Creation. But the times were changing. They didn't understand that they would nearly all have got the sack whether I'd continued or not. It was unsustainable and Sony were moving in to drastically change the way it was run. It was a glorious impractical love affair, and it was incredible really that it had lasted so long.

I hadn't meant to hurt anyone and I'm sorry if I did. But I'd never promised to be their dad.

Shutting early meant that the last Creation album, very appropriately, was by Primal Scream. *XTRMNTR*. Exterminator. It was released on 31 January 2000. We kept some people on till April to manage that record. But for most of the staff Creation was dead from January. I never went in again.

20: THE LIBERTINES

It was exciting to imagine how my new record company could be. Creation had become as corporate as a major by the end and I wanted to try to recapture some of the fun and energy of the label's first days, when we had been a small gang filled with passion. We had six months between the end of Creation and the start of Poptones, during which I'd kept busy with Malcolm for Mayor. Poptones was started with six people, with Joe Foster as a partner and the head of A&R, the very man who I'd first set up Creation with. (Dick Green went with Mark Bowen to start Wichita, which he still runs to this day, and which has had lots of success with Bloc Party, the Cribs, the Yeah Yeah Yeahs.) I was more and more interested in the internet. Joe Foster and I had been doing internet radio broadcasts at the end of Creation – great fun – and I wanted Poptones to be pioneering in the way it used the internet.

The initial idea for Poptones was exciting but too ahead of its time: a purely digital label. A website, MP3 downloads, a community and straight to the consumer without the need for record shops. I thought we could change the whole model. We were trying to do iTunes before iTunes had taken off. But the technology and the rest of the industry were lagging behind, and so we ended up pressing records as usual. Our first record was *Seventeen Stars* by the Montgolfier Brothers, a baroque, cinematic classic that almost no one has ever heard.

In September 2000 my daughter Charlie was born in the Portland hospital. We had music playing and she chose to come out to 'Higher Than The Sun'. It was an amazing moment. Watching a child being born and growing up humbles you. I was determined to be there for her, that this time things would go right. She's been the apple of my eye ever since.

Our first big band was the Hives in 2002. I saw them on German TV first actually, on Viva 2. I loved them and so did my young colleagues Ian Johnson and Al Hake, who knew every band known to man. It was just my thing, high energy garage rock. They found out they had two albums out but had only sold about 600 records worldwide. We put an album together from the two they had put out already and called it *Your New Favourite Band*. I chose the single, 'Hate to Say I Told You So', and that became their big record that made them famous. We broke them through TV shows, through the four biggest music shows in the UK including *Later . . . with Jools Holland*. Ended up selling about 400,000 copies. It was a hell of a start.

But ultimately Poptones never became what I'd hoped it would be, a forward looking company with the old Creation spirit. We didn't have the infrastructure and so we ended up doing a deal with Telstar. This was all right for a while; we sold another 200,000 Hives records.

During this time I missed out on selling 4 million records, something my colleague Ian probably still resents me for. He rang me up and said, 'Alan, I know this isn't your kind of thing, but I think they're going to be big and we should sign them.' It was a band with a sixteen-page feature in *Dazed & Confused*. 'Go on, put them on,' he said. It sounded pretty good to start with, a bit glam, a good riff, but then the vocals came in, a super camp, ultra-high-pitched falsetto: *I believe in a thing called love!* I just burst out laughing when I heard it.

'It's going to sell, it's going to sell. Let's do it,' Ian said.

'What are they called?' I asked.

'The Darkness,' he said.

So I did what I normally do when I need musical advice. I called up Bobby Gillespie and played it to him down the phone. He had the exact same reaction as I had, and started laughing his head off when he heard the singing. When I heard that I knew I couldn't sign them. I thought of the list of the great bands I'd worked with being topped off with a band called the Darkness. We had them ready to sign. Ian had found them. But I just couldn't bring myself to do it. Ian's their manager now. I'm sure they still fill decent sized venues and make a good living from it.

At the same time, I was tackling one of the hardest challenges I ever faced: managing the Libertines. It's a sad story.

I know I'm a good manager of bands. My skill has always been knowing how to convert things into cash, and this is why I still get offers to manage some of the biggest acts around. There are bands approaching me now who've been at the top of the industry for years, and when they look at their bank accounts they can't understand why they're so low. This is why they want me to come in. I'm ambitious and I'm not scared to ask for what I think a band is worth.

But the Libertines were something else. I still feel I could have done so much for them. My failure to get the best out of Pete Doherty is one of the things that I truly regret. Even though the album I worked on with them, *The Libertines*, was a number one, sold a million copies, and became their biggest ever record, it still feels to me like I have unfinished business with them; I never took the band to their full potential. I couldn't exert enough influence on Pete. Pete sober would be the biggest rock and roll star in the world, whether he was in the Libertines, or Babyshambles, or something else. I think his better bet is Babyshambles, simply because they all like each other, and would be a better support mechanism to each other. Whether Carl and he would make a better songwriting team, who can say?

He's got everything. Songs, lyrics, attitude. He's so sharp, so quick. He could be monumental. And he's still young, only thirty-four at the time of writing. When I was managing him he was only twenty-two.

But he's the most nihilistic man I've ever met, and in the end I didn't know how to reach him. I don't think we're ever going to find out how great he could have been.

*

I first became aware of the Libertines in 2002 when I was running my night Death Disco at the Nottingham Hill Arts Club (more on this later).

James Endeacott had signed the Libertines to Rough Trade – Rough Trade distribution had gone bust a decade ago but Rough Trade records were back with a bang after James had signed the Strokes for the UK. James gave Danny Watson at Rough Trade a copy of 'What a Waster' to play at the club. Straight away it made me stand up and take notice. I started playing it myself when I was DJing. I loved the lyrics, the energy, the attitude.

It turned out that before they signed to Rough Trade the band had been trying to get through to speak to me for ages at Poptones but no one had let them through. One of the problems with Poptones was that there were too many train-spotters there who thought they knew everything about music. These *reprobates* had been turned away every time because no one thought they were for real.

So I was a fan. I dropped by the studio when they were recording their great first album, *Up the Bracket*, in 2002. Pete Doherty and Carl Barât were the two front men and guitarists, two best friends and worst enemies who'd been running riot in London since Pete's sister introduced them. They wrote all the songs together and the lyrics were brilliant, very British, hedonistic and cocky. 'It's to the top of the world or the bottom of a canal,' Doherty said to Barât and both outcomes were equally possible. The bassist was John Hassall, brilliant, handsome, but told to stay in the background and let Pete and Carl shine. Their first manager Banny Poostchi knew they were the stars of the show who could make them massive. Gary Powell was a great drummer, originally from America, who joined the band in 2001.

The album was produced by Mick Jones from the Clash and he invited me to the album sessions because he knew I liked the band. As soon as I got there Pete Doherty dragged me into a side room and asked if I'd sign his friend's band. He was very charming, kept calling me Mr McGee, but I knew straight away it was an act.

Banny Poostchi had done a great job managing the band (and dealing with what I was about to have to deal with) but she resigned in 2003, and then James Endeacott started chasing me to be their manager. Pete Doherty had previously called me up and asked me to be *his* manager when it looked inevitable that the band was going to split, but I'd turned him down despite being tempted. Pete was already addicted to heroin and crack and was about to plead guilty to burgling Carl Barât's house. He'd kicked Carl's door down and nicked his stuff. Pete and Carl were so combustible together: they were like fire and petrol. If you put them in a room together you got explosive music, but there was always the chance someone was going to get hurt.

After a lot of encouragement from James Endeacott, I caught a taxi down to Crystal Palace where Pete was staying at his sister's place. Just as I was getting into the taxi, James said to me, 'Good luck. I'll be praying for you.'

I nearly jumped straight out. He'd persuaded me to get a

fifty-quid taxi miles away in South London and now he was telling me my life was in danger!

I liked Pete immediately when I arrived. Put on your five favourite records, he challenged me. I put on five Beatles songs. Put on *your* five favourites, I challenged back. He played me five Chas 'n' Dave records in a row! He was very funny, we got on well.

I was the first person who told him he was going to go to prison. It was obvious, he'd burgled a house. You have to do time.

'No one else is saying I'm going to prison,' he said. He was worried but couldn't really believe it would happen.

'You're going to prison,' I told him again.

The next Monday the judge sent him down for six months.

He served two months of his sentence. On the day he was released from prison, he was met at the gates by Carl Barât. They hugged and made up – although that was nowhere close to being the end of the animosity between them.

I was in New York on the day of his release. I didn't want to manage them! Everyone had told me they were bad news, pure chaos. But James had kept on at me: 'You're the only man who can do it.' They thought if I could handle Primal Scream's drug intake and self-destructiveness then I might have a chance of handling the Libertines.

This was in the two years when I'd started drinking again. I had a taste of red wine at the beginning of 2002, and I went straight back on the sauce again until I packed it in for good in 2004 when Kate gave me a yellow card and told me she wouldn't be married to a drunk. (I haven't touched a drop since.) But I was still drinking then, over in New York with my friend Nik Leman at Tribeca Grand. James Endeacott was on the phone: 'Pete's out – you have to come to the freedom gig!'

'I'm in New York!'

'Get a plane!'

'Fuck off!'

But when I did get back to England I couldn't resist any more. Pete Doherty wanted me there, and he was such an exciting talent. Even Geoff Travis, with whom I've never had a good relationship, wanted me to come and manage them. 'You're the only one who can do it,' I kept hearing, and it was too much of a challenge to resist.

When I first met Carl Barât he was wary of me. He was a bit macho. Someone from the entourage annoyed me and I threatened him. Then someone from the entourage annoyed Carl and Carl threatened him. It was a bit pathetic, but with that out of the way Carl really opened up. He's a lovely, kind man, and I loved him straight away. The challenge for me now was to find a way to heal his relationship with Pete Doherty and to put them in a room together to write songs. I had a great idea: I'd take them to the house I'd bought in the Welsh countryside, get them away from the temptations of London, and they'd write the next album in a nice peaceful setting.

I took them to the house I live in now, which I'd bought back in the mid-1990s when I was first seeing Kate. I'd bought her a car as a present. It was a little black car; that's how much

I know about cars. It was a sports car and she was a bit embarrassed about driving it. There she was, a good-looking woman in a flash car – a man in a white van threw a sandwich at her once. I've never learned to drive and so in some way I suppose the car was a present for me too, as it meant Kate could drive us out of London to the country. I'd bought her a cottage in a village called Crickhowell we could go to – I guess I must have been quite serious about her. Well, I know I was.

One day she asked me if I'd like to go to this bohemian little town, Hay-on-Wye, with loads of bookshops. I'd never heard of the place but it sounded fun, so we drove out there. It was the middle of the summer, August.

Hay is a weird little place. I was looking around and thinking, Yeah, I fucking love it here. I just had that feeling, I can't explain, like I was being energized by the place.

We walked past the estate agent, and I looked in the window. There was this big fuck-off house with eleven acres advertised for £350,000. Offer accepted.

'Can we go and see it?' I asked.

'Why?' Kate asked. 'Even if you wanted to buy it, and you don't, it's already been sold.'

'Can we go and see it?' I asked again. (I'm thinking *Led Zeppelin rock and roll mansion*.) This is not long after me banking the big chunk of Sony money I got in 1996.

So we went in and I managed to persuade the estate agent to ring up and arrange a viewing. We were shown in by a posh couple. The place was a wreck, an absolute state.

The posh couple, who turned out to be all right in the end, asked, 'What do you do?'

'I'm in the music business,' I said.

They found this hilarious. *Ha ha ha! Ha ha ha!* A bit patronizing, you know. I was thinking, *You cunts*. Very good.

So I had a good look round. The place probably needed hundreds of thousands of pounds' worth of work to make it liveable. But I just had this wonderful feeling about the place. I could imagine being completely relaxed there, on top of a hill, looking down over a Welsh valley.

I've got this great lawyer Kate Moss told me about, Howard Granville, who can buy houses in a day. He somehow cuts through all the shit. Kate Moss can beat anyone to buy a house because she found this amazing guy. It normally takes months. I don't know what he does. Perhaps he doesn't read the papers, but that doesn't seem very safe, so he must super-read the papers, who knows? He can put them through in a day.

Kate could see the look in my eye. She said to me, 'Please don't buy it.' She'd only been going out with me for a couple of years, and we were always falling out at this point. 'Please don't buy it. Please don't buy it.'

'Don't worry, I won't buy it,' I said.

So the next day I phoned up the estate agent. 'How much is the bid?'

'£350,000.'

'I'll pay £370,000.'

'Sold to you, Mr McGee!'

I told him I'd have all the legal stuff in order tomorrow and buy it then. The estate agent dude thought I was lying.

I phoned up Howard. On Thursday the place was mine. We had looked round it first on the bank holiday Monday.

I phoned up Kate then. 'I bought the house.'

'What!'

'I bought the house. It's mine.'

'What!'

'Yeah, I bought it. Will you do it up for me?'

So, after a bit of persuading, she did. It took her two years. Kate and I got married in 1998 and it was ready in 1999. She started doing it up in 1997.

And I just love the place. The solitude. The view over the hills. I don't have to see anybody I don't like. It's the island that Aleister Crowley speaks about: *find an island and fortify it.*

No matter what happens, I'll never move from here. There's a ley line under us, Strata Florida, which runs straight through the house, all the way from Glastonbury to Aberystwyth castle, with us in the middle. When I bought it, I just saw the house as a holiday home. I wasn't done with London yet, with the music industry. I was still burning to do something that was as fun as the early years.

And it was to this idyllic country retreat that I took Pete Doherty and Carl Barât.

I'll give Geoff Travis his props. He phoned me up privately beforehand and said, 'Do you know what you're getting involved with here?'

I said, 'I'll be fine, I've had Oasis.'

'Alan,' he said, 'this is not Oasis, this is way beyond anything you saw with them. Are you *sure* you want to take them to your house?'

I took the warning but thought he was maybe being a bit soft. And the first two days went quite well. They were talking, getting on, playing guitar and singing. I always saw Doherty as having the best initial ideas for the songs, but then Carl would come in and add something that made them better. Carl is more disciplined, adds some order to Pete's shambolics. It's a dynamite songwriting relationship, but unfortunately it's a dynamite relationship full stop.

Pete would be wandering around my house, putting all my first editions in his bag (he's a mad klepto when he's on the gear); Carl would be following him around slowly taking them out of his bag and putting them back on the shelves, because Carl's a good guy.

I went to sleep on the Wednesday, leaving them together, listening to 'Don't Look Back in Anger' on the stereo.

At quarter to ten the next morning, I was sitting in the lounge talking to the office when Carl came in. For about five seconds I thought he was wearing a Halloween mask, that it was a practical joke. And suddenly I realized that he wasn't wearing a mask, that it was his actual face.

His face was completely covered in dried blood, but what really shocked me was that one of his eyes was hanging completely out of the socket.

They'd had an argument, over a girl, I think, and said

some awful things to each other. It's a real love-hate relationship – because they were so intimate and shared everything
they know all of each other's secrets and exactly how to wound
each other the deepest. When Carl went back to his room he
headbutted the sink, twenty or thirty times, smashed his face
up and went to sleep. He did £400 of damage to my sink and
nearly lost an eye.

I thought Pete had done it to him. I thought he was going
to end up back in prison again.

I phoned up the farmer who rented some of my fields and
got him to drive us to Hereford hospital. Of course, when I
came in to the hospital with a guy looking like that, I was getting
asked some pretty interesting questions. No one believed that
someone could do this to himself. They were taking him to the
side trying to get him to admit that I'd beaten him up. We must
have seemed suspicious because we didn't want to tell them Pete
was staying at my house. He'd only just got out of prison and
everyone would have thought it was him. And we knew the
press would have a field day if they'd got hold of it. In the end
Carl confessed he'd done it to himself.

So that was my introduction to managing them, and that
was the end of the songwriting sessions, two days in. I had
to take Carl to Harley Street and pay for a specialist to look
at his eye. He would have lost it if I hadn't done that.

We tried again to put Pete and Carl together to write some
songs in Paris. I wasn't going to go with them this time, but
Carl came in to see me looking really anxious. He was on the

edge of some serious drug problems himself and was worried he was going to fall over the edge hanging out with Pete in Paris. So I offered to come with him and be his chaperone.

The look on Pete's face when he answered the door in Paris was classic: *Oh no, the manager's here.* It was the most disappointed look I'd ever seen.

The next day me and Carl went out and got absolutely pissed together in Paris. We met a band called the Parisiennes, who recognized us, and ended up back at a supermodel's house who Pete had made friends with. There was a tray going around with every kind of drug known to man. I knew then that I was never going to take drugs again, because I was out of my face on booze, and presented with every possible drug going, and I still didn't want any.

So we had fun, but there wasn't a great deal of songwriting going on. It was quite a quiet carriage on the way back home on the Eurostar and I suddenly noticed a funny smell just as we went into the tunnel. I turned round and there was Pete with his crack pipe lighting up. This really was going to be a challenge.

When we got back I booked them for three consecutive nights at the Forum. They hadn't been doing very big gigs so far, and I was trying to prove a point, that they were a bigger group than Rough Trade thought they were. They had such committed fans. If they were a cult band I knew they were a massive cult band. And we sold the gigs out quite easily.

One of the problems with booking gigs for them was having the anticipation for them undermined all the time by

Pete's guerrilla gigs. Pete was incredibly clever in the way he used the internet to talk to his fans – he'd post demos, chat to them and declare sudden gigs in his flat. He'd do these gigs for his drug money and charge a tenner at the door.

I'd booked them three consecutive nights at Brixton Academy by then, at 5,000 people a night. And to try to stop Pete from doing his guerrilla gigs I'd put him in the smallest flat imaginable. It was big enough for a bed and very little else. But somehow he'd still manage to fit fifty people in there on some nights. He'd do two gigs a night, make a grand and run off into the night to spend it all on crack.

They were such a shambles, Pete especially. On the Tuesday before their three-night run at Brixton Academy, Pete advertised another of his little gigs for that night – Meet at Whitechapel station at 7 p.m. He managed to rope Carl into doing it with him.

I saw Carl the next day, looking incredibly pissed off. 'What happened?' I asked. 'Only five people turned up,' he said. It sums the Libertines up perfectly, playing to 15,000 people at the weekend and five on the Tuesday before.

I was very involved in the making of the second album. Rough Trade, though they'll deny it, had pretty much handed them over to me by then. People were becoming more concerned about whether Pete was going to die than about whether or not he'd make another album. But I got them in the Metropole studio and for two months they recorded there.

It wasn't a normal recording session at all. I had to hire

two twins as bodyguards, each seven feet tall and three feet wide, mainly to keep Pete and Carl from killing each other. One was Pete's and the other was Carl's: whenever it kicked off between them the twins would pick up their Libertine and carry him to the opposite end of the room. Pete and Carl's feet would be pedalling around in the air, trying to kick out at the other.

For all of the two months, I think Pete showed up about six times. The hardest job I had was getting him to surrender the songs he'd written. I think he knew then that the relationship between him and Carl was unworkable and he was trying to save his songs for his next band. He really didn't care at all about the new album and if it was up to him it would have been filled with B-sides. He was at his worst stage, staying up every night, never eating.

I'd heard his new songs though – from the demos he'd post online – and I thought they were great. So when Pete arrived in the studio I'd wait until just after he'd done whatever he'd done in the toilets and say, 'Why don't we try this one with the band, Pete?' He'd go along with it then and we got some of the best songs of the second album that way, 'The Man Who Would Be King', 'What Katie Did', and 'Music When the Lights Go Out'. That was what saved the album. We got versions of the new songs really quickly, because the rest of the band were all such great musicians. John Hassall was one the best bassists I'd ever worked with, he was as good as Paul McCartney, and Gary Powell was an amazing drummer too. Carl's got a knack for really catchy guitar lines and John would quickly work out what to play alongside them and so it didn't really matter what Pete did on top with his guitar, or whether he was in a fit state to play it. Although, to be honest, you could give Pete ketamine and he could still play guitar; he has the constitution of an ox.

Mick Jones was a great producer, he was the vibe, kept the atmosphere going. I was the logistics, suggesting songs to record, stopping Pete and Carl from killing each other and trying to keep the hangers-on out of the studio. (Carl had as many of those as Pete; it was competitive. If Pete brought five one day Carl would bring six the next.) Rough Trade were paying for the session but were a bit petty. They were complaining about food bills. Food bills! It was a miracle these people were alive and they were concerned about food bills. Pete probably hadn't eaten for weeks anyway.

I think I did the best job I could have done on getting that second album into shape. Before I got Pete to contribute those extra songs we were heading to a really disappointing follow-up to their debut. The first album's definitely a better album, but the second has some great songs on it and sold a lot more copies. It's not a bad achievement for a band with a songwriting partnership who could barely talk to each other by then. I couldn't repair the band but even sticking them together with Sellotape was an achievement: they were always going to come apart again.

They were too much even for me, with my experience of the Jesus and Mary Chain and Primal Scream and the Gallagher brothers and Kevin Shields. I realized I'd taken on more than

I could handle on the British tour we went on. It was spring, March 2004. Each night I had genuinely no idea if we'd be able to play the next night on the tour. Each gig was like Dunkirk. We picked Doherty up at the beginning of that tour with one sock on, one sock off, no trousers. We'd been looking for him and found him in a crackhouse. He was in no state to walk so we wrapped him in a carpet and carried him into the van. Then we bought him some clothes on the way to Birmingham to play the first gig.

The next night, in Manchester, staying at the Britannia Hotel, Pete decided he was going to do a Keith Richards. He was with a Liverpool band at the time, the Bandits. We were all standing around in the hotel room. Pete was smacked off his tits and picked up this crap old TV. He staggered over towards the window and hurled it at it, but it hit the wooden frame in the middle, bounced back, hit him in the face and knocked him out cold.

I was sat over him, slapping his face – 'Are you alive?' I was quite worried. He was knocked out for about five minutes. Everyone else in the room was freaking out, going, 'He's fucking dead!' I was thinking how ironic it would be if it wasn't the drugs that killed him but the rock and roll.

I had some great times with the Libertines. Mad, mad moments. They were great fun to be with. But it was so hard to manage them. It wasn't just the drugs – it was Carl and Pete's relationship, how intense it was, how volatile and damaged.

One of the things that really helped blow that band up was

the support from the lads, the football fans. I suggested when Nick Love was filming *The Football Factory* that 'What a Waster' would make a perfect song for the soundtrack. Phonogram got in touch with me and asked me to find them music that 'sounded like acid house for 1998', whatever that meant. Can you sort it for us? I put in Mogwai, who I was managing then, to soundtrack the end of a blow job scene, and 'What a Waster' to soundtrack a scene where little thieves nick a character's phone and get kicked off the bus. Very Libertines. The central scene of the film really. The DVD sold 600,000 copies and suddenly all those football fans were interested in us.

We delivered the album, *The Libertines*, and then James Endeacott told me my next job was to try to get Pete sober. Well, that was clear to everyone at the time. It was Pete's business if he wanted to take drugs, but we all really thought he was going to die if he kept it up. He was so skinny that he looked malnourished. He was hanging around with Peter Perrett, an old punk and the lead singer of the Only Ones in the 1970s, a complete smack and crack fiend back in the day. I remember a gig they'd played together: Pete came out of the toilet and there was a mirror and a doorway next to each other. Pete tried to walk straight through the mirror and then slid down the wall. It was at that point I realized I didn't trust him to still be alive in a month. We all just thought we were going to lose him. It was really sad.

So we tried to rehab him in the Priory. I picked him up in a crackhouse, in bed with a girl, as ever. Hang on a minute, I've just got to chase this, he says, and finished burning a load of heroin, sucked it all up and blew it straight in my face. I couldn't move for about fifteen minutes. I could taste the heroin. My mind was floating off. I had to stick my head out of the window of the room we were in. Finally I landed back on earth and we took him off to the Priory.

A week later his mum rang me up to tell me he'd escaped. I found him in a crack hotel in the East End and then we put him back in the Priory again. The road leading to the place is called Rocks Lane and we found lots of rocks of crack on the back seat after we'd dropped him off. After eight days he clucked again and left. It was gutting. I knew what potential he had, how he could be the biggest star in the world. I still think he could. The Stones are too old. Bono's going blind, Chris Martin's a geography teacher. If the Libertines or Babyshambles came back with a straight Pete Doherty, or a straighter Pete Doherty, not totally sober, just functional, a Doherty that's transportable – it would be a clean-up job. Nearly all the world could be his. They won't let him into America, that's obvious. For now anyway. But once people get clean and have stayed clean for a while, then you can start to get lawyers in.

But he's done it over and over again. Got clean for a while then clucked. It's the heroin that's the real problem, and he loses it completely when he's taking it.

While we were trying to get Pete clean we had touring commitments we had to fulfil, and we did them with a replacement guitarist. We took a huge amount of flak from the fans for that, saying we were abandoning Pete. I was seen as evil

Machiavellian McGee who'd thrown Pete out of the band. So the gigs we honoured really harmed the band, and probably sealed the end of the Libertines. But I thought we had to do the gigs. We'd have been sued otherwise. It was a payday for everyone, including Pete, and there was no way on earth he would have survived the gigs. He was in no fit state to show up at the office, let alone go on an international tour.

One of the last gigs on that tour was to 20,000 people in Brazil, with Primal Scream as support. That many people even without Pete. With Pete, when he had his head together, they were the best live band in the world. The Saturday night at Brixton Academy was incredible. They had the world at their feet; we'd genuinely broken them worldwide. But when the tour ended that was that, there was no more Libertines.

The Libertines could only ever be Carl *and* Pete and reconciliation between them was impossible. Unless their personalities have changed a huge amount, I don't know how they could ever work together. When it was clear we couldn't get them together in the Libertines, it was tempting to manage Pete with Babyshambles. But there was no way I'd fuck Carl. Carl is such a fucking nice guy and I couldn't let him down. He'd be expecting me to let him down, and I wasn't going to do that to him. So Carl moved on to the next chapter with his new band Dirty Pretty Things, and I became their manager.

At Poptones, we had our big success with the Hives, and also did quite well with Cosmic Rough Riders, who went silver, and then Telstar went bust in 2004 – a disaster. This was when I was riding high managing the Libertines, and we attracted interest from Universal. It wasn't working out the way I'd hoped being independent and so we did a deal and licensed the Poptones' name to Lucian Grainge at Universal, the man who pretty much controls the whole music industry. He takes no prisoners, Lucian Grainge. His attitude is that A&R men are like oil fields; if they're not producing, shut them down. I was never at full speed when I worked for him. I came down with anaemia (the second Libertines manager in a row to get anaemia) and so I was working at full speed for only half of the year he gave me to prove himself. It was too short a time to find anything. After that, he tried to renegotiate the deal and we walked away.

It was a bad decision for Lucian Grainge to pull the plug so early. I discovered Glasvegas just after the deal had collapsed. James Allan's sister Denise kept getting in touch to tell me her brother was a genius and was going to change music from the working classes – I'd heard it all before. She heard I was in town mixing the Dirty Pretty Things album with Carl Barât and dragged me along to see them, in Glasgow in King Tut's again. He was a professional footballer at Dumbarton but they sacked him because of his song 'Stabbed', where he sings 'I'm going to get stabbed' over and over again. They got really good and years later in 2008 they got a deal and their first album *Glasvegas* was a hit.

But Lucian Grainge missed out on Glasvegas, and Boxer Rebellion, who we found that year too. They're both big bands, and he could have had the pair of them if he'd had more vision.

21: LOS ANGELES

I started escaping the English winters by going to Los Angeles every year for a few months. I went out there to mix the Dirty Pretty Things album with Dave Sardy in November 2005, and immediately remembered how much I loved the place. Maybe it's because I'm Scottish. The climate is the exact opposite to Glasgow, clear, bright and hot every single day. You could live a lifetime in Glasgow without seeing the sun you see in a month in Hollywood. I decided I'd stay there for the rest of the winter and was there – apart from some trips home to see the family – until April 2006. I did it every year for the next three years. Perhaps that was my midlife crisis.

I'd always go on my own and stay at the Standard on Sunset Boulevard in Hollywood. I'd been flying to Los Angeles for years by now and I had loads of pals out there. It was great not having to face the winter. The English pound was really high and it made it quite affordable.

Charlie was young enough so she didn't really mind me being away. One day, though, I was about to go out there again when she was seven and she grabbed my arm and said, *Don't go*. She was still young enough then that she would crawl into bed sometimes. You'd wake up and there she'd be, looking at you, *Hello*.

I don't want to miss her growing up. I like being there to say hello when she gets in from school, watching how she grows up. My whole life until Charlie was very indulgent – I just pleased myself. I used to think, if you're not pleasing yourself, then you're doing something wrong. I still do. But the best way to please yourself is by taking care of those you love.

On another rainy day in the valleys, I remember those Californian summers. There was a girl I was friends with called Nellie Kim, a stylist who used to go out with one of the Thrills. She phoned me up one evening before I was flying home and we arranged to go for dinner at Toi, a Thai restaurant on Sunset, where a lot of rock and rollers hang out.

She picked me up and while she was driving me there, she told me her friends wanted to meet me and could we go to theirs instead and get take-out? She mentioned the names of her friends, which I didn't recognize, and said they were in a band. I went along with it, fairly reluctantly, I must admit – the last thing I wanted to do was talk to some talentless band. She took me to a house with a studio in it and I was introduced to a guy called Joaquin and a guy called Antony Langdon. This guy Antony said he used to be in a band called Spacehog and he'd met me before when they supported Oasis. So we shook hands. I didn't really remember him but I went along with it.

The other guy, Joaquin, fancied himself as a musician. He played me seventeen songs. They were rubbish. Bombastic. They sounded like Pearl Jam. I took every single song apart. When I take a song apart, I fucking take it *apart. Marks out of ten: fucking zero*, that sort of thing. Halfway through the tenth song in a row I'd demolished, Joaquin was banging his feet on the floor, not with anger but with delight.

He was loving the way I was slaughtering his songs.

There was the hint of some decent songs under the production so I started to give him advice. I was like, *You take the drums off, you take all the electric guitars off and replace them with acoustics, you redo the vocals, maybe put some shaker on it* . . . I was telling him this when Kirsten Dunst came in and kissed this guy. I don't go to the movies and I don't watch TV but even I knew who Kirsten Dunst was. So I presumed the guy with the weird name was her boyfriend, or someone in her management.

By this time, the lad Joaquin had realized I really didn't know who he was. He'd thought I'd only been pretending not to know him at first, that it was my way of taking the piss out of him. He gave me his full name when I was leaving, Joaquin Phoenix, and I thought it must be something to do with River Phoenix, like maybe he's his brother?

Too many people were paying homage to the guy, he must be someone.

I was planning to google him when I got back to the Standard but before I arrived back I spotted his face on a massive billboard with his name in huge letters. He was currently starring in *Walk the Line* as Johnny Cash. I was the only person in Hollywood who didn't know who he was.

A week later, when I got back to London, I got a call from his friend Antony. He was in a diner with Joaquin beside him. This is winter, early 2006. 'We want you to produce the record.'

We made about three records, just as friends. Bits and pieces came out as Antony's solo record *Victoria*, but nothing under Joaquin's name.

We took it seriously though. I'd hum a melody and then we'd spend a day working out something around that.

Joaquin was completely wild. Carl Barât was in town one night and we were recording his second Dirty Pretty Things album with Nick Leman. Carl didn't believe that I knew Joaquin Phoenix and was winding me up. Go and get him then, he kept challenging me. So I rang up Joaquin and told him we were coming over. He was like, *Great*, bring them up. We ended up having the most bizarre night. It ended up in a big competition between Carl and Joaquin trying to prove to each other who was the crazier. Joaquin kept kung fu kicking Carl's guitar. But he was so hyped up he didn't realize he was actually kicking his own guitar. That was Joaquin being friendly. It's a good job it wasn't Carl's guitar because Carl's actually a really hard guy.

All the way through this I was sitting quietly and drinking Diet Coke in the corner of the room. Joaquin started pointing at my drink, going, '*You're fucking crazy! You're the most insane person in the room!*'

I thought that was a bit fucking much. *I'm* crazy? Compared to him and Carl, *I'm* crazy? I guess it's all a matter of perspective. Either way, I'm glad I met Joaquin and Antony. They were great friends, great fun, and they made LA for me.

I remember a party Joaquin threw on Independence Day 2007 in his house at the top of Mulholland. The party was in the garden. Me and my friend Belowsky were chipping a football over the dinner table where all the celebrities were eating. Chipping it just over their heads. We could both vaguely play football and could just about get away with not belting them in the face with it. They didn't know this at the table though. So we're winding them up, just for fun.

This Scottish woman piped up, 'Are you that Alan McGee?'

I'm thinking, Oh fuck, it's a Scots woman. 'I am that Alan McGee.'

'I'm Angela McCluskey.' She's a singer. I know who she is. She's mates with Courtney Love. So I had to stop playing football and sit down and talk to her.

There was an American woman at the table across from us, sitting in the shadow of a tree. When she realized I was involved in the music industry, she started firing questions at me, about digital royalties and Apple and what I think is a fair reward for musicians in the MP3 era. Very intense, knowledgeable questions.

So, I asked her, 'Are you in the business?'

She thought for a second and said, 'Yes, I am, my dad was Elvis.'

So that was how I met Lisa Marie Presley. We got along

really well – she and her husband Michael, a musican, are lovely – and she invited me to her birthday party. I thought it would be massive, but there was just me, her agent, her husband, her mum Priscilla Presley, her mum's boyfriend and her kids. They'd hired this huge place which seemed really empty. Then we were taken in a horse and carriage to see a band who one minute were Led Zeppelin and the next Gram Parsons. They could play 'Kashmir' and then 'Love Hurts'. Mental cover versions, absolutely bang on. There were eleven of us in a space for 400. Her son from her first marriage is a model. He turned around to face me and – shit! – it was Elvis. From the profile it wasn't obvious, but when he faced me, it was like looking at the man himself.

Lisa Marie was friends with Courtney Love too, who seemed to keep popping up in my life. It's been suggested to me on a number of occasions that I should sign Courtney Love. She called me out of the blue one summer in 2000. I'd met her only briefly when Teenage Fanclub were touring America.

'Hey Alan, it's Courtney.'

'Courtney who?'

'Courtney Love. Can we meet up?'

I was enjoying a quiet afternoon and immediately thought, How do I get out of this one? So I suggested we meet somewhere I thought she'd never find, Bill and Bill's record shop, just off Portobello Road. See you in fifteen minutes, Courtney.

I got there, ready to wait ten minutes and disappear, and of course she walked straight in.

We ended up spending the whole day together. We went to a pub in St John's Wood and when we walked in the entire place was silenced. Everyone's jaw dropped. She's a big celebrity of course, but it's more than that; people just look at her and they're struck by the force of her personality.

After a while the people in the pub began to get used to her. We were eating dinner when she suddenly said, 'Alan, I need to go outside and do some exercise.'

So then the whole pub watched as she went outside – you could see her straight through the window – and started kicking her leg up over her shoulder, doing gymnastics in high heels.

She called me up later and asked me to go to a West End play with her that Woody Harrelson was starring in. Okay, I said, and picked her up. As soon as the play started she fell straight asleep and began snoring, and she kept it up until the moment the applause began, when she leapt up and started cheering like mad. People had been turning round all the way through the performance, ready to wake her up, but no one had dared when they realized it was Courtney Love.

She's been to stay at my house in Wales. She's a keen horse rider, like Kate. You can ride out of my place for miles into the countryside. She lost a £40,000 bracelet when she fell off her horse up there and asked me to send out a search party. There's no way we would have found it. For all I know, there's still a £40,000 bracelet up the hill.

Courtney's such a force of nature but the nicest times I've had with her have been when she's been behaving normally.

I bumped into her in the Standard, my favourite hotel in LA, just after she'd been sectioned and released. She was calm and fun to talk to, and she was broke. Being broke was good for her. She did a deal shortly after that which made her $50 million and started behaving erratically again.

I think it was in the Standard that she introduced me to Paris Hilton. I was wearing a new hat that my friend Héctor Mijangos had bought me as a present. 'Hot hat,' she said. 'Hector,' I said to him later that night, 'the hat stays.'

I was watching TV with her once. Courtney was watching her favourite programme, *The Suze Orman Show*. Suze Orman is really big in America. She specializes in giving tips to black single mums with three kids on how to make ends meet. All of a sudden, Courtney said, 'That fucking bitch.'

'What's she done?' I asked.

'She took three weeks to get back to me.'

I was thinking, Why do you need tips on how to survive ghetto poverty? 'What did you ask her?'

'I wanted to know what I should do with ten million dollars,' she said. She wasn't joking at all.

'And what did she tell you?' I asked.

'Buy a big house and invest four million in stocks and shares.' The woman was meant to be saving impoverished kids and Courtney thinks she should be looking after her. Hollywood, what a place.

But I do respect Courtney. She's had a hard life. Can you imagine what it would be like to be a young woman with a one-year-old daughter and have your husband kill himself? The media obviously can't, the way they write about her. They like to blame her for Cobain's death – total bullshit. And then they make out that she didn't mourn him. It's not true. She loved him and she was in bits. She mourned her husband in her own way, immersing herself in touring. The media love to judge other people, but it's so sanctimonious. No one but Courtney will ever know what she went through, and no one has the right to make their mind up about her who doesn't know her. I know I really love Courtney. I think maybe that's because, like me, she's a square peg in a round hole.

It was in those days that I also met the last of my three greatest heroes and role models from the music industry. I had been lucky enough to be friends with Malcolm McLaren and Tony Wilson, and now I got to meet Andrew Loog Oldham.

I was DJing in Mexico City. Joe Foster knows him and told him I was going to be around in Mexico City for a couple of weeks and invited him over. He lives in Bogotá, Colombia, with the model he married. Andrew flew over and we got on like a house on fire.

We just hung out and it was brilliant. He told me his life story, which was crazy. By the time he was twenty-six he'd done it all. He'd snorted it all, he'd fucked them all, and then he fucked off to Studio 54, met his missus and fucked off to Columbia. He was a kid – they were kids – when he was managing the Rolling Stones. He was only thirty when he was in New York hanging out at Studio 54.

Andrew's a god. I'm just a guy who worked in the music

business and picked some good bands and brought out their records. Andrew put Mick Jagger and Keith Richards in a room and told them to write songs! He's a total artist.

The only time I ever missed Charlie's birthday was in 2007. She's never let me forget it. It was early September, she was turning seven and I was in Santa Monica, recording drums with Gary Powell of the Libertines for the second Dirty Pretty Things album. We came out, met the producer Nik Leman (who sadly died at Christmas 2012 of an overdose) and we were going towards one of those typical brilliant American restaurants, chicken and chips, portions the size of a table. Then something extraordinary happened, something para-normal – and at the time I was the most unspiritual human being you could come across. (There was certainly no room of interesting spiritual books, like I have now.)

Suddenly, the electrical wire us above started crackling and feeding back, and the street lights started flickering on and off, and we all backed off, worried we might be about to be electrocuted. Then the light went off completely.

It was silent, apart from the noise of crickets. Eerie. Area 51 is only up the road in Nevada. And across the sky, the fastest thing I've ever seen in my life traversed from the furthest left point of the horizon to the furthest right. Faster than any plane, much faster. This was going at three or four thousand miles an hour. A ball of light, about 12,000 feet up. It was completely silent. Gary couldn't see it but Nik and I both did straight away.

That was strange, because Nik and I described it to each other in exactly the same way. The thing we had in common though, me and Nik, was that we had both been drug addicts (or still was in Nik's case).

Now, I'm not saying it was aliens, more likely American military – some kind of secret weapon. Secret technology. But it couldn't have been powered by any natural fuel. That was the weird thing, the feedback on the street lights. It was 9 p.m. at night, and dark.

So when I got back to England I went to a party and started telling people. I told Bob Geldof and he started taking the monumental piss. 'You've fucking *lost it*, McGee! You fucking *loony*.' Even Joaquin Phoenix was telling me to get off the acid. And he's one of the most far-out humans on the planet.

Nevertheless, I couldn't stop thinking about what I'd seen, and reading up on the subject I quickly became obsessed with deep underground military bases. From finding out about this, I was led to Robert Anton Wilson and from there to Aleister Crowley, and then to Austin Osman Spare, and to automatic writing and then to the chaos magicians. It's a study of reversal of energy. I've been studying it for five years. I'm obsessed by it. It's good fun.

I know my readers now are thinking, This guy is genuinely off his rocker, but I'm willing to risk them thinking that. Geopolitics and metaphysics are very connected. What they call magic one year is science the next year.

Aleister Crowley is one of my heroes. His influence is

monumental. He changed society. Who do you think Sergeant Pepper was? That was Aleister Crowley. Crowley died in 1947, *Sergeant Pepper* came out in 1967. Twenty years ago today, who taught the band to play? The Beatles will never admit it, but he's on *Sergeant Pepper* twice. I suspect McCartney's obsessed by him – he just denies it so people don't think he's mad. I'm willing to risk it.

I think it was because I was friends with Courtney Love that the *News of the World* started to tap my phone. When the phone-tapping scandal broke in 2011 I got a phone call from the police to inform me that there was evidence suggesting someone connected with the *News of the World* had listened to some of my messages. The funny thing is that anyone who knew me knew I would never listen to my voice messages. They'd just stay there unlistened to and then be automatically wiped after a week. So they'd have got nothing juicy on there at all. It didn't stop me suing them and settling for an undisclosed sum. That felt good.

22: DJING

My DJing started towards the end of Creation. It had been a long time since I'd done the Living Room but I decided to try to put on nights again in 1998, when I was becoming bored with going through the motions at Creation. Me and Bobby Gillespie would DJ but no one would come. We were quite famous at this point, doing it in bars in Soho, and no one would show up. Perhaps because it was before the internet had taken off.

Then in 2000 in Notting Hill we started Radio 4 which turned into Death Disco in 2002 and it became a really popular night, 250 people inside and 500 outside trying to get in. It was a unique and weird club night with great live bands and it brought an unusual crowd together. To start with it was full of celebrities, Jude Law, Sadie Frost, that sort, but we lost a lot of them after the first year and the night became more interesting, full of extreme rock and rollers. You'd have people like Dave Grohl popping by too whenever he was in town.

We had tons of bands come through Death Disco. The Libertines, the Killers, the Brian Jonestown Massacre, Kasabian, Razorlight, the Hives, the Darkness, and loads more. It was a great scene.

It got me into DJing again, and it's been a really fun way to see the world. I seem to be able to get bookings all over the place, purely off the legend of Creation, and every country's really different.

You play Japan, for instance, and no one bats an eyelid if you switch from 'Jumpin' Jack Flash' to the Prodigy. I remember sharing a bill with Primal Scream at Summer Sonic, a festival in Osaka. They played to 17,000 people and I DJed to 5,000, playing Prodigy and Underworld records. I couldn't stop thinking, This is just two guys from King's Park Secondary.

Then in Italy you can switch between the Beatles, the Libertines, Oasis and Noel Gallagher, and the place goes so mental you can't hear the records for singing.

In Scandinavia I had a shock when I played 'Don't Look Back in Anger' and no one seemed interested. That one *always* works. So I stopped it and played 'Bohemian Rhapsody' and the place turned into a riot.

I DJed in Mexico with Carl Barât once. Héctor Mijangos, who I had given the second Libertines record to put out, phoned me up: 'It's a hit!' he said. 'Can you get them out here? Can you get Pete back in the band.' He ended up selling about 20,000 copies, which is a lot for Mexico considering that they bootleg *everything* over there.

I said, 'Héctor, it's not like Mexico here, I can't just tell people what to do.' I told him I could come out with Carl and we'd do an acoustic gig and some DJ shows.

We did a gig there just DJing in the Hard Rock Cafe to

about 1,000 people. I was the opening DJ. The place was going nuts with me just playing Oasis, drowning out the noise of the records. Carl then came on stage, and it was like a warzone: 200 kids were attacking four bouncers in the pit to get to him, and when they got through they'd get thrown off the two-metre-high stage and on to their heads. Pan-de-fucking-monium. Carl never put on one record. He'd just say to me, 'Velvets' or 'Smiths', and I'd drop 'I'm Waiting for the Man' or 'This Charming Man'.

The next gig was crazy. We borrowed a drummer, this mad jazz musician who could play any song. Should have been in Sun Ra or Miles Davis's band. There were about 1,000 people packed into a tiny bar, a really small DIY stage. Carl played his set and the place went mental. We ended up that night going back to a house. The party went on till about seven in the morning. Then we were in some kind of bus heading somewhere. There are a lot of drugs in the van. Not mine, but everyone else's. A police car went past and someone – I suspect Carl – gave them two fingers. Next thing we were pulled over and all had to continue on our way with considerably lighter pockets.

These days I don't travel nearly as much. I'm a family man, and I like the quiet of Wales. People come to see us.

Bill Clinton came to stay once. I was going to do a gig in New York in May 2001, and on AOL messenger Peter Florence, the director of Hay Festival, said, 'Hi, Alan, what are you doing next weekend?' When I said I was in America, the next question was, 'Can Bill Clinton stay in your house?'

I told Kate, and she was very excited. *What! Of course he can.*

I didn't particularly want Bill Clinton to stay at my house. American presidents, I know what their game is. Clinton's no different to the others, he's just really eloquent. But if Kate wanted it, that's okay: Clinton could stay.

The irony of all ironies was that Kate, who thought she was going to get to hang out with Clinton, wasn't even allowed to stay in her own house! She got kicked out and had to stay with Peter Florence's mum!

That was the end of being a hotel for the literature festival but it's still down the road every year. I spoke there in 2012 for an event based around Richard King's brilliant book *How Soon Is Now?*, a history of independent music in the UK. And Irvine Welsh texted me the other day to tell me he's doing the next festival. I met Irvine at the end of the 1990s. We all loved *Trainspotting* at Creation. Irvine would have fitted in very well with the Hackney days: he was always pissed or on an E. He'd come up to me and put his arm round me but he'd be so wrecked it was like being put in a headlock. He'd talk top speed in my ear while crushing my head like a vice. I imagine he's calmed down these days.

I've met many of my heroes through becoming well known in music. When I was living in Primrose Hill, I used to see Robert Plant wandering around. We'd just done Knebworth so we had stories to compare. In 2005 he phoned me up and asked me to DJ his son's wedding.

Well, you don't get more flattering offers than that, and I showed up at the wedding in Robert's place down the road in Kidderminster. Jimmy Page had just got sober and was wandering around. Jimmy Page is a god to me. I'd met him once before and rented him a floor of my office block.

I remember putting 'Lola' by the Kinks on as the first song and seeing Jimmy and Robert head to the dance floor and start dancing together. That was the absolute highlight of my DJing career!

23: 2013

I chucked music on 12 September 2008. No more management, no more record label. I'd become so bored with the music world. I'd been in it for thirty years since I moved to London with Andrew Innes, and I was convinced the world had more to offer. Three days later, 15 September, everything kicked off with the banks – and it felt like confirmation to me that I'd made the right decision, that we were getting out of the rat race at the right time. We decided to leave London then and settle for good in the house in Wales.

Here in Wales I seek nobody's attention, affection or friendship. It's my ongoing rehab from drink and drugs and rock and roll. I try to live a spiritual life here.

As I've got older I've realized that the thing that most annoys me in life is people. I was a social animal on drugs. When I was sober, I thought people were a bunch of twits. And I just don't have to deal with them here.

I've had a great five years, reading, teaching myself new things.

I've found out I have an eye for art, for instance. I started wandering into galleries when I went to London, buying paintings with the money I earned from DJing. I just bought art that appealed to me, that I wanted to put on my wall. Some of what I've bought is worthless in terms of money, it's just I like it. But Keith Vaughan has now become the biggest gay painter in the world. I used to have two of them in my office – I just liked them. My pal, who's gay, came in one day and asked, 'Do you know what these are?'

'Er, Keith Vaughans?' I didn't know anything about him.

'What do you think they're paintings of?' he asked me.

I said, 'Well, that one's depression, and that one's kind of, like, bleakness?'

'No, Alan,' he said, 'that one's a guy fucking another guy up the arse; and that one's a cowboy giving another cowboy a blow job.' I've been sitting in the office beneath all this gay erotic art for years and never noticed. *Now, I get it*. They're fucking good paintings.

I made a film in 2012 with my friend Dean Cavanagh, who shares my interest in occult thinkers and books. On a simple level *Kubricks* is about a director going mad trying to make a film at my house in Wales. We did it as an experiment to see if we could make a film and, incredibly, we could. It's a completely improvised film; I play myself. I don't act, I'm just myself. It's about quantum reality. I'm living in one reality but the main actor Roger Evans is living in another existence where he thinks he's shooting a movie. It took five days to shoot, all in my house and the grounds surrounding us. My friend Joanna Pickering is in it, a great actor and writer who one day should write the book about Death Disco. The premier screening was in Leeds in June 2013. Loads of my pals were there: Lee Mavers, Debbie Turner, James Allan. Mavers is a smart cookie: as soon as it started playing he came up to me, 'What's wrong with the screen?' He was right, it was too small so we were missing lots of what was happening on the edges. It's a film about someone living in two separate dimensions, and there was a whole third of the screen that was happening in a complete other dimension to the people in the room. I'd like to say it was intentional. But it was just a cock-up. The Creation ethos continues.

I'm in a film called *Svengali!* too which was written by my friend Jonny Owen. I play myself. People say to me I'm a good actor, to which I say, I've been acting since 1974. The real Alan McGee was left bleeding at the foot of the stairs in Glasgow; ever since then I've found it hard to know whether I'm playing a part, who's really there behind the appearance. There's a character called Alan McGee I've been playing for years, and I might play him a bit differently these days, but I can't promise I'm not still playing him all the same.

Taking a break from the music industry was necessary for me. I needed to refresh myself, follow my nose and discover what it is that inspires me. I've loved this time. I've had a five-year break from the music business but I've never forgotten about it, never been able to take my eye off what's going on out there, and now I feel ready to return.

A lot of the music I love has returned in 2013. There's the great new record by My Bloody Valentine. Primal Scream have their best album for years, back at their best. Even House of Love are back too, with Bickers back in the band and another really good album. When they were touring recently someone in the audience shouted to Chadwick, 'Take your clothes off!' Chadwick thought about it for a second. 'Those days are over,' he replied.

My hero has returned too. Who apart from David Bowie could record an album in secret, release a single overnight and have it the most talked-about record of the year?

I've got my music buzz back. Music has completely changed as a business and that for me is fantastic, because I'm interested in it again after having found it stale for so long. There is actually a huge amount of good unsigned bands around these days, because it's so hard to get signed. It's not hard to find good music. Whether you can penetrate the market with it is another question, but I'd like to find out. In one way it feels similar to when we first started in the 1980s. The record labels don't take risks any more so I think there's room for someone who will take a risk.

That's why I'm setting up 359 records with Iain McNay at Cherry Red. It feels good to be working with an independent again. I want the label to be a launchpad for new talent and some ignored older talent. But it won't be like it was running Creation or Poptones. My conditions for the deal are 1) I never have to go to another gig in London; 2) I never have to go to another marketing meeting; 3) I never have to go to another awards ceremony; 4) I will never come to your office again. Thank god for Ian McNay and Cherry Red! Who else would put up with those conditions?

I've signed a number of acts already. One of the first was Pete McLeod, who I'd met in 2007 and who had stayed in touch, badgering me to start up a label. He did more than anyone to get me back into music and I thank him. John Lennon McCullagh was another. He's only fifteen years old at the time of writing, and full of talent. I met his dad in Australia, a mad Oasis fan. He asked me to DJ in Rotherham which I thought was hilarious – you can't get a worse sounding gig than DJing in Rotherham – and I went along to see just how bad it could be. I had a great time in the end, but then John's dad told me he was putting his son on stage, and I thought, *Oh god*. A fourteen-year-old with a sixties haircut stepped up. I'm going to have to try and be polite here. But he played six Dylan songs and it was incredible. A superb voice, great guitar and harmonica playing. I told him to go away and write some songs of own, and he might have a career. When he came back with a bunch of his own I signed him up.

These days technology means I can run a record label from a BlackBerry in rural Wales. Or on the beach in Goa if I prefer. And actually, I think I can run a label better from here than I can in London. No one here cares about Oasis or Creation and I can focus on finding genuine talent.

In London, it's, 'Hey, how's the new label?'

'Hey, can I send you a tape?'

I don't mind that for ten minutes. Then I can't wait to get back home. It's so peaceful here, up on the hill. It has to be something special to bring me down.

Like managing one of my all time musical heroes, for instance. Perhaps I'll do that.

Joe Foster is in Glasgow and wants to leave. I've just bought a chapel and am thinking of doing civil marriages there. Joe Foster says he's an ordained minister. That would be a fitting ending – Joe Foster marrying people in my chapel in Wales. He'll always be a part of what I'm doing. When he gets too much, I just don't answer the emails.

Creation took its toll on all of us. Dick Green and I still have a publishing company together. Recently we were changing the company bank account and our adviser said to me, 'I've checked out both of your addresses, and you both live absolutely in the middle of nowhere. What is that about?'

'I suppose you had to be there,' I said.

It would be easy to think my life has become less interesting over the last decade but, if anything, it's the reverse. The journey has been worth it. Instead of being a yes man to a corporate boss, I've become a property dealer, an art collector, a DJ who travels the world, and now I'm writing this book. I love my family and I see them every day.

I remember buying my first guitar and deciding I wanted to be a punk rock star – I've travelled a long way from that teenager. Charlie's got a little guitar and sometimes I'll have a strum on it. She's picking it up, and she's a good piano player. We talk about music sometimes; she worries that One Direction might have gone off the boil, that the third album's been a long while coming. But mostly I try not to comment on anything musical to her, to let her find her own way. When I tell her she's a good piano player, she thinks, What does he know? She's like me, she wants something to rub up against. So I listen to her playing classical piano, thinking how good she is, and I keep really quiet.

INDEX